Frame Relay Applications

Business and Technology Case Studies

The Morgan Kaufmann Series in Networking
Series Editor, David Clark

Practical Computer Network Analysis and Design
James D. McCabe

Frame Relay Applications: Business and Technology Case Studies
James P. Cavanagh

High-Performance Communication Networks
Jean Walrand and Pravin Varaiya

Computer Networks: A Systems Approach
Larry L. Peterson and Bruce S. Davie

Forthcoming
Optical Networks
Rajiv Ramaswami and Kumar Sivarajan

The Art and Science of Network Design
Robert S. Cahn

Switching in the Internet
Yakov Rekhter, Bruce S. Davie, and Paul Doolan

Gigabit Workstations
Jonathan M. Smith, Bruce S. Davie, and C. Brendan Traw

Internet Payment Systems
Mark H. Linehan and Dan Schutzer

Advanced Cable Television Technology
Walter S. Ciciora, James O. Farmer, and David J. Large

ATM Applications: Business and Technology Case Studies
James P. Cavanagh

Multicasting
Lixia Zhang

Frame Relay Applications

Business and Technology Case Studies

James P. Cavanagh

Morgan Kaufmann Publishers, Inc.
SAN FRANCISCO, CALIFORNIA

Senior Editor	Jennifer Mann	Copyeditor	Ken DellaPenta
Production Manager	Yonie Overton	Proofreader	Jennifer McClain
Production Editor	Elisabeth Beller	Composition	Nancy Logan
Text Design	Mark Ong, Side by Side Studios	Illustration	RA
Cover Design	Ross Carron Design	Indexer	Valerie Robbins
Cover Photograph	Comstock, Inc.	Printer	Courier Corporation

Designations used by companies to distinguish their products are often claimed as trademarks or registered trademarks. In all instances where Morgan Kaufmann Publishers, Inc. is aware of a claim, the product names appear in initial capital or all capital letters. Readers, however, should contact the appropriate companies for more complete information regarding trademarks and registration.

Morgan Kaufmann Publishers, Inc.
Editorial and Sales Office
340 Pine Street, Sixth Floor
San Francisco, CA 94104-3205
USA

Telephone	415/392-2665
Facsimile	415/982-2665
Email	mkp@mkp.com
WWW	http://www.mkp.com

Order toll free 800/745-7323

Library of Congress Cataloging-in-Publication Data
Cavanagh, James P.
     Frame relay applications : business and technology case studies
/ James P. Cavanagh.
          p. cm.
     Includes bibliographical references and index.
     ISBN 1-55860-399-9
     1. Frame relay (Data transmission) 2. Business enterprises—Computer
networks—Case studies.   I. Title
TK5105.38.C38   1997
004.6'6—dc21   97-31803
                                                               CIP

Я посвящаю эту книгу, как и всю мою жизнь,
моей жене Ире, чья любовь, поддержка и постоянное поощрение
делают эту работу и многое другое возможной.

I dedicate this book, as I do my life,
to my wife, Ira, whose love, support, and constant encouragement
make this work, and so many other things, possible.

Foreword

Anthony Harris

BT Networks & Systems, U.K.

As information has become the lifeblood of manufacturing and service industries, so data networks have become their circulatory systems. Business processes would grind to a rapid halt without reliable data networks connecting people and equipment to companies' databanks and business applications. Many businesses would cease entirely without their data networks.

It is easy for the casual observer to assume that the Internet, with the Internet Protocol (IP) and its associated techniques, has taken over this world of data networking as we approach the year 2000. But those who have to maintain these networks know that many other technologies have combined to provide more and more capability over recent years without a corresponding increase in costs. Frame relay is one of these key technologies.

The genius of frame relay is that technically it is relatively simple. It is just one step more complex than leased circuits. It does just enough to enable different users to share the expensive long-distance bandwidth. It doesn't replace the more powerful higher-level protocols such as SNA, X.25, or IP, but can be used to upgrade their capabilities or make them more economical over long-distance circuits.

This book amply demonstrates the variety of data networks that can benefit from the introduction of frame relay. Jim Cavanagh has described real companies that have implemented frame relay to further their business. He presents some quite modest networks and a vast global network; companies who've installed their own frame relay switches and those who've taken frame relay service from one of the public carriers. Some companies have shown how frame relay and IP complement one another, while others show how frame relay prepares a network to move on to ATM, if that is the chosen strategic direction. Some of these networks look back, and show how frame relay can be used to modernise a "legacy" technology, while others point forward and are taking advantage of emerging capabilities for carrying voice over frame relay.

This book shows how frame relay technology can be of real benefit to different businesses, and it equips managers to assess its potential, and possible pitfalls, for their own situation. It is not intended to provide a comprehensive reference work on frame relay, but it provides enough information for the reader to appreciate the key decisions made by different companies in selecting and implementing data networking technology. This has been achieved by examining real installations, looking at both the business and technical issues that were taken into account and the lessons learnt. Here is an opportunity for commercially focused managers to understand how different network technologies can give the best value for the business as a whole and for engineers to better appreciate the commercial impact of the decisions that they are making.

The focus of this book is naturally on implementations in North America, since that is where the commercial and competitive forces driving frame relay have been strongest and have led to the strong growth and development of the technology. As the needs of users around the world demand more effective data networks, and telecommunications regulations continue to be relaxed, many of the principles applying now in North America will apply elsewhere.

Jim Cavanagh is well placed to chart this territory for he has been directly involved in setting up many frame relay networks over the past five years. I hope you find this account as illuminating and instructive as I have done. If you are responsible for the upgrade of a data network, then I'm sure you'll find many valuable pointers to issues and opportunities that you can apply in your own situation. This book will stimulate network providers as they consider the possibilities for new services. And it will stimulate network managers as they look for solutions to meet their users' demands for the twenty-first century.

Contents

Chapter 11   Global Multiservice Backbone Network   233

debis Systemhaus (Daimler-Benz)

Chapter 12   IP LAN Internetwork   259

UUNet Technologies, Inc.

Chapter 13 Data and Voice over Frame Relay 283

Allen Lund Company

Part 5   The Future 309

Chapter 14 The Future of Frame Relay 311

Preface

The project that became the bound pages that you are now holding began as the answer to some important questions. The questions are all simple ones about frame relay: What is it? Why use it? Who cares about the technology and its deployment? Where does it make the most sense and have the biggest business impact? How are the benefits derived? And when will it be deployed widely enough to truly have an impact? A quick survey of magazines, journal articles, and book projects released and underway at the time revealed easy answers to *what* and *when,* leaving us to ponder *why, who, where,* and *how.* I couldn't resist including my own version of *what* and *when,* but focused most of my attention on the other four.

Digging deeper into the early literature, it was clear that what little material was available was either highly technical—and therefore virtually unusable to the business community, which must approve expenditures, make investments, and assess results—or very benefit/marketing oriented—and therefore not usable to technical people actually trying to deploy frame relay technology. It was clear from the outset that a single book that merges both the business and technical aspects of frame relay implementation would be most helpful. And, because I have been applications-focused for the decade and a half of my career, a book that presented this information in an application case study format made the most sense. I saw this project as a chance to really look deeply into a variety of frame relay implementations and use the detailed understanding to draw some higher-level conclusions about the technology and its usefulness.

Book Objectives

For any specific situation, it is impossible to find an exact blueprint that can be implemented directly from the pages of a book. Therefore, this book has been written to show enough instances of frame relay applications for you to be able to draw meaningful conclusions about the technology and to find sufficient patterns and similarities to be able to reliably apply what you have learned in this book to your own situation. The objective of putting all of the business and technology information about frame relay applications in one place is to equip you to better understand frame relay in general as well as shortening the time frames needed to evaluate frame relay and its suitability in a given communications environment.

You will, of course, have your own objectives—objectives that are consistent with your own personal and professional missions. It might be a good idea to compare your own set of objectives with those general objectives we have established and used for guidance in the preparation of this book. Our general objectives are that after completing this book you will

- understand frame relay business benefits
- understand frame relay technologies and standards
- understand the interrelationship of both
- be able to avoid problems encountered by the case study companies in their implementations
- take advantage of the case study companies' experiences and hard-learned lessons.
- make intelligent decisions about the use of frame relay and other technologies in your own environment

This is a very good point at which to carefully consider these objectives and your own and to set some goals for yourself before reading this book. Doing so will keep your mind focused on the questions and problems that exist in your own environment that, we hope, will be solved as a result of reading this book.

Approach

Our approach to this book has been to exploit the information we have about case studies without repeating a lot of information available from other sources. We begin with two introductory chapters, one about business aspects of frame relay and the other about technology aspects. Both are designed specifically to provide a foundation for the case study information that comes later. These chapters are followed by four conceptual case studies that represent composites of needs from different companies Because elements of the case studies are pulled from many different companies, they become almost ideal examples that can very clearly represent pros and cons, features and benefits, and details that couldn't be attributed to any one company. The four conceptual case studies are followed by six case studies from real companies. The real world nature of these case studies allows us many opportunities to see how things really work, what can go right and what can go wrong, how the case study subject companies reacted and solved problems, and what problems remain. In many ways, these case studies are the most useful in considering how frame relay will work in a specific environment. In many other ways, however, they are the most frustrating because things like nondisclosure agreements or corporate policies keep us from publishing some of the details in any but summary form. But, taken together with the more academic conceptual case studies, they do paint a very full picture of frame relay and its business and technology aspects.

Target Audience

While writing this book, I tried to picture myself teaching the material directly to you in a one-on-one tutorial session. I tried to say things that were meaningful to you and to explain things in such a way that you would be able to take the information back and apply it to your own work situations. My vision of you changed from time to time as I tried to picture you and assess your needs. Who are you? Are you always anxious to learn, even after hours without breaks, objecting vehemently whenever our sessions are interrupted? Are you on schedule overload or always on call, but ready to set beeper and cell phone aside when we get to material of the most interest to you? Are you the Telecom or Project Manager, or are you the Planner, involved in the strategic, rather than tactical, aspects of technology deployment, or the Sales Consultant, a sponge for information because you need to wear many hats at different points in the sales cycle? Or are you the Master's Degree Candidate, the College Professor, the Corporate Chief Financial Officer or Chief Information Officer, the Technologist, the Internet/Intranet Planner, the Sales Executive, the Purchasing Supervisor, the Big Firm Consultant, even the Trade Press Writer, or maybe one of many others who appeared in my mind's eye as fingers contacted keys and this book took shape? Whichever of these people you are, I feel that there is a wealth of information here if you will take and put it to good use.

Web Site

One of the most frustrating aspects of developing any type of material is the inevitable decision about how to organize all of the information we have so that you may get the most benefit from it. I have tried to make available important information and frame-relay-related resources in the chapters of this book, in the appendix, and in a more dynamic form on the World Wide Web. The book's Web page can be reached via the Morgan Kaufmann Web site at `http://www.mkp.com`. The Web page contains such diverse items as questions that may be used for self-study or classroom study as a companion to this book, copies of related documents, and pointers to other frame relay resources. I hope you find it truly useful, and I welcome your feedback.

Acknowledgments

As a frequent reader of acknowledgments, I have always wondered where an author finds all of the names to include in this section. It was not until the conclusion of this project that I personally came to realize how many people impact the outcome of a book of this type and their various roles. In my own case, the reason why I was even in a position to write this book, with all due respect to my elementary school English teachers, was because of my long-time friend and former manager, Jerry Bahr. It was Jerry who gave me the confidence, encouragement, and opportunity to write my first published article and to do my first presentation at a technical symposium. And it is Jerry Bahr, and Phil Evans of Perot Systems, who have been trusted mentors, advisors, and guardian angels, both personally and professionally, over the course of many years.

There have been others who have made their mark on my life, as well. It is to Tom Johnson of Teletutor, Jim Brown and Susan Collins of *Net-*

work World, and Paul Berk formerly of Auerbach Publishers to whom I owe a deep debt of gratitude for all of the hours they each spent not only correcting my writing problems, but, more importantly, taking the time to explain *why*—in effect, taking this blob of clay that Jerry began to form and adding more definition and shape and hoping that a writer would appear, which is not quite what happened, but at least an engineer was made better able to communicate his thoughts.

Chris Heckart of TeleChoice, with whom I worked when she was at WilTel pioneering frame relay with Robert Gourley and Tom Pickren, and Stephen Taylor of Distributed Networking Associates both deserve special mention for the technical and philosophical guidance they provided in the crucial early days of the concept development and preparation of the first case studies for this book. Other reviewers of the book in various draft forms should also be recognized for their various contributions: Fred Knight of *Business Communications Review,* Curt Harler of *Communications News,* Jim Metzler of Strategic Networks Consulting, Mike Minnich of DuPont, Jeffrey Kipnis of Ameritech, Gerald Proctor and Bob Brown of Greyhound Lines, Tom Maurer and Rosemary Ede of Caliber Technology, Ken Lund of the Allen Lund Company, and Anthony Harris of British Telecom. Anthony, in addition to being our "international correspondent," was gracious enough to write the foreword for the book and to take this book project on as a personal task, providing insight and stewardship when it was most direly needed. I would also like to thank reviewers and case study subjects Allan Taffel and Kevin Boyne of UUNET, who, even though our encounter was measured in mere hours, enlightened me in many ways and changed many of my philosophical paradigms about the world of advanced networking technologies and their deployment and impact.

Lest we forget the many behind-the-scenes people who made this project come to fruition—and we won't forget—we should mention the superb orchestration of the production process, which was coordinated by Yonie Overton and Elisabeth Beller of Morgan Kaufmann, the surgical accuracy of the copyedit by Ken DellaPenta, and the thorough, precise, and timely support and administrative assistance of Jane Elliott, who, like the proverbial Northern Star, was always there, and the superb efforts of Christine Corliss of AT&T and Clare Whitecross of StrataCom (now a part of Cisco Systems, Inc.). Special recognition also goes to Jeanette Sanwald and Bob Etzel of Telecommunications Research Associates (TRA). Jeanette worked tirelessly to create the beautiful graphics that fill this book from some simple line art I provided, and Bob has been very supportive of this project and will oversee the development of a class based upon this book, which will be a part of the repertoire of TRA and be coupled with the existing Understanding Frame Relay curriculum.

And last, and most importantly, I would like to acknowledge the unflagging, constant, and complete support of Jennifer Mann, my editor at Morgan Kaufmann Publishers, who both weathered the storms and celebrated the successes that we encountered in the spirit of true partnership and toiling together toward mutual goals. Without the dedication and support of Jennifer Mann, neither this volume nor any that will follow it in the Technology Applications: Business and Technology Case Studies series would be even remotely possible.

I have tried to put every bit of information into these pages that space considerations and nondisclosure agreements would allow, hoping to make this a truly useful text. You, the reader, are now tasked with going forward and applying this information to your own job situation and for your own gain and benefit. Good luck in your mission.

PART ONE

Frame Relay Overview

CHAPTER ONE

Frame Relay in Perspective

Frame relay represents one of the most important paradigm shifts in modern telecommunications: a shift away from network-based intelligence and complexity toward a simplified, streamlined network infrastructure that provides simple, cost-effective, multiplexed information paths between intelligent devices. The most important indicators of frame relay's success have been overwhelming market acceptance and near global availability from a wide variety of public network carriers and service providers as well as in several private networking variations.

Numerous articles, books, videos, and computer-based training packages exist that explain the basic mechanisms of frame relay, its history, and standardization. But this book goes beyond the basics and delves into the intricacies of frame relay through ten case studies: four conceptual case studies representing a combination of requirements from several companies and six real-life case studies that chronicle the efforts of individual companies in their implementation of frame relay. The six individual company case studies represent a rare opportunity for you to look closely at the issues and problems that real companies encountered in their implementation of frame relay and the solutions they derived. In many cases these solutions may be generalized to your own situation, but in just as many cases the solutions will be directly applicable to your specific requirements.

1.1   What Is Frame Relay?

What is frame relay? The answer to this question depends upon whom you ask. If you pose this question to the corporate telecom manager or vice president of enterprise networking, you may get answers as wide ranging as "a cost-saving data transport technology," "a single, globally unifying information transport technology," "a new communications system that allows cost-effective data and voice networking," "a bridge to asynchronous transfer mode (ATM) and other cost-effective high-speed information transport systems of the future," or "something we've started using because we need networking flexibility and ATM isn't ready yet." The network administrator or telecom engineer might answer in a more technical way, often ignoring the cost-saving aspects and focusing instead on other aspects of frame relay. Network administrators or telecom engineers might provide answers such as "a new networking technology that allows multiple logical paths to be connected via a single access line to form virtual meshed networks," "a new way of sharing network bandwidth that provides flexibility and higher effective throughputs through oversubscription and instantaneous dynamic bandwidth allocation," "one of three emerging broadband technologies currently available in the marketplace," or even "the heir apparent to X.25 and older public networking systems."

Whatever the answer, it is clear that the "usual answer" does not take into account both the business and technical aspects of frame relay. In fact, most articles, white papers, and books written about frame relay have taken into account only business or only technology aspects. But in the telecommunications marketplace both the business and technical aspects of any technology must be well understood before a new technology is widely adopted.

What is the "right answer" to the question "What is frame relay?" While the "right answer" will highlight the specific individual's area of interest and background, one "right answer" might include both business and technology aspects: "Frame relay is an emerging technology, available in both public and private networking implementations, that provides configuration flexibility, high-speed interfaces, and a framework for integrating traditional SNA and packet data, bursty LAN data, Internet connectivity, and, under some circumstances, voice and/or video communications in a cost-effective manner. Frame relay is being used by many companies to implement their tactical and strategic plans today as well as to provide a bridge to future technologies such as asynchronous transfer mode."

1.2 What Isn't Frame Relay?

Frame relay isn't an instant solution to all networking problems: many problems that existed before frame relay will continue to exist after the implementation of frame relay. Delays caused by components outside the network, slow host computer response, or poor applications software design, for example, will not be eliminated by the implementation of frame relay, nor will it solve problems related to poor training or inexperience of personnel using communications systems.

Even though frame relay is suitable for use in a wide range of applications, it is not right for everyone. And, in many cases, older, traditional, existing systems are doing a very adequate job at a very reasonable cost. In these cases the cost of upgrades plus the cost of migration does not make a move to frame relay justifiable. The determination to move to any new system, whether it be frame relay or any other technology, should be based on an expectation, grounded on real facts, that the technology will contribute in some measurable way to the overall goals and objectives of the organization.

1.3 Frame Relay's Life Cycle

All technologies generally go through four distinct phases of their life cycle: (1) new technology introduction, (2) early adoption, (3) general acceptance, and (4) legacy. We will discuss each of the four phases of technology life cycles as it relates to frame relay in an attempt to develop a better understanding of frame relay and how it has evolved and will continue to evolve. We will look first at factors affecting the duration of each phase of technology evolution and then look at the phases themselves.

1.3.1 Duration of Technology Life Cycle Phases

The duration of each phase of the life cycle of a new technology is very important from both a business and a technology perspective. From a technology perspective, the anticipated duration of each phase indicates to technologists and standards makers both the impact of their efforts and how resources should be allocated for further development and refinement.

If a technology is a very-short-duration solution to a problem that exists in transitioning between two technology phases, then not a lot of time and effort is justified. On the other hand, if a new technology or potential technology allows a sweeping new architectural approach that revolutionizes the marketplace and enables new capabilities not even dreamed of previously, then the technology is worth a large investment of human and financial resources to further develop and refine. Likewise, from a business perspective, companies are reluctant to spend their money on temporary measures and would rather make longer-term investments in sound technologies that will continue to deliver their desired results for the long term.

The length of time a technology is in each phase is affected by many factors, such as

- marketplace requirements
- impact in solving new problems or replacing existing technology
- direct applicability of new technology
- speed of market entry of competing technologies
- marketplace acceptance

In order to better understand each of these key points generally, and their importance in the frame relay context specifically, we will look at each of these reasons in more depth.

Marketplace Requirements

A new technology may appear promising, but if it does not address the true needs of the marketplace, as determined through testing and "after the sale" performance, it will be short-lived. Frame relay addresses several true needs of the marketplace, such as cost savings in a simple and streamlined package, domestic and international standards compliance, and near global availability, and the timing of its arrival has been fortuitous both for users as well as product manufacturers and service providers. Frame relay represents more than just a bridge between older technologies and a future filled with asynchronous transfer mode, wave division multiplexing, and photonic switching; frame relay represents a simple, streamlined transport technology that operates in a manner the marketplace can easily understand and is simple to implement, compared to other technologies.

Impact in Solving New Problems or Replacing Existing Technology

New "breakthrough" technologies are often adopted much more quickly if they offer solutions to long-standing problems than if they simply replace existing solutions. Because frame relay is a replacement technology (replacing X.25 and leased lines), it is being adopted much more slowly than if it was truly a breakthrough technology delivering capabilities never before available. The cost savings aspects of frame relay have greatly helped justify adoption, but still some companies considering the use of frame relay are occasionally reluctant to move away from their existing working, well-understood systems, regardless of possible cost savings.

Direct Applicability of New Technology

The easier it is for the marketplace to understand the direct applicability of a new technology and to determine where and how to use it, the better the technology will fare in the marketplace in terms of adoption and a long, profitable life cycle. Frame relay is a fairly straightforward technology that counts among its many benefits simpler installation and operation than some prior technologies it is replacing, such as X.25, and lower cost and leveraging of shared bandwidth networks not possible with some other technologies being replaced (i.e., leased lines, satellite networks, and similar systems and services).

Speed of Market Entry of Competing Technologies

The decades-old marketing concept of FUD (fear, uncertainty, and doubt) plays an important role in the adoption, and rate of adoption, of any new technology. As in the personal computer marketplace, it is possible to remain reluctant to purchase a new technology until its life cycle has passed entirely. The fear of buying something that will be outdated tomorrow is ever present in the telecommunications marketplace. Frame relay suffered early on from the "should I buy frame relay today or wait until ATM comes along" delay until the position of frame relay in the low- to medium-speed (64 Kbits/second to 55 Mbits/second) space was clearly understood and plans for frame-relay-to-ATM interworking were clearly enumerated.

Marketplace Acceptance

A widespread adoption of a new technology is also a reason to continue to support it, update it, and create new versions of it. The size of the installed base of a technology is an important factor in determining the length of time it will be viable in the marketplace. One place where we are seeing this factor come into play strongly is with time division multiplexing (TDM) systems. Customers clearly understand the benefits of moving away from the older circuit-switched TDM systems (which apportion bandwidth in fixed channels) to a cell relay or high-speed packet or frame-switching system (which allows true dynamic bandwidth-on-demand, oversubscription of port and trunk bandwidth, and enhanced rerouting inside the network), but they are tied by several factors to their older, less-capable TDM technology. Some of the many factors are substantial financial investments in the installed equipment base, extensive experience with the operation and management of these systems, and investment in test systems and training.

Frame relay has been adopted in many different companies across a wide range of industries and is realizing the depth of penetration that is possible as these companies begin to use frame relay in a wider range of applications. Because frame relay's user base is growing and frame relay is being used more and more frequently in both support and mission-critical systems, it will be difficult for the next technology in the door to dislodge frame relay, just as TDM is embedded and difficult to dislodge, even when the drawbacks are obvious. This trend indicates that frame relay's general acceptance phase may be a very long one.

1.3.2   Technology Life Cycle

We will now look at the four phases in the life cycle of frame relay. We will discuss the new technology introduction phase and early adoption phase historically because frame relay has already gone through these phases. We will discuss the general acceptance phase in the present tense because that is the phase in which we currently find frame relay, and a phase in which it will be for some time to come. We will then try to make some educated guesses about the future of frame relay and the technology and market forces that will cause its legacy phase to begin.

Phase 1: New Technology Introduction

Many industry pundits described frame relay early on as a "solution looking for a problem." While this was certainly true of frame relay when it was still tightly coupled with the baseband Integrated Services Digital Network (ISDN) standards, the early marketers of ISDN-independent frame relay were certainly very clear and accurate in their positioning of frame relay for LAN internetworking. While certainly far more capable than simply as a "WAN for LANs," frame relay's initial market introduction in the area of LAN internetworking and interconnection solved many problems: market acceptance, carrier acceptance, and shortening the uptake cycle.

The first problem was one of market acceptance. Frame relay had been decoupled from the baseband ISDN standards and developed by Strata-Com (now part of Cisco Systems, Inc.) as a new interface that was complementary to their proprietary baseband ATM switching architecture, which was widely used at the time in private networks. When StrataCom's frame relay product had been successfully deployed in a public network variation and was first introduced as a service by Williams Telecommunciations (WilTel) as WilPak in January 1991, the marketplace did not really know what frame relay was or from where it had come. It fell, therefore, to the marketing department at WilTel to craft a good frame relay story, establish competitors to battle against, and create a market. I had the good fortune of being heavily involved with these pioneering efforts as well as assisting in the design and implementation of a network to meet the goals of the marketers and helping to paint the picture created in the minds of the first potential customers.

Even though the typical, and very lucrative, leased-line market was a clear candidate for a first attack, this was strategically and tactically unwise because WilTel was at the time "the carriers' carrier," and the customers for WilTel's fledgling frame relay service could come from no other source than the customer base of WilTel's customers. WilTel still stood to offend their customers, but less strongly, with a foray into the LAN interconnect/LAN internetworking marketplace: a marketplace served by leased lines as well as X.25 packet-switching and infant frame-switched router internetworks. It was also an application that did not have an acceptable solution at that time. WilTel's marketers quickly developed a strong message about the applicability of frame relay for connecting LANs, cast X.25 and SMDS as the primary competitors, and rolled out the WilPak service in January 1991.

The second big hurdle for frame relay was carrier acceptance. While it would appear that WilTel's interests would best be served by occupying the frame relay market space as the sole provider, and thereby dominating this new technology with a 100% market share, this was not so. Single-vendor, proprietary solutions did not last long in the early 1990s and have even shorter life spans in the standards-focused late 1990s. In order to assure long-term acceptance of frame relay, it was necessary for WilTel to join others with a vested interest in the success of this newly introduced technology and push the technology into as many corners of the marketplace as possible. WilTel, StrataCom, DEC, and Northern Telecom hoped that this initiative to build an open frame relay marketplace would attract large investments by competitors and therefore legitimize the market and focus customer attention on frame relay, regardless of which provider supplied the service or products.

Standardization, market education, and industry acceptance were the main ideas behind the inauguration of the Frame Relay Forum, of which WilTel was a charter member, by Cisco Systems, Digital Equipment Corporation, Northern Telecom (now Nortel), and StrataCom. The Frame Relay Forum now numbers several hundred members and includes carriers, users, manufacturers, consultants, standards writers, and academicians. It was not philosophically easy for other carriers to develop frame relay service offerings because they had existing end user leased-line bases; they saw it as a cannibalization of their own revenues, but market realities, such as customer demand and the need to maintain a technology leadership, forced a rethinking of their positions. Some of the smaller, more flexible, and aggressive carriers announced early and looked to the leased-line bases of their larger adversaries for customers, while the larger carriers considered frame relay service offerings as a necessary defensive weapon.

While frame relay itself was conceived in Europe as a part of the International Telecommunications Union–Telecommunications Section (formerly CCITT) standardization efforts, it was born in its independent public and private networking versions in the United States. It was clear from the beginning that, for frame relay to be universally accepted, it must play an important role in domestic networks in countries other than the United States as well as linking multiple domestic networks into international or global networks. Fortunately for frame relay its introduction was contemporaneous with deregulation and privatization of communications monopolies and postal, telephone, and telegraph authorities around the world. Just before or during the same era as frame relay was first widely introduced, the global marketplace saw the creation of international and multinational carriers such as Concert, the partnership between MCI and British Telecom, both of which were, interestingly, by-products of deregulation and privatization, and a vehicle to take frame relay international.

The third big problem was shortening the uptake cycle of the new product offerings and thereby assuring the long-term survival of frame relay in the marketplace—that is, establishing a large market presence before the introduction of important competing technologies like ATM. This was accomplished by advertising the simplicity of frame relay and the flexibility it offered over other alternatives. By attaching sites to a large, robust, resilient backbone network via an access circuit that could be shared by logical connections going to multiple destinations, many of the problems of traditional leased lines, such as their inability to provide dynamic bandwidth sharing and their dedicated, point-to-point nature and associated lower reliability, could be overcome. This is the same model that had been introduced by X.25 network designers 25 years before, but which was problematic with X.25 technology when scaled to larger bandwidths. The problems in scalability are due primarily to higher network latencies caused by more packet-processing overhead, coupled with lower backbone trunk rates and lower access line rates. These scalability problems rendered X.25 incapable of meeting the multimegabit future head-on, even though X.25 still represents an important international public data networking paradigm.

Phase 2: Early Adoption

After the three main barriers of frame relay's new technology introduction phase had been passed, it was time for some actual revenue-generating users of frame relay to emerge. Those who were first to deploy frame relay in their own networks were the pioneers, or early adopters, who took the biggest risks and made the biggest sacrifices to field-test this new technology and pave the way for the users who followed.

The early adopters often had the most knowledge about the interoperation of all of the components of the frame relay service but were woefully inadequate in transmitting this information from their labs to the field engineers and end users who would be involved in the implementation process. Though the early frame relay networks were generally built on sound platforms using good engineering practices, the first paying users were plagued by a lack of knowledge on their own part and on the part of their suppliers and service providers. Consultants with any real experience in frame relay implementation were nonexistent, as were books, white papers, installation guidelines, or any other form of meaningful formal documentation. Although the manufacturers of the frame relay switches and other backbone hardware were generally knowledgeable about their own equipment, they were often completely unaware of the expectations of the customers or the service offerings of their carrier customers. The carriers, in general, only understood the most rudimentary operations of the frame relay switches. Purveyors of routers and other frame relay access devices were generally unaware of any aspect of frame relay except for how their systems had been configured during lab testing and certification, and often with a different manufacturer's switch products than they met in their initial installation attempts in the field. And the end users for the most part were only aware of the fact that the process was supposed to be easy and that the carrier assured them during the pre-sales phase that there would be a high degree of hand-holding during installation and start-up. The first installation or two were closely supervised, and though plodding and difficult, they eventually worked. The subsequent installations often dragged on for a very long time, frequently requiring attention from the lab crew who had performed the initial testing and certification of frame relay interfaces and products.

Phase 3: General Acceptance

Frame relay moved relatively quickly from its introduction in January 1991 through the early adoption phase and into general acceptance around the spring of 1993 or so. Today the most common business benefits of frame relay—lower cost and increased flexibility—are well known, as are many of the technical aspects of frame relay implementation in the most common application area, router networks. Frame relay is generally accepted as an option when looking at different wide area networking technologies.

Important questions remain: "How long will frame relay technology be viable, and will it be displaced by some other technology?" In other words, "How long is frame relay likely to be in the general acceptance phase?" and "What factors might cause it to be moved to the legacy phase?" These questions are more than an academic exercise; they are very important to companies adopting frame relay now in terms of deciding how heavily to rely on frame relay or to what extent to reserve budget dollars for newer technologies. In many ways these two activities are closely related: If purchasers of products and services make increasing financial commitments to frame relay, then frame relay will thrive and will be around longer. On the other hand, if the shrinking budget dollars are reserved for some newer technologies, then frame relay will move through its phases and become obsolete more quickly.

Phase 4: Legacy

The only up-and-coming technology that has looked as though it might hasten frame relay's move toward its legacy phase was asynchronous transfer mode, the switching of multimedia information flows in small, efficient, fixed-length units called "cells." This was, however, before ATM and frame relay, as well as the relationship between frame relay and ATM, were well understood by the marketplace. In the early days of the 1990s, it appeared as though the "frame relay versus ATM" decision was an either/or decision. In the enlightened latter part of the 1990s, most decision makers realize that each has an important role and that those roles are best realized through the adoption of a dual frame relay and ATM strategy, where each is used where its strengths may best be realized: frame relay as a low- to medium-speed access technology and ATM as a high-speed backbone and access technology, with frame-relay-to-ATM interworking providing the bridge between the two. The frame-relay-to-ATM internetworking initiative alone has extended the technology life cycle of frame relay well into the 21st century, as well as making ATM adoption feasible in many organizations requiring an integrated frame/ATM strategy.

Another aspect of the "ATM versus frame relay" debate that was not clearly understood by the marketplace in the earlier days of this decade is also now known: the shifting definition of what is required to provide a multimedia network. It was previously thought that ATM was required for "true" multimedia networking and that frame relay was relegated to data-only networks, something that many suspected would survive only another 10 years or so. But this was not to be the fate of "data-only" networks. Advances in compression and digitization technologies for packet- and frame-based video and voice, fueled in large part by the immense jump in popularity of the multimedia Internet and private corporate intranets, made everything appear to be "data" and slowed the advances of multimedia ATM infrastructures. Many carriers of packet/frame data eschew the use of ATM even when they are forced to use ATM to break the 55-Mbits/second boundaries presently imposed by frame relay. This additional consideration has pushed the arrival of the legacy phase of frame relay out several more years and has provided additional incentive for research and development and standardization efforts for bigger, faster, more capable frame relay.

1.4 Conclusion

Frame relay is a widely accepted and promising new communications technology that is revolutionizing the way we move information. Traditional data, LAN data, and even voice and video are being packed into frames and transmitted over public and private frame relay networks. The next two chapters of this book will provide important background material for a complete understanding of the business and technical aspects of frame relay. Even though you may feel that you are knowledgeable in the "basics" of frame relay, you would be well advised to read these background chapters thoroughly as they provide an important foundation for the rest of the book. Beyond the two following chapters lie the ten case study chapters that form the core of this book, followed by a chapter on the future of frame relay and how it relates to other technologies. Read on, pausing frequently to think about how what you are reading applies directly to your own situation, as well as how the knowledge and experience contained in these pages may be generalized and applied.

PART TWO

Frame Relay Business and Technology Aspects

Frame Relay Business Aspects

It does not matter if the currency units are dollars, marks, francs, pounds, yen, guilders, or rubles, one fact is consistent on a global scale: companies large and small are trying to do more with less and are leveraging telecommunications products and services to extend their business reach. This chapter investigates the potential financial incentives of a move to frame-relay-based networks and highlights some of the methods used to estimate the financial impact of such moves. The second part of this chapter is a review of the frame relay marketplace.

It is also noteworthy that all of the benefits stated in this chapter are true to some extent of a transition to any packet, frame, or cell transport technology when compared to leased lines or time division multiplexing. In keeping with the theme of this book, however, the examples are specific to frame relay.

2.1 The Business Case for Frame Relay

In today's highly cost-conscious business environment, no effort is undertaken unless it is cost justifiable, and a transition to frame relay products and services is no exception. Based on estimated frame relay services revenues of $1.3 billion for 1996 (Vertical Systems Group 1995), it is impossible to ignore frame relay as a potent financial force in the marketplace. Even if frame relay is not the final choice, it is imperative that it at least be in the list of candidate technologies being considered by any organization.

Frame relay costs continue to fall, and such regular changes would certainly make any generalized pricing obsolete very quickly. For this reason, cost comparisons in the cost models in this chapter will be treated in the abstract, and no implication of actual pricing examples will be made, even though specific pricing is used in the case studies, where appropriate. In the case studies we will look in depth at the alternatives to frame relay and their respective pros and cons, but in this chapter we will make the assumption that only frame relay is being analyzed or, where appropriate, that the alternative for comparative purposes is traditional leased lines or time division multiplexing. Unless otherwise stated, we will assume that a public frame relay network service will be the basis of our comparison, as opposed to a private frame relay network.

2.2   Frame Relay Cost Justification Models

There are several variations on the cost justification theme, and several thematic nuances within each, based upon an individual's experience inside an organization and/or personal preferences. In this chapter we will categorize the primary financial approaches to assessing the fiscal impact of frame relay on an organization's telecommunications budget. We will not cover any methodology for assessing the need for telecommunications within a modern organization, though this is an important step that should be accomplished before determining what *kind* of products or services are needed. It is recommended that an organization perform an audit of their needs and applications prior to moving ahead with any type of telecommunications system since telecom represents a substantial part of any organizational budget.

2.2.1   "Raw" Cost Savings Model

The "raw" cost savings model is one of the simplest and most straightforward methods of determining the feasibility of adopting a new procedure or approach. The assumptions of this model are that an investment of some amount of money is applied to a recurring cost such that the recurring cost is reduced. The cost savings analysis takes into account the costs and the savings and estimates a point in the future when the costs will have been repaid (the break-even point). From the break-even point to the end of the useful life of the new system, all of the savings will be returned as a bottom-line contribution that can be applied to any number of possible areas, including profitability.

Let's look at a typical case with frame relay and apply some specific rules of thumb. In this example, an organization presently has 100 56-Kbits/second point-to-point leased lines in a star configuration from various geographic locations to a central computer center. The stated objective from management is pure cost savings, but not at the sacrifice of performance or reliability (as opposed to strategic positioning, consolidation to a single communications transport, or some other objective). The clear statement of objectives at the outset is very important because it drives the process and makes it possible for individuals at the operational level to make decisions about ways to proceed.

Frame Relay Costs Rule of Thumb

An analysis of the present leased lines shows that 3% of the leased lines are to points within the same Local Access Transport Area (LATA) as the data center, another 7% are outside of the LATA but within 300 miles of the data center, 84% are beyond 300 circuit miles but within the continental United States, and 6% are international.

One rule of thumb regarding cost-effective frame relay pricing applies very clearly here. It has three distinct parts:

1. Frame relay may or may not be cost competitive within the LATA (this varies by LATA).
2. Leased lines are generally more cost competitive from the edge of the LATA out to a distance of approximately 300 miles.
3. Beyond 300 miles, frame relay is typically more cost competitive (all the way to the extent of including global networks).

The main reason why this rule of thumb works is that leased lines are priced on a distance-sensitive basis, while frame relay pricing is generally distance insensitive. While it is possible to charge for frame relay permanent virtual connections (PVCs) on a distance-sensitive basis, most carriers have adopted the distance-insensitive pricing model, which is easier and preferred by most customers. The only area of frame relay pricing that might be found that is distance sensitive is the pricing of local access circuits.

Because the cost of a leased line is distance sensitive, the price rises as a function of distance, while the price of a frame relay PVC is flat for a given bandwidth; the lines cross at about 300 miles of leased-line distance. Said a different way, a leased line from Atlanta, Georgia, to Detroit, Michigan (a distance of about 600 miles) is more expensive than a leased line from Atlanta, Georgia, to Charlotte, North Carolina (a distance of about 230 miles) because leased lines are priced based primarily on circuit miles. A frame relay PVC from Atlanta to Detroit and from Atlanta to Charlotte would cost the same (assuming that the same bandwidth were guaranteed to each PVC), regardless of the distances involved, because frame relay is typically priced based upon the cost of connecting to the backbone network plus some allocated piece of the total cost of the shared "bandwidth pool" to be used by the customer.

It is also possible for carriers to offer "tiered" or "banded" pricing, which may provide one price for PVC connections within a country and another price for international PVCs. It is also possible in some cases to have the international pricing divided on the basis of intracontinental and intercontinental traffic.

Frame relay pricing may either be fixed or, if it is variable, the variable is traffic dependent and not distance dependent. This is one of the most important aspects of frame relay pricing when considering cost savings versus leased lines.

Returning to our example, we will leave the metropolitan area discussion alone (because of all of the possible local variations) and concentrate on the 90% of the circuits that are greater than 300 miles in length. A comparison of the total cost of the 56-Kbits/second leased lines versus 56-Kbits/second frame relay shows that straight replacement will yield a cost savings in excess of 50%. But the objectives stated that we must save costs without sacrificing performance or reliability. Let's look at each separately: we will look at reliability first, and then performance.

Reliability Issues

The reliability of frame relay is actually better than that of traditional leased lines because public frame relay networks ordinarily offer rerouting within the network in case of network failures (this should, of course, be verified with the carrier or service provider because rerouting within the network is a feature of the service offerings and is not mandated by frame relay standards). If a leased line fails, then it is down until it is repaired. The only alternative in this case is to wait or to provide a dial backup connection. It must also be stressed here that the architecture of frame relay is such that the rerouting around a failure only occurs if the failure is in the network itself and that frame relay is still subject to failures of the local access loop (a problem that can be solved with dial backup).

Performance Issues

Regarding performance, leased lines and frame relay are two fundamentally different approaches to moving information. Leased lines are dedicated pathways that provide a constant and very low delay while bits are moved sequentially across the wire from one location to the other. Frame relay moves variable-length packages of bits through shared circuits and intermediate switching devices, and this process introduces variable and sometimes very large delays. Because leased lines are dedicated, they can always be expected to deliver the same performance every time, but because frame relay is based upon sharing of intermediate facilities, delay is a by-product of the cost savings. The general rule of thumb in this case is to provide higher bandwidths. Typically bandwidth is thought of for capacity purposes (the traditional view), but increasingly there is a paradigm shift to thinking about bandwidth for speed. This is especially true when substantially larger bandwidths in the access and backbone parts of a network can be used in a broadband fashion by lower-speed logical circuits in such a way that information can burst to some peak and that the peak speeds achieved during information transport can offset delays.

As an example, let's consider a 64-Kbits/second leased line. On the leased line, 64,000 bits every second will move across the wire, and their movement will be locked to a clock such that one bit moves each 1/64,000th of a second. If there are fewer than 64,000 bits of real information to send, then some filler bits will be inserted to make up the proper number of bits in the line of bits moving from sender to receiver. If there are more than 64,000 bits of real information during a second, the bits will simply have to wait their turn in the line of bits moving at a rate of 64,000 each second. If more capacity is required, it will be necessary to change the clock speed upward to move more bits each second, and conversely if less capacity is needed, the clock speed may be adjusted downward to move fewer bits per second. This is clearly bandwidth used for capacity purposes.

Now let's look at frame relay. Let's say that in our frame relay example we have a logical connection (which is the term we will use in lieu of "circuit") of 64 Kbits/second. A logical circuit simply means that we expect to send an average of 64,000 bits per second. If a logical 64-Kbits/second connection does not have 64,000 bits of real information to send each second, no problem, other logical circuits sharing the network may use the bandwidth. Because we are considering the 64-Kbits/second connection as an average, it is possible that it will send fewer than 64,000 bits per second, but it is also possible that it may send more than 64,000 bits per second. In order for the average to be about 64 Kbits/second, we also must have some way of sending more than 64,000 bits per second. We do this by establishing the 64-Kbits/second connection on a network that provides greater than 64-Kbits/second circuits inside the network and a greater than 64-Kbits/second access circuit to the network. As an example, let's say that the access to the network is 128 Kbits/second and that the network's internal trunks are at least operating at the T1 rate of 1.5 Mbits/second.

When our anticipated 64,000 bits of information per second is sent, it is actually sent at the access rate of 128,000 bits per second and therefore gets into the network in half a second (half a second faster than the 64-Kbits/second circuit could possibly do it), and then, once inside the network, our bits travel at the network speed of 1.5 million bits per second, or 1/24 the time the 64 Kbits/second circuit requires. So, what do we do with all of the time we've saved by transmitting information at the faster access and network internal trunk speeds? The bits do travel faster when they travel, but they are also delayed more often as well, and the net effect is a similar performance, at the lower speeds, when the access rate is double that of the connection rate.

What this means for our example is that even though a one-for-one frame relay replacement at 56 Kbits/second of the 56-Kbits/second leased lines would yield the greatest cost savings, this is not feasible from a performance standpoint. In fact, based on our rule of thumb, replacing the 56-Kbits/second leased lines with 64-Kbits/second PVCs over 128-Kbits/second frame relay access circuits will yield a slightly better performance at a cost savings of 30–40% over the leased lines.

Cost Savings Model Example

Other factors that now need to be taken into account are the costs of additional software or hardware needed to adapt the existing systems to use the frame relay network as well as costs of migration, including downtime, personnel costs, interim costs of running the old and new system in parallel (if needed), training, and any other costs.

Another financial impact that can be taken into account would be the costs of any personnel who might be reassigned as a result of a move to a frame relay public network managed in whole or in part by the carrier. The assumption for this example will be that two network engineers would be made available for other duties and that their reassignment represents a

Table 2.1   **Cost Savings Example**

Analysis of Recurring (Monthly) Costs

Present leased-line costs	$100,000 per month
Frame relay costs	60,000 per month
Personnel cost savings	10,000 per month
Savings on recurring costs	50,000 per month

Analysis of One-Time Costs

Additional equipment costs	$250,000 one time
(could be special routers, SNA-to-frame-relay conversion equipment, DSU/CSU equipment, etc.)	
Additional training	20,000 one time
Installation of frame relay	80,000 one time
Deinstallation of leased lines	45,000 one time
Total one-time costs	395,000 one time

Cost Recovery Analysis

One-time costs	$395,000
Divided by	50,000 savings per month
Equals	7.9 months before the savings pay for the one-time costs

cost savings because they displace two new persons who would otherwise have had to be hired to fill two open job requisitions.

Table 2.1 shows one example of how this analysis would be performed conceptually. This analysis, while not based on actual costs, is representative in terms of the cost recovery period. Companies often demand that a cost-saving change be paid for within the first 12 months of operation, and 9- to 11-month payback periods for the type of transitions to frame relay discussed here are typical. The variables are present leased-line costs and the new frame relay costs, cost of new equipment, training, installation, and related costs, and will, of course, vary by specific instance, but the ratios will be approximately as stated in this example.

Some additional calculations may be applied here to fine-tune the estimate even further, such as calculating the additional impact of borrowing the money for the one-time costs and repaying the loan over the payback period and other similar things, which will be left to the accountants and actuaries. There is one more step, however, that we might wish to take to show our cost savings in the best possible light: the Kriensian bottom-line contribution model.

2.2.2   Kriensian Bottom-Line Contribution Model

Assuming all of the calculations of the prior example have been performed twice and found to be correct, most managers, salespeople, or network administrators trying to cost-justify a move to frame relay (or any new system) would simply stop and submit their findings to upper management for approval. But there is one more step that can be performed that can highlight the true positive impact of the cost savings on the organization's bottom line.

Let's assume that the organization is a profit-making entity and that the organization's profit margin is 50%. What this means is that for each dollar the organization brings in, 50 cents goes to profit and 50 cents goes to overhead, cost of goods or services, and so on. In the prior example, after the first 7.9 months, the move to frame relay is causing the organization not to have to spend $50,000 per month. If the profit margin is 50%, then the $50,000 per month represents the same bottom-line contribution that $100,000 in sales per month would make. Twice as impressive as $50,000 per month, but that is assuming that the profit margin is 50%. In businesses where the profit margin is even smaller, like 10%, the difference in impact of the same figures is even more impressive: $500,000 in sales! And if the bottom-line contribution is annualized, it is possible to say that "the bottom-line impact of moving to the frame relay network, assuming a 10% profit margin, would be the same as increasing sales by $6 million annually."

2.2.3   Productivity Improvement Model

The productivity improvement model evaluates the positive impact on productivity (and its resulting financial impact) as a result of the introduction of some new system or methodology. The assumptions of this model are that the actual costs of each human whose productivity is being positively affected is known and that the financial impact of any improvement can thereby be quantified. This is a common method of cost justification for movement to a new frame relay system, but it can be problematic because real productivity increases are often difficult to judge. As an example, it is possible to do something faster or more efficiently and not have a net positive financial impact. Picture a small rural office of an insurance company. The fact that an insurance claim takes five hours to process by

hand and one hour to process by the new computer system is hardly important financially if the office only processes one claim per week. The resulting time savings do not benefit the insurance company if the time saved is
not applied to other meaningful work. (It is possible, however, to make a
good case for the positive impact of improved customer service, especially
if there is competition in town, but this is another justification we will
discuss later.)

Now, instead of a single five-hour transaction without another in the
queue behind it to be done, let's discuss the positive impact on productivity of a series of very short transactions. Let's look at a customer service
center with distributed sites that rely on a central, remote computer center
for product data. If each request to the remote computer for product data
takes 30 seconds, and it is possible to improve the speed of retrieval by
improved communications between the remote and central systems such
that the retrieval time is cut to 20 seconds, then a 33% time savings results.
And because there are callers waiting in the queue immediately behind the
present callers, there will be something to do with the time that has been
saved.

If the average call is three minutes before the improvements to the communication system, and each average call requires three retrievals, it is
possible to determine the cost savings due to the improvements in the communications system. Let's make some further assumptions. Let's assume
an average call center operator providing first-line assistance to callers costs
$20 per hour, including salary, insurance, their computer terminal, and
other overhead costs. And let's assume that there are enough calls to keep
the call center busy. These assumptions would be used for the calculations
in Table 2.2.

Based on the results shown in Table 2.2, it is possible to multiply 16%
by the total budget for call center operators to determine a net savings, but
that is only possible if the hourly call center operators go home 16% early
and do not service the additional calls, or if the call center staff is reduced
by 16%, a more likely approach. We have demonstrated a cost saving, but
with no clear bottom-line impact to the company, simply handling more
customer assistance calls, which is important, but still an overhead cost
and not one that contributes to the bottom line directly. Only by reducing
staff and keeping call volumes constant can we show a savings. This statement is true if management has not been considering additional expenditures to increase call center staff. If they have, we can look at the cost
displacement model.

Table 2.2   **Sample Productivity Increase Cost Justification**

Analysis of Present Average Call	
Average time	3 minutes
Average number of remote retrievals	3 per call
Average time per retrieval	30 seconds
Average total retrieval time	90 seconds
Average calls per hour per operator	20 calls/hour
Cost per call center operator	$20 per hour or $1 per call
Cost per 3-minute 800 call	$ .30
Average cost per call	$1.30

Analysis of Average Call after New System Installation	
Average time (30-second savings due to savings of 10 seconds per retrieval over existing system × 3 average retrievals per call)	2.5 minutes
Average number of remote retrievals	3 per call
Average time per retrieval	20 seconds
Average total retrieval time	60 seconds
Average calls per hour per operator	24 calls/hour
Cost per call center operator	$20 per hour or $ .84 per call
Cost per 2.5-minute 800 call	$ .25
Average cost per call	$1.09

Cost Savings Analysis	
Cost for existing system	$1.30 per call
Cost for new system	$1.09 per call
Savings per operator	$ .21 per call or 16%

2.2.4   Cost Displacement Model

The cost displacement model assumes that additional expenditures were going to be made and that the improvements in a system or procedure that result will either eliminate, or at least greatly reduce, the additional expenditures. Usually a one-time investment will be used to reduce or eliminate a recurring cost. Looking back at the prior example, the case of a customer service call center, if management were going to increase computer terminal positions and staff in order to handle more calls and it were possible to make a one-time investment to reduce the monthly cost for people and equipment, the savings might be very attractive. In this case, our 16% savings could be viewed as a way of getting 16% more work from the same group of people. If the plans were to expand the call center by 15%, then they would not have to expand the call center at all as a result of the productivity increases. On the other hand, if the plans were to expand the center by 30%, half the cost would be displaced by improvements and 16% of the remaining half would not be required either, assuming the 30% increase were calculated based on old efficiencies and per call averages.

2.2.5 Increased Sales or Revenues Model

The assumptions to this point have been that the call center in question is an overhead function and that questions are being answered free of charge for existing customers on a toll-free 800 or 888 service. If we change the model around and assume that callers are either purchasing products or are being charged for the technical assistance that they are getting, the 16% increase in efficiency would represent additional sales or revenue, and we could then use the increased sales or revenues model.

The increased sales or revenues model assumes that sales or service revenues are being generated and that an improvement in a system or procedures will also improve the sales or revenues directly. Will leasing cell phones for salespeople in the field increase sales?

The answer is yes if the cell phones allow them to make more customer contacts during otherwise wasted time (such as driving or commuting on the train). But the answer is no if the cellular phones simply allow the salespeople to talk to each other during these "otherwise wasted times" about how bad their compensation plans are. In our prior example, if the call center is generating revenues, it would obviously be beneficial to increase efficiencies and call center operator positions until customer wait times were minimized and queue depths averaged one caller waiting per operator position. (Even though we would like to say that it is beneficial to eliminate caller waiting entirely, it is actually better to have the incoming caller wait briefly than to have the call center operators idle for any period of time.)

In the increased sales or revenues model, we would simply take any resulting efficiencies and multiply times present sales or revenue volumes to determine the positive impact. Sales of $1 million per year would translate in our case into sales of $1.16 million per year, assuming that the present system could not handle all of the calls and that callers were either not calling back or were calling competitors. Callers calling back during less busy times would not figure into this equation because their revenues would be counted already, but it would be a part of the "intangible" enhanced customer service model.

2.2.6 Intangibles Model

One of the very best things any department within an organization can do from a planning standpoint is to get in line with an organization's mission statement. The question that each department must ask is, What is the primary goal or focus of this organization, and how can we support it? The answer to this question is very important in looking at the possible intangible benefits of new technologies or procedures and how they will benefit the organization.

Competitive Advantage

Competitive advantage is an intangible, or "soft," benefit because it is impossible to determine, at least in advance, the impact of a competitive advantage. Car rental companies, for instance, that provide roving clerks with handheld wireless terminals have a competitive advantage over those that don't, but is the cost for the people, hardware, and software worth the competitive advantage? Is the additional revenue going to justify the investment? And what happens when the competitors adopt similar systems? Is there another way to stay ahead?

These questions are all very important ones to answer, but there is one additional hurdle that must be overcome when looking at the competitive advantages provided by a technology like frame relay that is not readily visible to the customer in the way that wandering employees with handheld terminals are. In the case of frame relay, it is necessary to translate the results of using frame relay into clear competitive benefits. In one case, a manufacturer of commercial and residential lighting had an older PC-based system used by lighting designers and construction engineers to order lighting components. The system would dial the local warehouse and determine inventory levels. If there was insufficient inventory at the local warehouse, the system would drop the call and place another call to the next warehouse, and it would do this in a round-robin fashion until all nine regional warehouses were called. This system was not unlike systems provided by their competitors (and which were even run on the same PC), but the PC operator soon learned that when the second dialing sequence was heard on the PC speaker that it was dialing a second warehouse, and the PC operator would halt the program (because the process of the PC redialing to several warehouses takes time to do and extra time to ship from a remote warehouse) and use a competitor's program until inventory was located at some warehouse on the first call. In order to provide a competitive advantage, the lighting manufacturer realized that it would be necessary to provide an affirmative response on the first call. The lighting manufacturer networked all of their warehouses and production facilities via frame relay so that only one dial-up call was made, even though all warehouses (and the manufacturing management system in the production department) were being checked. The result was to give the customer an affirmative response and a delivery date in over 90% of the cases.

Even though it was not possible to assess the positive impact prior to implementation, the manufacturer felt that the system would pay for itself and was willing to make the investment simply to provide the best customer service. The manufacturer was confident that the best customer service yields the most business. And they were right.

One important note about frame relay as it relates to other technologies; after reading the foregoing example, it is possible to ask why the manufacturer waited so long to network their warehouses, or why frame relay was used instead of leased lines, or why the example worked out so well—and is it a real example? Yes, it is a real example. Remember that frame relay is typically more cost-effective than leased lines. In this case specifically, leased lines were cost prohibitive, and the manufacturer found the cost of the leased-line approach daunting, while frame relay costs were reasonable. Also, the manufacturer was less savvy about the benefits of long-distance data communications at the time they evaluated leased lines than when they looked at frame relay. In the initial evaluation the manufacturer did not realize the difference between the more costly leased-line approach and the dial-up approach: both put a remote customer in touch with information about products they needed, and in the dial-up case the cost of the calls was borne by the customer. It seemed ideal at the time.

Enabling Technology and Strategic Positioning

In many cases an organization has made a decision to move to some new information management approach, such as image processing, client-server, newer automation, and tracking systems, but it lacks the bandwidth to implement the new initiative effectively. Frame relay very often can provide the bandwidth needed at a reasonable cost. Frame relay must, of course, be evaluated along with other technology alternatives, and it is possible that a combination of communications technologies may be required to provide the entire solution.

It is also possible that an organization has embraced broadband communications and technologies (such as SMDS, frame relay, and ATM) as a future direction and wishes to position itself for the emerging ATM world. Using frame relay for this strategic positioning purpose makes a great deal of sense because frame relay, SMDS, and ATM all have a similar logical model, that of multiplexed physical interfaces being used to provide shared access for multiple logical connections to a pool of bandwidth, and frame relay operates on transport units that do not require the adaptation at the edge of the network required by ATM. In other words, frame relay transports variable-length packages of bits by simply adding some limited frame relay information to the beginning and end of the package; ATM chops up, or parses, the variable-length package of bits into small, efficient fixed-length cells, a somewhat more complex process. And, as we discuss in more depth later in the chapter, it is likely that frame relay will be around for a long time, so the use of frame relay for strategic positioning purposes makes very good business sense. This brings us to the last of the intangible benefits: network simplification or consolidation.

Network Simplification or Consolidation

One final "intangible" area, though one whose benefits could at least be estimated with a lot of hard work and many assumptions, is in the area of network simplification and consolidation. Historically the use of technology for this purpose has been put into the cost savings or cost offset category, but history has also shown that sufficiently little is understood about the cost trade-offs of network simplification and/or consolidation that it might be best to just take it on faith that network simplification or consolidation will reward the effort in many ways: cost savings, improved network efficiencies, and network reliability.

Network simplification or consolidation is, quite simply, putting a single new technology, such as frame relay, in place and consolidating the functions of several other older networks onto the single new network. The new network will very likely cost more than any one of the single older networks but less than the sum of the costs of the older networks being replaced. Companies are using frame relay to consolidate older, separate SNA or other legacy computer system terminal networks, LAN interconnections, and, increasingly, internal company telephony networks. The newly created frame-relay-based network requires fewer people to operate than all of the networks being replaced and represents fewer overall components and fewer points of failure, thereby increasing overall network reliability.

2.2.7 Combining Multiple Approaches

While one of the above approaches may make absolute sense for a given situation, it is usually a combination of many approaches to cost justification that makes the final case and garners approval from upper management. The guidelines for presentation of cost justifications for any system (and this is especially true of new frame relay network initiatives) are fairly simple:

- State the benefits in clear, concise business terms.
- Be prepared to support any claims with sound evidence (but do not necessarily present your evidence as a part of the main presentation: provide it as a follow-up to the meeting or have it on slides that you may not use, or provide it as an appendix to a written justification).
- Present benefits and cost savings in decreasing order of interest to the audience (biggest items first, least important last, and take into account your audience's special interests).
- Make good use of graphics and analogies to clearly make points.
- Give examples of other companies who have been successful and their results.

And, most importantly, pick and choose from the approaches suggested here, use your own creative spin, and be aware of any standardized forms or formats that might be used within your company. And do you know of another project that has been approved? It might be beneficial to at least review their approach and get a briefing on areas of special concern or interest on the part of the approvers that might be highlighted in your own presentation.

2.3 Frame Relay Marketplace

In comparison to many technologies, frame relay has not been in the marketplace for very long. Though it has been known of since the late 1970s, the infrastructure to support it was not yet in place. It was not until 1989 that a product was envisioned, and not until 1990 that the product came to market, and not until 1991 that the first public networking service based upon frame relay was announced. In order to better understand the market forces and competitive influences shaping frame relay, we will take a look at the evolution of the competitive landscape and the primary product differentiators and areas of customer emphasis over frame relay's short life span.

2.3.1 Evolution of Competitive Landscape

There have been two common threads throughout the entire history of frame relay: cost savings and frame relay's relationship with ATM (see Figure 2.1). The cost question has always been consistent: does frame relay offer enough cost savings or other quantifiable benefits to justify its use? As competitive pressures have forced the price of frame relay farther and farther down, more and more companies have been able to say "yes" to this question.

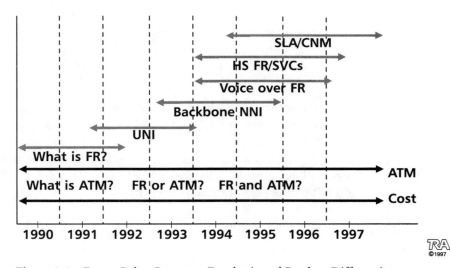

Figure 2.1 Frame Relay Customer Emphasis and Product Differentiators

It is also important to point out that frame relay pricing has been very volatile and is likely to rise again after settling down to an artificially low point, a point below which the carriers and service providers can make a profit, and after some consolidation of suppliers has occurred in the marketplace. Competition is driving prices, especially on very large networks, to points below cost, and in the final analysis it will be discovered that the thousands of smaller networks are subsidizing the attractive pricing given to the largest users. Table 2.3 shows the general decline in list prices of two comparative networks priced by *Data Communications* magazine in 1995 and 1996 (Gareiss 1996). Both Network A and Network B are fully meshed networks with sites in Atlanta, Chicago, New York, and San Francisco, and both have had three-year term discounts applied. Network A uses 1.024-Mbits/second access rates, with a committed information rate (CIR) of 320 Kbits/second per PVC. Network B is based on 56-Kbits/second access rates with 16K CIRs. Large networks of the type and size now migrating to frame relay (typically in the hundreds of sites and many times in the thousands) will see substantial discounts as carriers and service providers fight for revenues and big wins that can be announced with great flourish to further fuel their growth.

The relationship with ATM, the second question, has also been a constant issue, but the answer seems to have changed over the years. The first step was for the market to develop a fundamental understanding of frame relay, ATM, and the main differences and similarities between the two. Frame relay was viewed in the beginning primarily as a data-only transport for the wide area, well suited to bursty LAN-to-LAN traffic but also capable to some degree of transporting legacy frame and packet traffic. Frame relay's applicability to voice and video was strongly questioned, and certainly was questionable, in the early days of the decade of the 1990s. ATM, on the other hand, was viewed as the perfect solution for everything: an information transport panacea. It was typical to hear ATM being called the equivalent of a "single world religion" in communications because of its near universal acceptance or to hear people say, "ATM is the answer, what's the question?" Frame relay predominates today in large part because of the large cost differences in initial implementations of ATM (the more expensive choice) and frame relay, and the time lag between the earlier commercial introduction of frame relay and later availability of ATM. The cost difference and time lag allowed the marketplace to develop a better understanding of both technologies and for the multimedia aspects of frame relay, as they relate to voice and video, to emerge.

Table 2.3   **Frame Relay Pricing Comparison**

	Network A 1996	Network A 1995	Network B 1996	Network B 1995
AT&T	$9,940	$8,870	$1,290	$1,300
Cable & Wireless	9,120 256K CIR	13,910 256K CIR	2,315	2,245
Compuserve	11,230	12,800	1,210	3,380
LCI	6,240	7,885	700	735
LDDS Worldcom	7,180	10,180	890	1,160
MCI	5,770–7,630	9,575	850–970	1,690
MFS Telecom	8,740	11,310	1,105	1,130
Sprint	10,060	10,635	1,320	1,420
Unispan	10,775	5,900	1,420	1,010

After the marketplace developed this fundamental understanding, the next question, and it seemed like an obvious one, was "Should I use frame relay now or wait for ATM to come along ?" This question was driven in large part by manufacturers who, at the time, offered one or the other and by the two distinct consortiums that support each: the Frame Relay Forum and the ATM Forum. A more mature, and carrier/service provider driven, market is beginning to understand that the ideal answer is to use frame relay where it makes sense as one of possibly many service interfaces to a high-speed, multiservice/multimedia backbone network based on ATM. This is the model the carriers and service providers are using, and many customers are adopting it as their own strategy as well.

The "What Is Frame Relay?" Era

Early frame relay sales and marketing work, circa 1990–1991, was primarily missionary work: converting the great masses whose mind-set was firmly fixed in the orderly, guaranteed-delivery leased line and traditional X.25 packet-switching era to a technology that solved network congestion and data corruption problems by throwing frames away and relying on higher OSI layers to retransmit the information if needed, and wooing the LAN interconnection and LAN interworking community with a new WAN technology dubbed early on as a "wide area network for LANs." The early days were also full of free trials and offers of migration and technical support to get customers to just take a look at the budding new technology. After

Table 2.3	*continued*				
	Price Includes Local Loop?	Distance Sensitive?	Usage Based?	Simplex or Duplex PVC?	Includes CPE?
AT&T	no	no	no	duplex	no
Cable & Wireless	yes	no	no	duplex	CSU-DSU
Compuserve	no	no	no	duplex	no
LCI	no	no	no	duplex	no
LDDS Worldcom	no	no	no	simplex	no
MCI	no	no	yes	simplex	no
MFS Telecom	yes	no	no	duplex	no
Sprint	no	no	no	duplex	no
Unispan	yes	no	no	duplex	no

customers began to understand frame relay, they needed a point of comparison to allow for the selection of the "right" product or service. This initial point of differentiation was the user-to-network interface (UNI).

The "Does the UNI Comply with Standards?" Era

Following the development of a market understanding of frame relay came the UNI compliance era. Requests for proposal for frame relay products or services in the years 1992–1993 invariably contained an exhaustive list of all possible options for the physical and logical support of frame relay on the UNI, and vendor and service provider answers were carefully scrutinized and evaluated. The end result of these tedious and exhausting exercises was to determine that all devices adhering to the Frame Relay Forum Implementation Agreement 1 (FRF.1) would interoperate. (This level of simplicity comes in large part from lessons learned in the highly complex world of X.25 interface standards, and it is also these experiences that caused users to fall back on this methodology of selection.) After it was realized that the frame relay interface was fairly simple—and that multiple pages of questions, and 10 times as many pages of answers, could be reduced to simply asking, "Does your product or service comply with FRF.1, and which of the optional local management interface specifications do you use, if any?"—the fallback position was to choose products and services based on price. It was also during this period that the users knew what the carriers and service providers already knew—that public frame relay networks made much more sense financially and operationally than private networks. With that knowledge the market turned its attention to looking at the backbone networks provided by the carriers to transport the frame relay data.

The "Carrier Backbone Engineering and NNI" Era

After the UNI faded away to the status of a box or two to be checked on the evaluation sheet, the backbone network and network-to-network interfaces (NNIs) became a primary point of differentiation. This area of customer focus characterized the years 1993–1995. There are three primary backbone choices: TDM/circuit switching, frame switching, and cell switching/ATM.

With the exception of private TDM networks, circuit switching was never considered a valid transport for frame relay information and was never utilized in any public network. The main reason is that circuit switching uses fixed-bandwidth dedicated circuits that are not capable of responding to instantaneous bandwidth allocation needs to support bursty data in a cost-efficient manner. This left frame and cell switching to battle it out. During this phase of frame relay feature differentiation, the customers wanted to be provided with minute levels of technical detail that the carriers and service providers were reluctant to part with—for both competitive and time constraint reasons. Prospective users demanded backbone operational details and specifications about network-to-network interfaces and how they operated. Carriers and service providers, on the other hand, wanted to focus the attention of users on the use of frame relay as a service, with the service provider or carrier assuring that the backbone they provided would provide the service level for which the user contracted.

The market soon learned that, while the choice of backbone was a very important decision, it was a far more important decision for the provider of the network than for the users of the network because both packet/frame switching and cell relay/ATM backbones can provide the same levels of service at the edge of the network. The biggest difference was the operational efficiency, and therefore cost, of the backbone network. The two biggest effects of this realization were that customers again fell back to price as the primary method of comparing different service offerings and increasingly relied on formal, written service level agreements, or similar language embedded in service contracts, to guarantee certain levels of reliability and performance from the network.

Toward the middle of the backbone/NNI era, customers again began to become concerned about frame relay and its ability to handle applications for which they had found ATM desirable: voice, high-speed data and video services, and switched virtual circuits. ATM was not yet widely available in cost-effective forms, frame relay was already widely implemented and well understood, and it would be desirable if frame relay could be used for a wider set of applications.

The "Voice over Frame Relay" Era

The next important era in the frame relay market evolution was the "voice over frame relay" era, during the years 1995–1997. During this period, customer focus was shifted away from carrier backbone engineering and NNIs to the more multimedia aspects of frame relay. This period also parallels the period of strong interest in voice over IP in the Internet/intranet community.

While still not as good as traditional toll-quality voice, several technology advances have allowed companies to begin to make fairly widespread use of frame relay for carrying voice traffic. Voice over frame relay is important because it provides a further level of communications consolidation and cost savings to an already very attractive technology and helps fuel the move toward packet voice—a complete shift in both technology paradigms and cost when considering traditional telephony. Recent advances in packet voice generally, and voice over frame relay specifically, have moved packetized/frame voice from the realm of sounding like talking with the first astronauts on the moon to a normal phone call with very slight delays at the beginning of voice bursts.

Voice over frame relay has also become a major service differentiator, with early adopters purchasing their own equipment and installing their own systems, and others waiting for the service to be offered by their carrier or service provider.

High-Speed Frame Relay and Switched Virtual Connections

The years 1994–1997 saw another shift in customer focus. With acceptable answers, or at least efforts being made toward achieving acceptable answers, in other areas, customers began to look at high-speed frame relay and switched virtual connection availability as product and service differentiators.

Frame relay was originally standardized at a maximum access speed of 2.048 Mbits/second (European E1 rates). Initial market projections and studies indicated that the primary use of frame relay would be for "high-speed" (at the time) LAN interconnection at 1–1.5 Mbits/second. We were all quite surprised to find that almost two-thirds of frame relay connections today are 64Kbits/second or below. What this did was to cause an initial focus on the lower-speed connections (of which there were the most) and on special aggregation and multiplexing equipment that could be used to provide those low-speed connections at even lower prices. After the needs of lower-speed connections were met, it was realized that the aggregation of dozens, hundreds, or even thousands of low-speed connections into a very few data centers was driving the need for very high-speed frame relay. The aggregation of all of the lower-speed traffic now mandated frame relay interfaces to be standardized at 45-Mbits/second North American T3 rates and at 32-Mbits/second European E3 rates as well as 55-Mbits/second High Speed Serial Interface rates for both UNI support between customers' data center sites and public networks as well as NNIs between networks.

Along with the need for higher-speed interfaces came the need to have switched connections (the frame relay equivalent of phone calls) to supplement the already existing permanent virtual connections (the frame relay equivalent of leased lines, though they only use bandwidth as needed and are not fully allocated or "nailed up" prior to use).

Customers argue that switched virtual connections (SVCs) allow them to use virtual connections, and therefore be charged, only when they are actually required to send real information. As opposed to investing large sums of money to support SVCs for this reason, most carriers responded with special pricing schemes for low-usage PVCs.

The second argument as to why customers need SVCs is as a method of gaining connectivity beyond the present addressing limitations by reusing the same virtual connection dynamically to connect to different destinations. Although 992 PVCs are available for customers to use as specified by standards, the real limitation is lower, as defined by a given manufacturer's hardware implementation. In the absence of SVCs, this problem was solved by providing tiers of routers or other devices such that networks greater than 992 could be created. Full mesh networks are rare anyway, and the use of mesh-connected stars to create a tiered-type network has solved the problem.

Even though all major service providers have announced plans to support SVCs in the future, they have been slow to do so, and it remains to be seen if SVCs will ever really catch on in the frame relay space.

Service Level Agreements and Customer Network Management

The two issues in frame relay today (1995–1998) receiving the most customer attention, and which will be discussed in more depth in Section 2.3.2, are service level agreements and customer network management. *Service level agreements* are contractual obligations, with penalties in most cases, that guarantee a certain level of service from a frame relay carrier or service provider to a customer. *Customer network management* is the ability for a customer, *initially*, to have visibility of events within the network that affect their frame relay service, and *eventually* to have monitoring and configuration capability of the portions of the public network that carry their traffic. The configuration aspects are still some time off because of the network reliability and security issues that arise from each customer having the ability to modify the network.

2.3.2 Hot Issues in Frame Relay

The biggest problem with a book, rather than magazine articles or other periodic publications, is that some issues are "hot" today and "cold" tomorrow. For that reason we will discuss the following topics in a somewhat generic manner so that the information we provide will be valid and accurate whether these topics are "hot" or "cold" in the future. In fact, regardless of their "hot" or "cold" status, they will still be issues.

Public versus Private Networks

This is the classic "build or buy" decision. Carriers and service providers today provide very reliable frame relay backbones on a global basis, and many will even pay the cost of back-hauling domestic U.S. traffic from any location to the nearest network connection point in order to be able to make a claim of "ubiquitous service." In keeping with the trend toward the focus of organizations on their core competencies, letting a carrier, service provider, or even typical outsourcing company handle the frame relay network makes a great deal of sense. The only thing to keep in mind to assure success is that regardless of the size of the project or the extent to which the network and its operation is turned over to another group outside the company, it is absolutely imperative to retain sufficient staff to monitor the network and to act as a liaison between the customer and network provider.

The desire to hand everything over to a competent network provider and take a completely hands-off approach to the network operation is strong. It is critical, however, to maintain enough people to monitor the network provider's performance, warn of impending doom, and be sure that contractual obligations are met. This cannot be a lawyer or actuary, but must be a full-time employee who is a seasoned telecom professional, who understands the issues and knows the impact on the company, and who represents the needs of the company first and foremost.

The result of dozens of computer modeling exercises, hundreds of customer network implementations, and thousands of consulting hours and sales calls yields a single statement about public versus private frame relay networks. With the exception of some very special cases, there are only two types of networks that might be implemented more cost-effectively as private networks; all others are much better off as public network implementations. The two types of networks that might be better implemented as private networks are very small networks and very large, multiservice, multimedia networks.

Small internetworks   Small networks, typically five to seven sites and in many cases using only router technology, are very often better implemented (depending upon distances, locations, etc.) as small private networks, and in many cases they do not even need the added complexities of frame relay. Full or partially meshed networks of this size very often can be kept very simple and can be very stable and require little fine-tuning in the long run by keeping the number of variables to an absolute minimum. For instance, LAN internetworks using simple routing protocols over fully or partially meshed leased lines (and possibly based on just one protocol suite, such as TCP/IP) can be very easy to administer and can be highly reliable. This is a case where the monthly cost might be modestly less for a frame relay network but where the added complexity may not be justified.

Multimedia/multiservice backbones   The only type of network where a private frame relay implementation, or more realistically a hybrid public/private implementation, might make sense is when an organization provides an information transport backbone that provides their internal users with voice, video, and data service, in effect making the internal network organization an "internal carrier." This is a situation where a private or public/private implementation might make a lot of sense, and frame relay is only a part of the picture.

The most common large private or public/private hybrid network types are either an ATM or STM (synchronous transfer mode, basically high-speed TDM circuit switching) backbone with multiple interfaces, such as frame relay, voice, video, and other interfaces. The scale of these networks and the cost savings that can be realized by the sheer volume of the network often make these types of networks feasible versus a strictly public network implementation.

The security issue   The only other argument that has been used successfully to justify a medium-sized private frame relay network has been the "security" argument. In the final evaluation, it was learned that the biggest "security" concern on the part of the engineering staff who wrote and supported the justification was "job security." The security argument is usually based upon the fact that an organization can manage their own network, be sure that their data is not compromised, and can be responsible for their own destiny. The facts are the following:

- Most information theft is done from the inside.
- A private network's data is more vulnerable and easily identifiable as it crosses carrier facilities in discrete, identifiable circuits (as opposed to being mixed in with everything else on a public network).
- Carriers with their large staffs and large transport capacities are in a better position to service a small to medium-sized customer than they are capable of doing themselves.

These facts weaken the traditional security argument.

"Outsourcing"

"Outsourcing" is a very important buzzword in today's management circles. Everything from office garbage collection to running prisons is being outsourced. In terms of frame relay, there are three distinct levels of outsourcing that are possible: The first is to let a carrier or service provider provide frame relay public network services, in which case they manage the transport infrastructure. The second is to let the carrier or service provider provide a combination of frame relay public network services and customer-located equipment (routers, CSU/DSU, etc.), in which case they manage all network-related services. The third is to allow an outsourcing firm to implement and/or manage a complete frame relay network and all LANs and peripherals.

Carrier/service provider services   Using a carrier or service provider to provision and support a public frame relay network is the most common path for most companies today. This level still requires knowledgeable staff on the part of the customer but provides the most control and is consistent with most companies' level of risk acceptance. This is typically considered a service that provides all OSI Layer 1 and Layer 2 services for use by an organization.

Managed network services   Managed network service providers typically provide everything a carrier/service provider does with the addition of management of routers, SNA frame relay adapters, LAN bridges, and any other devices needed to provide the networking aspect of the customer's computing environment. Managed network services companies typically have a strong expertise in routers and internetworking, including Internet security and interconnectivity, and very often can alleviate the need for the customer to maintain staff with expertise in these areas. Managed network services typically include OSI Layers 1, 2, and 3.

True outsourcing   True outsourcing is just what the name implies: giving an outside firm control of all aspects of network provisioning and operation as well as workstations, applications, servers, or some subset of this. True outsourcing can be all-encompassing and can include all seven OSI layers.

   Regardless of the level to which a company puts their networking destiny in the hands of an outside firm, the ability to view the status of the public network and, eventually, to directly command and control portions of the network is very important. All of these aspects are encompassed by the term "customer network management" (CNM). CNM is an issue currently of great importance and will be for years into the future.

Customer Network Management

Table 2.4 shows the current state of customer network management, not the ideal state where customers would like to see it (Gareiss 1996). Ideally the public part of the network should appear as a seamless extension of the customer's private network (LANs, building networks, campus networks, etc.), with the customer able to receive instantaneous updates of status and able to configure and control the parts of the network for which they are paying. There is a large gap between what the customer wants and needs and what is available.

Taking the first column, SNMP feeds, as an example, what customers want is an instantaneous update of status; what carriers are offering is delays of up to an hour for status to be provided. In many cases, problems have already occurred and been reported by users via telephone, and often repaired, before they are reported. Lags of an hour are actually worse than no visibility at all because it can delay a customer's operations team from being aware of some problems for up to an hour—problems that may have been already repaired by the time they are made aware of a problem's existence.

Different carriers provide a mixed bag of other reporting and information services, but the most crucial, until true customer visibility and command and control materialize, is the ability for customers to set custom thresholds for reporting purposes so that alarms reported are exception conditions worthy of the customer's attention and the customer is not deluged with problems that do not require intervention.

It is also possible to negotiate capabilities not normally offered, depending on the size of the network and the amount of profit a carrier is making. This is an instance where the lowest possible price is not always the "best deal"; sometimes, in order to get custom concessions on the very important CNM area, a customer must pay a bit more, but the trade-offs can be well worth the investment.

It is also possible for a customer to utilize network monitors, specialized CSU/DSU equipment, and other important (though costly) methods of implying what is going on inside the network based upon statistics and settings of certain key bits in the header of the frame relay frame. These systems are outside the normal network products provided by most carriers, but many carriers are aware of these systems, and some have special capabilities to make these systems easier to implement.

Service Level Agreements

In the early days of frame relay, customers and prospects demanded to know all of the intricate details of the internal engineering of the carriers' frame relay networks. The carriers' response was, "Trust us. We're providing a service, not a leased line or telephone service; it's a whole new world." The compromise is the now fairly common service level agreement (SLA). The SLA is often incorporated into a contract for service, but in just as many cases, it is "incorporated by reference," which means that an entirely separate document is made a part of the legal contract by name and, technically and legally, becomes a part of the contract.

Table 2.4   **Network Performance Reporting**

	SNMP Feeds	Real-Time Alarms	Paper Reports	Electronic Reports	Util per Port per PVC	DE Traffic
Ameritech	15 min	no	yes	yes	yes	no
AT&T	1–2 hr	yes	yes	yes	yes	yes
AT&T Canada	1 hr	yes	yes	no	yes	yes
Cable & Wireless	15 min	yes	yes	no	yes	yes
Compuserve	1 hr	yes	yes	yes	yes	yes
ICI	1 hr	yes	yes	yes	yes	yes
LCI	none	no	yes	yes	yes	yes
LDDS Worldcom	1 hr	yes	yes	yes	yes	yes
MCI	5 min	yes	yes	yes	yes	yes
MFS Telecom	15 min	no	no	no	no	no
SBC	15 min	yes	no	no	no	no
Sprint	15 min	yes	yes	no	yes	yes
Stentor	1 hr	yes	no	yes	yes	yes
US West	15 min	yes	yes	no	yes	yes

As with any type of agreement, an SLA can contain any types of guarantees and any types of penalties, but there are some general guidelines that have emerged. Guarantees tend to be based either on service reliability/availability and/or performance (such as transit delay or frame delivery), and penalties tend to be modest, though some can be fairly large, especially when they are based upon actual outages or percentages of service cost.

There are many possible metrics that can be used to determine if there are problems in frame relay performance and that can be used as the basis for initiating trouble tickets and subsequently invoking penalties under SLAs. The two primary measurements are performance based. They are round-trip delay and frame loss, both of which affect the actual throughput of information across the frame relay network.

Round-trip delay   Frame relay networks that are global in scope typically have a banded approach to maximum (worst-case) round-trip delay (RTD)

Table 2.4   *continued*

	Overall Util	Bursts to Port Speed	Custom Thresholds	Price/ Month	Reports/ SNMP
Ameritech	yes	no	no	$2.50	PVC for both
AT&T	no	no	yes	$5 $5	port port
AT&T Canada	no	no	yes	4% of port costs	7% of port costs
Cable & Wireless	yes	yes	yes	$200	$200
Compuserve	no	yes	yes	free	free
ICI	yes	yes	yes	free	5–7% of monthly frame charge +$125
LCI	no	yes	no	free	none
LDDS Worldcom	no	no	no	free	free
MCI	no	no	yes	free	free
MFS Telecom	no	no	yes	none	$200
SBC	no	no	no	none	$40 per user ID +$250
Sprint	no	yes	yes	free	free
Stentor	yes	no	yes	$80–250	$475
US West	no	no	no	$25	$65

values that are used to benchmark service performance. The biggest issue becomes the size of the geographic bands that provides a sufficiently representative value without being too narrow such that it incorrectly causes problems to be indicated where there are none simply because of modest delay variations. Typical geographic bands are "in country," "in continent," and "global" and have upper-limit RTD values specified in milliseconds. More narrow bands are technically possible, but the delay variations within the bands are sufficiently small to not require differentiation except for very specific applications.

Round-trip delay can be measured within the IP environment by PINGs, several of which can be performed sequentially to develop a statistical average, minimum, and maximum. PINGs are a realistic means of measuring instantaneous performance of frame relay networks and associated higher-layer facilities and systems such as routers or other frame relay access devices.

Table 2.5   **Service Guarantees and Objectives**

	Minimum Network Available	Minimum Frame Delivery	Maximum Transit Delay	Mean Time to Repair
Ameritech	99.75	none	none	none
AT&T	99.96	none	none	none
AT&T Canada	99.84	99.99	none	3 hrs
Cable & Wireless	99.99	99.9 CIR 0 DE	300 ms	4 hrs
ICI	99.5	99.5 CIR 99 DE	250 ms 256 bytes	4 hrs
LCI	none	none	none	4 hrs
MCI	99.5	99.5 CIR 99 DE	70 ms US 250 inter.	4 hrs
Nynex	99.875	none	none	none
SBC	99.95	none	none	2 hrs
Sprint	99	none	none	none
Stentor	99.998	99.9 CIR DE nego.	54 ms	2.5 hrs
US West	99.9	99.99 all	28.5 ms	2–8 hrs

Frame loss   Frame loss is a metric that is typically used to determine network performance and can be measured and compared over time. Frame loss is impossible to determine precisely; the measurement most commonly referred to as "frame loss" is determined by subtracting the number of frames delivered at the egress point of the network from the number of frames presented at the ingress point of the network. It is not common to include the UNI/local loop in the calculation, but this may be done simply by using frame-delivered/frame-presented numbers from the frame relay access devices, as opposed to the starting and terminating network switches.

Because of the manner in which higher-layer protocols outside of the frame relay network operate, there is usually not "frame loss," but rather "frame retransmission." The metric called "frame loss" is actually a measurement of the number of times a frame is presented to the network for retransmission and is a measurable way of assessing delays due to multiple attempts to transmit frames because of discard. As an example, if 120

Table 2.5   *continued*

	New Order Install	Change Ports or PVCs	Penalties
Ameritech	30 days	5 days	20% of install
AT&T	21 days 20 days	30 mins 5 days	case by case case by case
AT&T Canada	(56–64) 31 days T1		
Cable & Wireless	50 days	21 days	case by case
ICI	21–28 days	2 days	10% of monthly charges
LCI	29 days	1–2 days	$1,000 credit
MCI	28 days	3 days	5%–15% of monthly charges
Nynex	15 days	5 days	none
SBC	4–5 days	1 day	none
Sprint	30 days	10 days	increase CIR free
Stentor	21 days	1 hr–3 days	none
US West	10–41 days	2 days	none

frames were sent and 100 frames were received, this would indicate that 20% of the frames had been retransmitted, assuming that a reliable higher-layer protocol, such as TCP, were being used. Only if a reliable protocol were not being used would this number represent actual frames lost in transit and never actually delivered.

Table 2.5 outlines some representative guarantees and objectives (Gareiss 1996). Guarantees, those items shaded on the chart, differ from the unshaded objectives in that guarantees have an associated penalty for nonperformance, while objectives do not.

One item that is not listed in this table but that shows up from time to time in SLAs is a provision where a carrier or service provider will pay all or part of migration costs of moving a customer to another service if contracted service levels are not met for more than a certain percentage of the sites for more than a certain percentage of the time. This clause is much less common now than in the beginning but might be a good one to include when dealing with some of the smaller or newer service providers.

2.4 Waiting for ATM?

Though asynchronous transfer mode was once thought of as a single common technology that could be deployed across all networks, be they local, metropolitan, or wide area networks, ATM has seen some major setbacks in recent times. Because of its small, efficient, fixed-length cell format, which allows high-speed switching to be performed in hardware, and its ability to uniformly carry all types of traffic (voice, video, image, traditional data, and bursty LAN data), ATM was originally developed for high-speed carrier backbones but soon found wide acceptance in other areas of networking. In the LAN space, high-speed Ethernet, first at 100 Mbits/second and by the mid- to late 1998 time frame to be standardized to 1 Gbit/second, has largely recaptured the imaginations and budget dollars of network managers. ATM, which had been gaining ground as a campus backbone to replace FDDI/CDDI networks, as well as some high-speed workstation applications, is being rolled back or moved out in lieu of high-speed Ethernet.

ATM is still the transport of choice in the metropolitan area networking (MAN) environment and is used in the physical layer of the Switched Multimegabit Data Service (SMDS), but SMDS revenues still represent only a small percentage of the broadband services marketplace. This leaves the WAN arena as the remaining place for ATM to establish a strong foothold, and, quite interestingly, ATM has done so because of frame relay. The majority of frame relay frames are parsed into cells at the edge of the network and travel across the long-distance backbones as ATM cells. This approach gives carriers the "ATM advantage" but does not provide direct UNI interfaces to customers, but this is coming. In fact, of 11 long-distance carriers and value-added networks and 8 local carriers surveyed, only 4 said they had no plans to provide interoperability between frame relay and ATM.

The final area of adoption for ATM—its original role in carrier backbones—is happening slowly, and, as indicated by Figure 2.2, it is felt that frame relay growth will outpace ATM for many years to come. It is difficult to look at current data and determine where ATM will begin to predominate.

The answer appears to be clear: don't wait. Use frame relay now where it makes sense, use multiple frame relay connections (including high-speed UNIs up to 55 Mbits/second), and fill in with ATM when it becomes available. ATM-to-frame-relay interoperability will assure that an investment

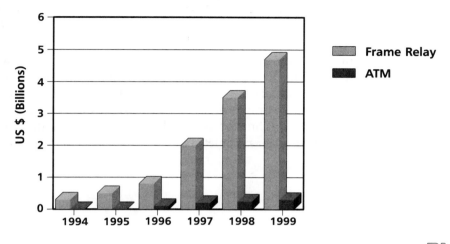

Source: International Data Corp.

Figure 2.2 Frame Relay versus ATM Market Growth

in frame relay today is justified and will have a long life. ATM-to-frame-relay interoperability will allow customers to use frame relay in the areas where it is best suited (low-speed multiple sites that are aggregated into larger data centers) and ATM where it will have the most impact (as an entry point to the larger data centers used by the multiple lower-speed sites and as a backbone transport technology).

2.5 Conclusion

The business aspects of frame relay are varied but eventually return to one single point: cost savings. Regardless of how the justification is made or which model is used, the single most important point to know about frame relay is that it is the cost savings aspect that has driven its adoption and that will continue to fuel its growth. With break-even points of typically 9 to 12 months and the strong competitive nature of today's business environment, every minute wasted is money lost. For this reason alone, you should probably initiate a frame relay project before moving on to the next chapter.

In the next chapter, we will look at the technology aspects of frame relay, at its standardization, operation, and interoperation with ATM. Even though some of the content of the next chapter may seem somewhat daunting to the nontechnologist, you should make every effort to read through it and to understand it in the light of the business aspects of frame relay discussed in this chapter. This chapter presented the answers to the questions of why companies are embracing frame relay. The next chapter explains the technical basis for the features and benefits of frame relay and is important to a complete understanding of the subject area.

CHAPTER THREE

Frame Relay Technology Aspects

Though a simple technology when compared with its predecessors, frame relay does have its own unique vocabulary, operational characteristics, and associated standards. In this chapter, we will further present a comprehensive explanation of frame relay technology and standardization in support of our ultimate objective: a complete understanding of the application of frame relay technology to real-life problems. A comprehensive discussion also follows of the "world of broadband" model, first put forth by Dr. John McQuillan as a model for organizing the various elements of the emerging world of broadband technologies. Although abandoned by many in the intervening years since its introduction, it is still an important organizational model. An explanation of frame relay's role in the International Standards Organization's Open System Interconnection (OSI) model, as well as a background on the OSI model, are also included in this chapter because a complete understanding of frame relay's relationship to other protocols is critical to a complete understanding of how frame relay works together with other elements within a telecommunications system.

3.1 Frame Relay: The Technical Definition

Technically, the definition of frame relay is somewhat more involved than a cost-savings-based business definition. From a more technical point of view, frame relay is a streamlined, high-speed delivery system for variable-length units of transport called *frames* (closely related to packets). Frame relay frames are susceptible to large transit delays, and to large variations in those delays, and are therefore not suitable for transport of raw, unmodified voice or circuit video traffic. Increasingly, however, manufacturers are introducing systems that give bursty characteristics to voice and video on the transport network and maintain their circuit characteristics on the port side. Special encoding makes voice and video suitable for transport over frame relay and packet-based IP transports.

With each passing day, the distinctions blur, and it is becoming increasingly difficult to distinguish between different types of data and suitable transports. The main reason is that all types of information (voice, data, video, image) can be represented as digital ones and zeros. Sophisticated compression techniques are giving the digitally coded information a bursty, variable-demand aspect when the information is transmitted across a network switching fabric, and this approach works very well with frame relay's technical strengths and low-overhead variable-length transport unit.

3.2 Frame Relay in Perspective

We will now put frame relay in perspective as it relates to other important communications technologies, standards, and services. We will begin by reviewing the traditional seven-layer OSI model and discuss frame relay in the context of its functions in Layer 2, the data link layer. We will then introduce an organizational framework that is unique to the emerging broadband networking technologies, called the "world of broadband" model.

3.2.1 ISO/OSI Reference Model

The International Standards Organization (ISO) seven-layer OSI reference model is the most widely used conceptual framework for discussing the functions of communications (see Figure 3.1). The model has created a

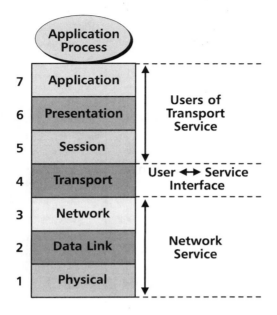

Figure 3.1   Seven-Layer OSI Reference Model

special shorthand so that communications professionals referring to "Layer 2 functions," for instance, in discussion are all aware that they are discussing the functions of synchronization and error control for information transmitted over the physical link, or data link—functions normally associated with LAN bridges or the synchronous data link control protocol (SDLC), high-speed data link control protocol (HDLC), point-to-point protocol (PPP), or even frame relay protocol. In case you do not use this system frequently, and therefore do not have instant recall of the concepts and functions of the layers, we will review the layers briefly.

The layers are numbered from the bottom to the top from 1 to 7 and represent "peer" functions, with the seven-layer model being replicated on both sides of the communication (see Figure 3.2). These are the two communicating systems, referred to in OSI nomenclature as "end systems" (ES). It is also possible (and in the cases of frame relay networks, router networks, and packet-switching networks, mandatory) to have relaying or switching systems between the end systems, called "intermediate systems" (IS).

The work on the OSI model began almost 20 years ago to provide foundational, internationally accepted concepts for communications. Even

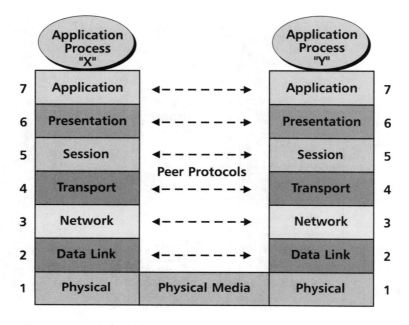

Figure 3.2   OSI Model Communications between Two End Systems

though it is not mandatory for every manufacturer or systems developer to architect their communications protocols to exactly match this model, the concepts form a common thread through all modern communications. The choice of seven layers was, in fact, arbitrary, but it did meet the requirements that the model be neither too complex nor too simple, and it is not mandatory to specify all seven layers of functionality if they are not needed for a meaningful communications exchange to occur.

The application process at the top of the model resides within the local computing environment of the specific communicating device. The OSI model is a conceptual framework and, therefore, independent of operating system or computer processor type. The application process communicates with Layer 7 of the OSI model, the application layer, even though the title "application liaison layer" may better describe its functions because Layer 7 is not the application itself, merely a link between the application and the layered communications process. The application layer establishes the association between the two communicating applications processes, the local application (shown in Figure 3.2 as Application Process "X") and the remote application process (shown as Application Process "Y") as well as supporting actions of the communication such as file transfer, virtual terminal access, transaction processing, and electronic mail.

The presentation layer (Layer 6) provides the services that allow the application processes to interpret the meaning of the information exchanged. The presentation layer identifies and negotiates the transfer syntax used for the communication to assure that a common information coding scheme is used. As an example, the presentation layer might be responsible in a given instance for translating the Extended Binary Coded Decimal Interchange Code (EBCDIC) common to IBM mainframe computer systems to and from the American Standard Code for Information Interchange (ASCII) common to minicomputers and personal computers. In another instance, the presentation layer might be responsible for encrypting information to assure authentication and reduce the likelihood of its being understood if the information is intercepted while in transit. Or both.

The session layer (Layer 5) manages the dialog between the cooperating application processes, binding and unbinding them to create an association between them.

Taken together, the application, presentation, and session layers are considered the users of the information transport service. The three upper layers ensure a full and meaningful communication and ensure that information delivered to the destination is understandable and can be readily processed. The lower four layers are concerned with the movement of information between the systems and are often referred to as the "bit pipe" over which information flows between the communicating end systems via intermediate systems, where appropriate.

The transport layer (Layer 4) provides end-to-end control and information exchange with the level of reliability that is needed for the application. The services provided to the upper layers are independent of the underlying network implementation. The transport layer is, therefore, the liaison between the upper three layers and the lower three layers. The most readily recognized Layer 4 protocol is TCP, of the TCP/IP protocol suite. TCP (Transmission Control Protocol) provides a reliable communications link between Layer 4 of the two communicating end systems. TCP is responsible for providing reliable communications via retransmission of missing or damaged information transfer frames as well as adapting dynamically to the communications environment. Another, less readily recognized Layer 4 protocol is UDP (User Datagram Protocol). UDP, like TCP, operates at Layer 4, but, unlike TCP, UDP sends datagrams without regard to sequence or missing datagrams; in other words, UDP provides an unreliable communication environment. While both TCP and UDP operate at Layer 4, they provide different levels of reliability, as required by the higher-layer protocols. TCP is useful for session-oriented applications, like remote terminal emulation, where it is important for everything that is being sent to arrive in order to provide a meaningful communication, while UDP is more useful for periodic, broadcast-type messages that are fully self-contained, such as user authentication messages.

The network layer (Layer 3) is responsible for the creation of end-to-end paths over which the information being transmitted will flow. The most common devices to associate with Layer 3 are routers, but X.25 packet switches and other types of packet switching operate at Layer 3 as well.

The data link layer (Layer 2) provides synchronization and error control for the information transmitted over the physical link. Frame relay is a Layer 2 protocol, as are PPP, SDLC, and HDLC, as previously mentioned. Frame relay varies from the typical protocols found in Layer 2 in that the traditional Layer 2 connection exists between adjacent systems only and has no end-to-end significance. Frame relay represents a hybrid because the UNI and NNI specifications describe connections between adjacent systems, but the switched and permanent virtual connections that use the UNI and NNI actually provide an end-to-end path over which information flows.

As shown in Figure 3.3, the Layer 2 address of the LAN world, the Media Access Control, or MAC address, is mapped by the router to the frame relay Layer 2 address, called the data link connection identifier (described in detail later in this chapter) for transmission of the frame across whatever physical infrastructure is used by frame relay. Frame relay is implemented by and between intermediate systems, often called relaying systems, and exists in both the routers or other frame relay access devices (FRAD) and the switches.

The physical layer (Layer 1) provides the functions to activate, maintain, and deactivate the physical circuits interconnecting the communicating end systems and intermediate systems that actually move the bits. The physical layer may be either electrical or optical and includes wire, fiber optic cables, radio transmissions, and any other means of moving bits. While all seven layers are present in the end systems, only the lower three layers are present in intermediate systems.

With this general information about the OSI model, we now know quite a bit about frame relay. For instance, because frame relay operates at Layer 2 of the OSI model, we know that frame relay is responsible for synchronization and error control for the information transmitted over the

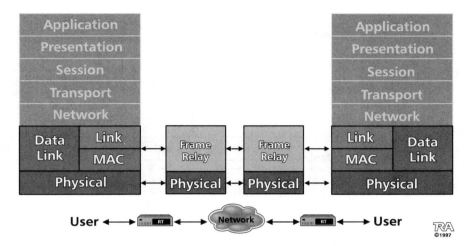

Figure 3.3 Frame Relay OSI Operation

physical link. We will learn more later about how frame relay synchronizes information and assures that it will go to its proper destination, as well as the simple mechanism that frame relay employs to assure that errors are handled at the point of detection and not propagated through the system.

If someone were to ask whether frame relay translates between different information coding systems, we would already know that it does not, because that is the job of Layer 6, the presentation layer, if the job needs to be done at all. And if our present network is an IBM network and the synchronous data link control (SDLC) protocol is our present Layer 2 protocol, we know that frame relay, if we adopt it, will replace SDLC at Layer 2. These are but a few of the things we can infer about frame relay from our basic understanding of the OSI reference model.

3.2.2 "World of Broadband" Model

Frame relay, cell relay/ATM, and SMDS all fall under the major umbrella of "broadband networking." Broadband networking, in general, defines methodologies for building multiservice networks that provide a common switching fabric for voice, traditional "legacy" data, bursty LAN data, image, and video, which operate over low bit error rate communications facilities at high speeds. Broadband is making a substantial impact in both public and private networking, and a complete understanding of frame

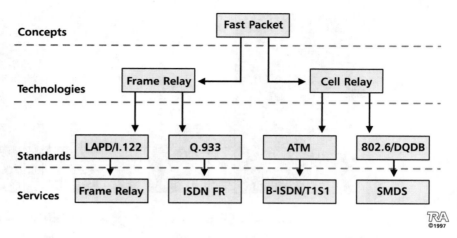

Figure 3.4   "World of Broadband" Conceptual Broadband Hierarchy

relay includes not only understanding where frame relay fits into the traditional seven-layer OSI reference model, but also understanding where it fits into the broadband model.

One of the most commonly misunderstood aspects of emerging broadband network technology is the relationship of concepts, technologies, standards, and the service offerings in which they are packaged. Figure 3.4 shows those key relationships. A clear understanding of frame relay's role in the hierarchy of broadband switching elements will foster an appreciation of frame relay and its application to public and private networking.

While commonly used interchangeably with ATM and cell relay, "fast packet" is an overall term referring to many of the general concepts of broadband networking. The foundational concepts for all fast-packet technologies, standards, and services are

- intelligent end systems
- inherently reliable, low bit error rate digital transmission facilities
- high-speed communication

Modern end systems such as personal computers and UNIX workstations can operate sophisticated protocol stacks. Resident protocol stacks allow end systems to detect errors in transmission and to either correct simple errors or request retransmission. This is a stark contrast to more traditional systems that used "dumb" terminal equipment. The coupling of "dumb" terminal equipment and unreliable communications facilities requires pre-fast-packet networks to have a great deal of communications intelligence. They are, therefore, very slow when compared to fast-packet networks.

In addition to intelligent end systems, fast-packet networks require low bit error rate digital transmission facilities that are inherently reliable and can operate at high speeds. The combination of intelligent end systems and reliable high-speed communications facilities enables fast-packet networks to be simple and fast.

Frame relay and cell relay are the two divisions of fast-packet technologies. Frame relay and cell relay both require intelligent end systems, reliable digital transmission facilities, and high bandwidth capacities. The major differences between frame relay and cell relay are the units of information transferred and the place in the network the protocol is employed. Frame relay transfers information in variable-length "frames." Cell relay transfers information in fixed-length "cells." The frame relay interface is an access arrangement, like X.25, and was designed for use at the edges of the network: to provide access to the backbone network. Cell relay is used to develop a common integrated switching fabric for a variety of types of information (including frame relay) and is used at the core of the network, even though we are seeing a proliferation of cell-relay-based standards and services (such as ATM) in all areas of network operation—WANs, MANs, and LANs.

In the area of frame relay standards, LAP-D, LAP-E/Q.922 (often referred to colloquially as LAP-F), and I.122 define PVC-based frame relay services. The Q.933 standards define call setup procedures for switched virtual circuit frame relay services. Link Access Procedure-D (LAP-D) is a set of OSI Layer 2 (link layer) specifications for use with the ISDN D channel. LAP-D is the basis for the frame relay standards for information transfer. LAP-D is defined by ITU-T I.441/Q.921 standards. Link Access Procedure-Extended (LAP-E) and Link Access Procedure-Frame Relay (LAP-F) are common names applied to an enhanced LAP-D specification that is defined in the ITU-T Q.922 standard.

In the bottom level of the conceptual broadband hierarchy are the service offerings that are the vehicle for delivery of the standards and technologies to the end user. Service offerings shown in Figure 3.4 that are important to this description of the frame relay interface are "frame relay" and "ISDN frame relay." Frame relay services are currently public or private network PVC-based or SVC-based offerings, while ISDN frame relay represents the source of the original frame relay standards: a bearer mode data service for use with ISDN. Public and private service PVC or SVC offerings are identical in their use of the frame relay interface protocols, varying only in areas such as who owns pieces of equipment, where devices are located, who performs network management, and how a customer is billed for the service.

Even though Figure 3.4 is not a comprehensive compendium of all standards and services, it does provide a much needed outline of fast-packet networking and clearly shows where the frame relay interface fits. This organizational model, also called the "world of broadband" model, was originally introduced by John McQuillan in the early days of this decade (McQuillan 1990). The "world of broadband" model is not widely used (certainly not as widely as the OSI model), but it provides a much needed organizational framework for understanding this complicated area.

3.3 History and Standards Activity

For a technology with such a profound impact on the communications industry, frame relay has had a fairly short history. Frame switching and framed data communications have been standard fare for the past two decades. However, the work that has become the frame relay interface was not initiated until the mid-1980s. What is now known as the frame relay interface began as a part of the digital multiplexed interface (DMI) standards, specifically as DMI Mode 3 (bursty data). DMI was originally intended to be a means of integrating bursty data support with voice on private branch exchange (PBX) equipment. Standardization efforts for DMI were initiated in 1987 by the now defunct ANSI T1D1 work group. Several elements were borrowed from work done earlier by ITU-T (CCITT at the time) and other standards bodies on the use of the ISDN B (bearer) channels for the transmission of bursty data.

There are a number of driving forces supporting the implementation of frame relay: the remarkably influential Frame Relay Forum (founded by Cisco, DEC, StrataCom, and Northern Telecom), large end user organizations, government agencies, public carriers wishing to provide frame relay services, and numerous domestic and international standards bodies. Table 3.1 describes the bulk of present standards activity. In addition to the historical and foundational standards, there are two other parts of the frame relay story that contribute to a complete understanding of frame relay's technological development and market acceptance: frame relay's commercialization and uniform implementation across multiple vendors and platforms.

Table 3.1 **Frame Relay and Related Standards**

Organization	Standard	Description
ANSI	T1.606-1990	Architectural Framework and Service Description for Frame Relaying Bearer Service
ANSI	T1.606a	Architectural Framework and Service Description for Frame Relaying Bearer Service
ANSI	T1.606b	Network-to-Network Interface Requirements—Frame Relay Bearer Service Architectural Framework and Service Description
ANSI	T1.617	Frame Relay Bearer Service—Architectural Framework and Service Description
ANSI	T1.617a	DSS1—Signaling Specification for Frame Relay Bearer Service
ANSI	T1.618	Frame Relay Bearer Service for DSS1 (Protocol Encapsulation and PICS)
ANSI	T1.633	DSS1—Core Aspects of Frame Protocol for Use with Frame Relay Bearer Service
ITU-T	E.164	Numbering Plan for the ISDN Era
ITU-T	I.122	Framework for Providing Additional Packet Mode Bearer Services
ITU-T	I.233.1	Frame Relay Bearer Services
ITU-T	I.365.1	Frame Relaying Bearer Service Specific Convergence Sublayer (FR-SSCS)
ITU-T	I.370	Congestion Management in Frame Relaying Networks
ITU-T	I.372	Frame Mode Bearer Services Network-to-Network Interface Requirements
ITU-T	I.431	Primary (1544,2048 Kbits/second) ISDN Interface
ITU-T	I.555	Frame Relaying Bearer Service Interworking
ITU-T	I.610	B-ISDN Operations and Maintenance Principles and Maintenance-Proposed Text on Loopback Capability
ITU-T	Q.921	ISDN Digital Subscriber Signaling System No. 1 (DSS1 1), Data Link Layer
ITU-T	Q.922	ISDN Data Link Layer Specification for Frame Mode Bearer Service
ITU-T	Q.931	ISDN Network Protocol
ITU-T	Q.933	ISDN Signaling Specification for Frame Mode Bearer Services

Table 3.1   *continued*

Organization	Standard	Description
ITU-T	Q.933 (Revised)	ISDN Signaling Specifications for Frame Mode Switched and Permanent Virtual Connections Control and Status Monitoring
ITU-T	Q.951	Stage 3 Service Description for Number Identification Supplementary Services Using DSS1
ITU-T	X.6	Multicast Service Definition
ITU-T	X.121	International Numbering Plan for Public Data Networks

Even though many different organizations contributed to the development of frame relay standards by performing many computer modeling efforts, writing academic papers, and publishing core research on frame relay, it was a California-based multiplexer manufacturer named Strata-Com, Inc., now a part of Cisco Systems, Inc., that developed and released the first working frame relay hardware and software. And it was the then-obscure telecommunications carrier Williams Telecommunications (WilTel), now a part of WorldCom, Inc., that exploited the benefits of frame relay in the public network in the incarnation of WilPak, the world's first public frame relay network. StrataCom originally developed the frame relay interface hardware for its IPX line of cell-based multiplexers because frame relay represented an ideal new interface to the usage-sensitive multiplexing and switching fabric of their ATM-like switching fabric. WilTel seized the opportunity to use this product in the public network space, as many of the early visionaries, such as WilTel's Robert Gourley, the undisputed "father of public relay," had seen frame relay as the next generation of X.25—stripped of the burden of the Layer 3 processing required by earlier analog transmission networks, streamlined, and ready to usher in the next era in public networking: fast-packet networks.

Not only did the industry wish to emulate the gigantic success of X.25, so, too, it wished to avoid some of the pitfalls and problems that had occurred with X.25. The very simplicity of frame relay, possible because much of the complexity could now lie outside the network in intelligent intermediate systems and end systems rather than in very costly network-based switches, made it possible to avoid some, but not all, of the interoperation difficulties of X.25. The one step that avoided the rest of interoperability problems and the translation of the many standards into working, interoperable products was the formation of the Frame Relay Implementer's Forum, which is known today as the Frame Relay Forum.

Table 3.2   **Frame Relay Forum Implementation Agreements**

Number	Date	Description
FRF 1.1	1/19/96	User-to-Network Implementation Agreement (UNI)
FRF.2	8/15/92	Network-to-Network Interface Phase 1
FRF 3.1	6/22/95	Multiprotocol Encapsulation Implementation Agreement
FRF.4	1/5/94	Frame Relay User-to-Network SVC Implementation Agreement
FRF.5	12/20/94	Frame Relay/ATM PVC Network Interworking Implementation Agreement
FRF.6	3/25/94	Frame Relay Service Customer Network Management Implementation Agreement
FRF.7	10/21/94	Frame Relay PVC Multicast Service and Protocol Description IA
FRF.8	4/14/95	Frame Relay/ATM PVC Service Interworking Implementation Agreement
FRF.9	1/15/96	Data Compression over Frame Relay

The Frame Relay Forum's four founding members (known as the "Gang of Four" and drawn as the Four Musketeers with upraised swords in a *Telephony Magazine* cartoon of that era) were intended to represent the cross section of the computer and telecommunications industry. Strata-Com represented private networking, Northern Telecom (now Nortel) represented the carriers and large public networks, cisco (now Cisco) represented LAN internetworking, and DEC represented computing. The Frame Relay Forum, from those humble beginnings, has grown into a very influential industry force and has been responsible for industry awareness, market development, and the publication of a number of very important documents, called Implementation Agreements. The Implementation Agreements, while not standards per se, guide manufacturers and service providers in creating interoperable products. Table 3.2 shows the Frame Relay Forum Implementation Agreements.

There are two last organizations whose interests intersect with those of the Frame Relay Forum. And, like the Frame Relay Forum, neither of these organizations have official standard-making authority, though they do perform a very important function in terms of assuring interoperability between frame relay and ATM, and frame relay and the Internet. These organizations are the ATM Forum and the Internet Engineering Task Force (IETF), respectively, and their primary contributions to the literature that impact on frame relay are listed in Table 3.3.

Table 3.3   **Frame Relay Related ATM Forum Implementation Agreements and IETF Requests for Comments (RFCs)**

Organization	Document	Description
ATM Forum	—	UNI Specification Document (Version 3.0)
ATM Forum	—	B-ICI Specification Document (Version 1.0)
IETF	RFC 1213	Management Information Base for Network Management of TCP/IP-based Internets—MIB-II
IETF	RFC 1315	Management Information Base for Frame Relay DTEs
IETF	RFC 1442	Structure of Management Information for Ver. 2 of the Simple Network Management Protocol (SNMPv2)
IETF	RFC 1445	Administrative Model for Ver. 2 of the Simple Network Management Protocol (SNMPv2)
IETF	RFC 1448	Protocol Operations for Ver. 2 of the Simple Network Management Protocol (SNMPv2)
IETF	RFC 1483	Multiprotocol Encapsulation over ATM Adaptation Layer 5
IETF	RFC 1490	Multiprotocol Interconnect over Frame Relay
IETF	RFC 1604	Definitions of Managed Objects for Frame Relay Service

3.4 Frame Relay Function and Format

One important characteristic of traditional synchronous data communications is a fixed physical connection between both ends of a circuit. In order to assure the continued presence of the communications connection, information is exchanged periodically between end points, even in the absence of actual data. This overhead function, while necessary for less reliable analog transmission facilities, is unnecessary in emerging highly reliable, high-throughput fast-packet networks. Rather than transferring bits between fixed locations, as a circuit does, a frame relay interface acts like a wide area LAN. A sending device simply has to place an addressed frame into the network, and it is transported quickly to its destination. Utilizing a single physical frame relay interface, a LAN interconnection device, such as a router, or any other frame-relay-equipped device may send data directly to any other device in the network by specifying the destination's address.

Since the frame relay interface recognizes frames that are to be transmitted, the rate of transfer, theoretically, is under the control of the sender, up to the access rate (the maximum clocked rate at which the network can accept input). If the sender has a large burst of data to send (very characteristic of LANs), the bandwidth is made available and the data is moved into the network for transmission. If little or no information is to be transmitted, little or no bandwidth is utilized. The capability of a network to absorb data as it needs to be transmitted without a flow control mechanism is called instantaneous "bandwidth-on-demand." The backbone network to which a frame relay interface is connected must provide instantaneous bandwidth-on-demand in order for a user of frame relay to realize all of the benefits of frame relay.

There are practical considerations in implementing a network that provides instantaneous bandwidth-on-demand. Among the practical considerations are handling of congestion inside the network, handling bandwidth contention at the periphery of the network, optimizing throughput, and enforcing a system of equitable sharing between multiple users. These aspects of frame relay are covered in more depth later.

Providing LAN-to-LAN connectivity is emerging as a primary data application. The concept of connecting many LANs with routers to make one large, virtual enterprisewide LAN is simple and easy to support for a small number of LANs. When it is desirable to connect many LANs in this fashion, performance drops off sharply, costs climb exponentially, and the collection of interconnected equipment that results is almost unmanageable.

Figure 3.5 shows a traditional WAN/LAN internetwork. Without frame relay, a full mesh interconnection is required to guarantee low latencies (by reducing the number of hops to a minimum) and to assure alternate routes in case of failures. The number of paths required for a fully mesh-interconnected network rises at the rate of $(n(n-1))/2$, where n is the number of devices being interconnected. The cost model deteriorates, and performance and manageability collapse, in configurations with more than five to six remote LANs.

The alternative to a physical mesh internetwork, as shown in Figure 3.5, is a logical mesh network, as shown in Figure 3.6. LAN interconnection with frame relay is achieved by providing a single multiplexed physical connection for each LAN device to a very high-speed backbone. Each single physical connection carries many logical connections that can be used to create a logical mesh internetwork.

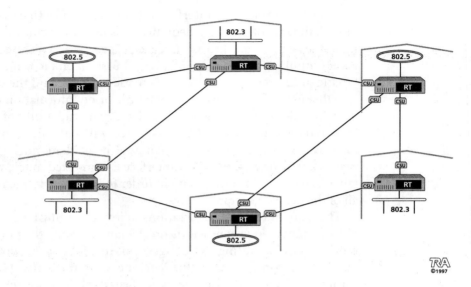

Figure 3.5   Traditional WAN/LAN Internetwork

The frame relay design approach in Figure 3.6 reduces total recurring costs, reduces network-induced latency, and increases reliability. Recurring costs are reduced because a single, higher-capacity connection to a common network backbone carries all traffic regardless of destination. When used with an efficient, high-speed bandwidth-on-demand cell relay backbone, network-induced latency is reduced because hop counts decrease and available bandwidth increases. Reliability can also be increased because the backbone networks supporting frame relay interfaces are often implemented using redundant hardware and high-speed alternate routing capabilities.

Frame relay is a standardized interface protocol, like X.25, and does not define the backbone switching protocols or topologies. The fundamental assumptions of broadband networking (reliability, high speed, and intelligent end systems) must be met for the frame relay interface implementation to be successful. It will, therefore, be assumed for the rest of this discussion that an efficient, high-speed, bandwidth-on-demand cell relay transmission network is used.

The frame relay user-network interface (UNI) is asymmetrical. As shown in Figure 3.7, devices on both sides of the UNI have different roles. Routers, bridges, front-end processors, and other controller devices are defined as frame relay access devices. The intelligent nodal processors at

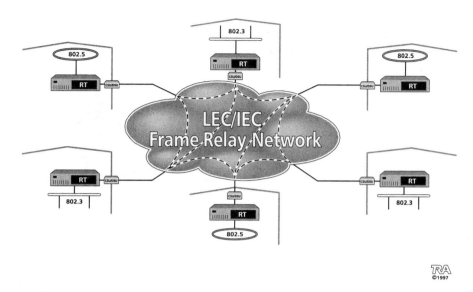

Figure 3.6   Logical Mesh Internetwork

the other end of the UNI are defined as frame relay network devices (or often as frame relay switches or nodes). Frame relay standards describe an OSI Layer 2 data transfer protocol that operates between frame relay access devices and frame relay network devices. Transport of data from one end of the network to the other is achieved using either a standard or proprietary backbone switching protocol, but is independent of frame relay standards. A second Layer 2 protocol, the control protocol, is also defined between the access device (router, etc.) and the network device (nodal processor).

One implication of an asymmetrical interface is that two frame relay network devices cannot be directly connected. This is of importance when implementing a hybrid public/private frame relay network. Unless a symmetrical internetwork protocol (such as the network-to-network interface described in Frame Relay Forum Implementation Agreement FRF.2) is being used, two frame relay network devices must be terminated on a common frame relay access device, and logical connections must be bridged by the access device. In the case of a LAN internetwork, for instance, a public and a private frame relay connection would be made to a single router, and the router would be responsible for mapping logical connections between the two networks.

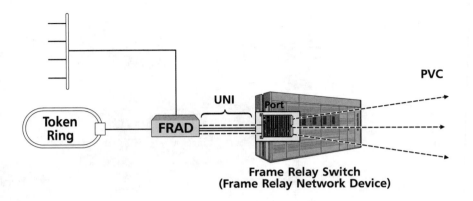

Figure 3.7   Frame Relay User-to-Network Interface

The frame relay interface presents its data to the transmission network in a format that is consistent with LAP-D framing. The version of LAP-D that is specific to frame relay has been called both LAP-D+ and LAP-F, but it is generally being referred to now as LAP-E. The transmission network recognizes three core elements of LAP-E frames: the frame delimiters (flags), an addressing mechanism called the *data link connection identifier* (DLCI), and a two-byte cyclical redundant check (CRC) called the *frame check sequence* (FCS).

When a frame is received from the source (access device), the network device looks at the address field and decodes the destination. The frame is then transmitted across the backbone and replayed to the destination device. Only correct frames are relayed to the destination; frames with incorrect FCSs are discarded, and it is assumed they will be retransmitted by a higher-layer protocol, if needed.

The frame relay standards designate frames formatted as shown in Figure 3.8. The fields are formatted and used according to the following conventions.

3.4.1 Flags

Flags are used for delimiting frames. In order to ensure no bit patterns in the payload portion of the frame inadvertently match the 01111110 pat-

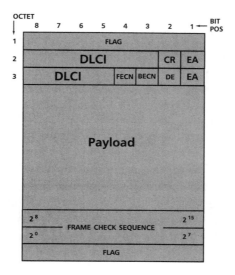

Figure 3.8 Frame Relay Frame Format

tern of the delimiting flags, frame relay performs zero insertion. When the frame relay access device is transmitting data that is between the opening and closing flags of a frame, it will insert a 0 bit after all sequences of five contiguous 1 bits. These extra 0 bits are removed at the receiving end of the connection by zero bit extraction.

3.4.2 DLCI

The data link connection identifier (DLCI) is the addressing mechanism of frame relay. The DLCI consists of the six most significant bits of the second octet plus the four most significant bits of the third octet of the frame relay frame. Additional bits, dependent upon the value of the extended address (EA) bit, may be used to form a complete DLCI. While two-, three-, and four-octet forms of the frame relay address field format exist, only the two-octet version shown here is presently implemented. The three- and four-octet forms defined in standards will allow the frame relay address space to be extended beyond its present 10-bit size (1,024 addresses) to 16 bits (65,536 addresses/three-octet format) or 23 bits (8,388,608 addresses/four-octet format) if needed.

Under present implementations of frame relay, there are several restrictions placed on the assignment of DLCIs. DLCI 0 is reserved for in channel call control signaling as defined by ITU-T Q.931/ANSI T1.6fr standards. ITU-T Q.931 and ANSI T1.6fr are particularly well suited to SVC frame relay and do not apply to the present implementations of frame relay. DLCIs 1 through 15 and 1,008 through 1,022 are reserved for future use, and DLCI 1,023 is reserved for local management interface (LMI) communications. This leaves the 992 DLCIs from 16 through and including 1,007 available for frame relay PVCs.

It is important to note that DLCIs only have local significance in standard frame relay implementations. A frame relay connection that goes from Chicago to Atlanta may (and very likely will) have a different DLCI on the UNI at each end of the connection. It is also likely that a specific DLCI number, say, 42, will identify two different connections on two different UNIs. For instance, DLCI 42 on a Los Angeles UNI may point to Denver while DLCI 42 on a Chicago UNI may point to Atlanta. The only exception to DLCI local significance is if the frame relay network is using global addressing, in which case DLCI 42 would mean the same destination wherever it is used.

3.4.3   BECN and FECN

The backward explicit congestion notification (BECN) bit, if implemented, may be set by a congested network to notify a frame relay access device that congestion avoidance procedures should be initiated. As a frame relay frame travels through a network, it may encounter congestion. It is the responsibility of the network to recognize this condition and set the forward explicit congestion notification (FECN) bit.

When the receiving frame relay access device detects that the FECN bit is set for a given PVC, it must then set the BECN bit for frames being transmitted back to the source of the frame containing an FECN bit.

This all sounds very complicated, but is really very simple. Frame relay is bidirectional. For a PVC from A to B, there is an A-to-B side of the connection and a B-to-A side of the connection. The traffic requirements on the A-to-B side are independent of the traffic requirements on the B-to-A side. This would be analogous to a two-lane highway.

If A were a terminal and B were a host, a very small transaction (request, query, etc.) from A to B would be sufficient to cause a very large information transfer from B to A. A frame traveling from A to B, therefore, might not encounter any congestion, while a frame traveling from B to A might encounter severe congestion.

Table 3.4   **State Tables for FECN and BECN Bits**

	Traffic	FECN	BECN
No Congestion	A → B	0	0
	B → A	0	0
Congestion A → B and B → A	A → B	1	1
	B → A	1	1
Congestion A → B; No Congestion B → A	A → B	1	0
	B → A	0	1
Congestion B → A; No Congestion A → B	A → B	0	1
	B → A	1	0

Let's consider the state tables in Table 3.4. The first two, on top, are fairly straightforward. If there is no congestion in the network, then neither the FECN nor the BECN are set for either PVC. If there is congestion in both directions, then all FECN and BECN bits are set. The state table for "Congestion A → B; No Congestion B → A" shows the FECN bit is set for A → B and the BECN bit is set for B → A. The FECN from A → B tells the frame relay access device at B that the BECN bit should be set for frames being sent to A to notify A there is congestion somewhere in the A → B path. A similar situation, but just the opposite, exists for the fourth state table. "Congestion B → A; No Congestion A → B" shows an FECN of 1 from B to A, which notifies the frame relay access device at A that congestion was encountered. The BECN of 1 from A to B is A's way of notifying B of the congestion situation.

3.4.4 Discard Eligibility

The discard eligibility (DE) bit is used to indicate a frame's suitability for discard in network congestion situations. In theory, the frame relay network would discard frames with a DE bit set to 1 instead of frames with a DE bit set to 0 when the network became congested and could no longer carry all the data being presented to it. A frame, for instance, that contains a LAN server broadcast message could have its DE bit set to 1 by a router as the frame was being built for transmission. If the LAN server broadcast message only reaches its destination some of the time, this would be OK because of the nature of LAN server broadcast messages—they are informational and are sent out every few seconds. Another instance where a DE bit might be set is when a PVC exceeds its committed burst size, guaranteed burst capability, or B_c, for more than the committed rate measurement interval. In this case, the DE bit might be set; this would lower the likelihood of delivery at the destination boundary of the network, but would be better than not sending the frame at all. The important thing to remember when considering frame discard, however, is the communication is assumed to be occurring between intelligent senders and receivers. It is assumed any data discarded by the network will be retransmitted, if needed, by a higher-layer protocol. The net effect is usually diminished performance as opposed to truly lost data.

3.4.5 Extended Address

The extended address (EA) bit is the low-order bit (bit 1) of the octets comprising the frame relay address field. In current implementations only a two-octet address field is utilized. In this case, the EA bit in the first octet of the address field (second octet of the frame) is set to 0, and the EA bit in the second octet of the address field (third octet of the frame) is set to 1. For further explanation of the use of the EA bit in three- and four-octet address fields, please refer to the description of the DLCI (Section 3.4.2).

3.4.6 Command/Response

The command/response (C/R) indication bit is not used by the frame relay data link protocol and may be set to either 1 or 0 by the frame relay access device. The C/R bit is carried transparently by the frame relay network.

3.4.7 Frame Check Sequence

The frame check sequence (FCS) is a two-octet field that follows the user data field and precedes the closing flag. The FCS is the result of applying the ITU-T cyclic redundancy checking (CRC) polynomial to the frame relay frame from, and including, the first bit of the address field to the last bit of the user data field. It is important to note that FCS is calculated by the source frame relay access device and recalculated by the destination frame relay access device. If the two FCSs do not match, then the frame is discarded; recall there is not a method to request retransmission within frame relay. Retransmission will be handled, if needed, by a higher-layer protocol. FCS is used to verify that a frame is not corrupted during transmission. Frame relay will not deliver corrupted frames.

3.5 Virtual Connections

Frame relay allows use of either permanent or switched virtual connections. Virtual connections in the frame relay context are used for connectivity and addressing. It is assumed that all traffic for a particular virtual connection uses the same path through the backbone network, or that some other mechanism besides frame relay is used to assure the arrival of transmitted frames in the same order in which they were transmitted, because there is no such thing as a sequence or serial number for frames in frame relay. Virtual circuits consume no resources when they are not active, but can instantaneously carry up to 53 Mbits/second of traffic if using a High Speed Serial Interface (HSSI).

A protocol for dynamically setting up virtual circuits is described in several standards and in the Frame Relay Forum Implementation Agreement FRF.4. Frame relay SVCs are established across frame relay UNIs using procedures based upon Q.933 standards. The Q.933 call establishment and call termination signaling messages will operate over a reliable Q.922 transport protocol using DLCI 0. Frame relay SVCs may operate over a variety of permanent and switched frame relay connections including T1/E1, T3/E3, HSSI, and ISDN connections. There are two numbering plans that may be used for frame relay SVCs: X.121 and E.164. The X.121 standard describes an international numbering plan for data networks and is the numbering plan used exclusively by X.25 networks, while E.164 describes a "numbering plan for the ISDN era" that is applicable to both telephony and data networks. The E.164 standard is the international ITU-T standard upon which both SMDS and the North American Telephony Numbering Plan are based. The choice of numbering plan used will be dependent upon the service provider.

Even though SVC standards exist and are already implemented in many manufacturers' frame relay products, it remains to be seen if switched virtual connections in a frame relay context will be in great enough demand to merit the effort and cost required to implement them in public frame relay networks. There are four areas where there is demand for SVCs:

- Customer networks with greater than 992 frame relay interconnected sites
- Customers wishing to save money by using frame relay connections only periodically
- Services desiring dynamic connections (switched versus full period access)
- Network-to-network interface resiliency

For customer networks with greater than 992 frame relay interconnected sites, it is possible to solve the maximum address issue by simply using interconnect routers to terminate UNIs from each of two or more "maximum 992 site" networks and interconnecting multiple "maximum 992 site" groups together at OSI Layer 3. This limitation is actually not in the number of data link connection identifier addresses as much as it is in interconnection equipment. Because the 992 DLCI addresses are locally significant (that is to say each frame relay UNI may use up to 992 DLCIs to address up to 992 other sites), the total number of interconnected sites may exceed 992, unless the sites are *fully mesh interconnected.* In reality the limitation is more based upon the maximum number of PVCs that can be supported by a given interconnect device, such as a router. A router may be limited to a dozen PVCs, 50 PVCs, or 100 PVCs, but the number is typically well below the maximum 992 number. It is important to keep in mind the fact that in many router architectures a frame relay virtual connection is treated in much the same way as a physical port was treated prior to the idea of logical ports addressable by DLCIs and that most routing architectures were not designed with enough buffer space or processor power for several hundred ports. For all of these reasons, it is more likely that some creative network design and engineering, and possibly sending traffic through an intermediate router, will be the solution to these problems before SVCs are.

In the second case, some customers wish to use SVCs to save money, especially in cases where a connection might cover a large geographic distance but not be used very frequently. As a way of making customers happy, without the expense and difficulty of implementing SVCs in their networks, some carriers have responded to this customer need simply by discounting PVCs with less than a certain threshold of traffic per month. This is a very good solution because it meets customer needs with a minimum of cost and disruption and achieves the same result without a great investment in time and equipment.

In the third case, customers would like to make dynamic, switched connections to other sites within their own company or those of suppliers or customers. This could be as a part of a full-period leased-line frame relay UNI or as a part of a switched access UNI. In either case, it would be desirable to make a dynamic connection, much like those made via TCP/IP Telnet connections or X.25 sessions. In fact, there are presently work-arounds using a combination of TCP/IP or other higher-layer protocols and underlying preestablished frame relay PVC connections that are usable for the time being. It is possible to identify work-arounds on a case-by-case basis, dependent on the specific network architecture, and to still avoid the cost and difficulty of a carrier implementing SVCs.

The only area where there is no real alternative to SVCs, or some other call setup based upon standardized signaling, is in the area of connections that go between the frame relay networks of different carriers and/or customers and quite potentially between networks based upon different manufacturers: the network-to-network interfaces. This is one area where we may very well see SVCs implemented. Today, NNIs are not resilient: there is no rerouting across the NNI, even though most frame relay backbones, which comprise the networks on either side of the NNI, do have rerouting within their own backbone. The reason is that the switching architecture within the entire frame relay backbone is controlled by a single manufacturer or network provider, and they may implement any proprietary or homegrown methodology they would like to realize that a problem exists and reroute around the problem, but a vendor-independent, standards-based approach is required at the NNI.

3.6 Link Management

Some kinds of protocol devices perform regular link management with receiver ready (RR) polling and acknowledgments at the link layer. This is common with HDLC LAP and LAP-B/X.25 and SNA/SDLC sessions. An extension to the frame relay interface standards that performs a similar function for frame relay is the local management interface (LMI). LMI is an optional extension that allows "keep-alive" messages, configuration information, and congestion status to be exchanged across the UNI between the access device and the network device.

The LMI message begins with a DLCI of 1,023 (the highest possible DLCI in a two-octet header) if using the pre-standards StrataCom-Cisco LMI or ITU-T Annex D LMI, or a DLCI of 0 if using the ANSI Annex A LMI. The 1,023 or 0 DLCI combined with an unnumbered information frame type and protocol discriminator of 00001001 identifies this as an LMI frame. A null call reference octet is used to maintain compliance with other standards, thereby limiting difficulty of implementation. The balance of the frame consists of a message type and a number of information elements (IEs). The IEs carry the actual information of the message.

3.7 Application to Public and Private Networking

There are many benefits that frame relay can deliver to the public and private network. The multiplexed physical interface can reduce the number of ports required on expensive bridge, router, and controller equipment, as well as reducing the number of expensive communications facilities required to interconnect the bridges, routers, and controllers. Frame relay's DLCI addressing can allow a single frame relay access device to communicate as if directly attached to almost 1,000 other access devices. The bandwidth-on-demand characteristics can give end systems and intermediate systems the appearance of having far more bandwidth available than they physically have dedicated, and the optional LMI extensions can greatly simplify the configuration and management of frame-relay-based networks. Even considering this impressive list of benefits, there is one benefit that seems to be having a far greater impact than the rest: even though the idea of raw cost reduction comes to mind, the benefit is reduction of network latency, which has a positive performance impact and also a cost reduction element.

Historically, network designers and engineers have worked on increasing the number of bits per second that could be transferred between two points. This work has included developing new compression schemes, streamlining protocols, improving the line encoding to increase the number of bits that could be represented per baud, and other similar activities. The new trend, and one that emerging broadband networks are capitalizing on, is the reduction of the number of seconds required to move a specified number of bytes—in other words, instead of increasing the number

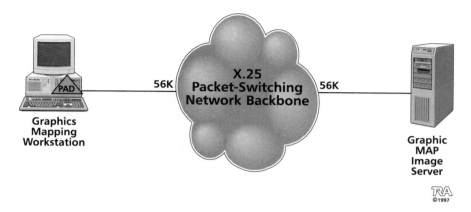

Figure 3.9   X.25 Network-Based Mapping Application

of bits per second, reducing the number of seconds per bit. These two approaches, when applied simultaneously in frame relay networks, can have substantial impact. Put a different way, frame relay can optimize the low-latency/higher-bandwidth applications that have typically been ideal for TDM circuit-switching systems and the more bursty multiple destination applications that have typically required packet-switching systems.

One application that clearly showcases latency reduction through the use of the frame relay interface is a raw file transfer application. One such sample application is the transfer of topographic map files between graphic-oriented "map stations" on geographically disbursed LANs. Each map file would average 588 kilobytes in length.

In the initial configuration (Figure 3.9), each of the 588-kilobyte map files would take approximately 3 minutes 50 seconds to transmit. The key points to note about Figure 3.9 are that the use of an X.25 network, which has a maximum access speed of 56 Kbits/second, requires full buffering and interpretation of OSI Layers 1, 2, and 3 at each intermediate node and handles information in units of packets.

In a possible "Phase 2" configuration (Figure 3.10), the X.25 network is replaced with a T1 backbone and nodal processors that provide T1 speed ATM as a backbone switching fabric. The access speed remains at 56 Kbits/second, and the point-to-point protocol (PPP) router firmware replaces the X.25 firmware. T1 trunks are used within the backbone. The average transfer time for a map file drops from 3 minutes 50 seconds to 1 minute 45 seconds, a decrease of 2 minutes 5 seconds, or 54%. At this point,

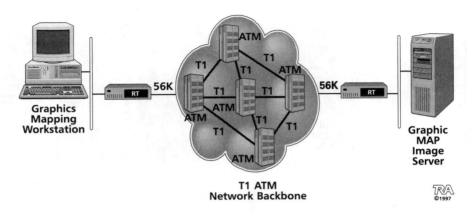

Figure 3.10   Graphic Mapping Application with T1 ATM Backbone

frame relay has not yet been implemented. The latency reduction associated with using dedicated 56-Kbits/second facilities instead of X.25 at 56 Kbits/second is all that has been realized. In the Phase 2 implementation, there is minimal buffering of data inside the network and no OSI Layer 2 and Layer 3 processing latency at intermediate nodes resulting from a heavyweight packet-switching protocol—just a clear 56 Kbits/second path from source router to destination router.

In migrating from Phase 2 to Phase 3, frame relay is implemented on the same T1 cell relay backbone as Phase 2. The frame relay physical access bandwidth utilizes a fractional T1 with 12 DS0s and provides 768 Kbits/second of access bandwidth. The individual connections from router to router are still defined at 56 Kbits/second, but now have the ability to instantaneously burst to the maximum bandwidth of 768 Kbits/second when needed. Special software mechanisms are in place to enforce fairness on the interface and ensure one connection does not "hog" all of the bandwidth when multiple connections require bandwidth. When all users need bandwidth (the worst-case scenario and one that is statistically unlikely on a properly sized frame relay interface), they will each be given only their committed information rate (CIR), or exactly what they have subscribed for. When only one user needs bandwidth, they will be given bandwidth up to the maximum available, even if it exceeds their CIR. Even with these mechanisms being enforced and a CIR of 56 Kbits/second, this application, with no contention from other PVCs, realized an effective throughput of approximately 378 Kbits/second.

Phase 3 further reduces average transfer time to 11 seconds, which is only 10.5% of Phase 2's average and 4.8% of the time required in Phase 1. By increasing the amount of bandwidth available to transfer the information, the amount of time required has been reduced. The key points, though, are that the bandwidth has been substantially increased in such a way that overall network recurring costs have been reduced and several logical connections may cost-effectively share a single multiplexed physical connection. A more subtle aspect of this application is that it uses several products from different manufacturers that match a common standard.

3.8 Frame-Relay-to-ATM Interworking

One of the big questions for the last several years has been "Should I implement frame relay now or wait for ATM to come along?" We have addressed the business aspects of this question in Chapter 2. Here we will look at the technical aspects. We will look briefly at frame-relay-only cases, at ATM-only cases, and at the two varieties of frame-relay-to-ATM interworking: service interworking, which allows frame relay devices to communicate with ATM devices and vice versa, and network interworking, which uses high-speed ATM as a transport for information between frame-relay-capable devices.

3.8.1 The Roles of Frame Relay and ATM

In most cases, remote sites have fairly low bandwidth requirements, and there are a lot of them. The reverse is true of data centers: they tend to have high bandwidth requirements, often due to the aggregation of the many small requirements from the remote sites, and there tend to be very few of them. In cases where the applications requirements at the remote sites are for data and/or frame-based voice or video only and there are not that many remote sites—that is, the aggregate of remote traffic is low—frame relay will provide an ideal solution, and there is no reason to even consider the use of ATM. In cases where bandwidth requirements are great at both the remote sites and the host site(s), as is often the case with medical imaging, computer-aided engineering, or computer modeling applications, ATM makes sense for both the remote and host sites because of multimedia and bandwidth concerns.

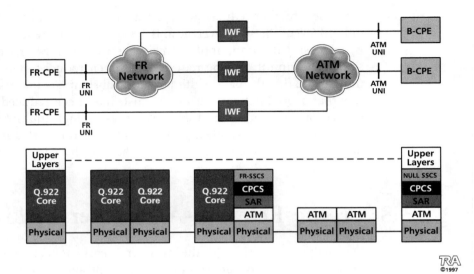

Figure 3.11 Frame-Relay-to-ATM Service Interworking. Source: *Frame Relay Forum Implementation Agreement Number 8 (FRF.8), "Frame Relay/ATM PVC Service Interworking Implementation Agreement," April 1995.*

However, in cases where the remote bandwidth requirements are low and those of the central site are high, it makes sense to use frame-relay-to-ATM service interworking. Where it is desirable to carry frame relay across an ATM switching fabric, as is often desirable in a carrier or service provider infrastructure that must be able to carry a variety of types of data besides frame relay, the use of frame-relay-to-ATM network interworking is advisable.

Frame-relay-to-ATM service interworking is shown in Figure 3.11. The frame relay customer premise equipment (CPE), or frame relay access device, on the left side of the figure communicates with the ATM-capable CPE on the right side of the figure via an interworking function (IWF) that translates between frames and cells.

The upper OSI layers in the FRAD equipment on the left side of Figure 3.11 use a frame relay UNI to connect to the ATM network, either directly via an IWF or indirectly via a frame relay network and then through an IWF. The IWF performs a gateway function and converts the Q.922 core functions to the ATM frame relay service-specific convergence sublayer (FR-SSCS), which in turn uses the common part convergence sublayer (CPCS), segmentation and reassembly (SAR), and asynchronous transfer mode (ATM) layers to access the ATM switching fabric. The various sub-layers within the IWF communicate with their peers in the ATM-capable end system or intermediate system on the extreme right side.

The biggest difference between service interworking and network interworking is that service interworking delivers cells to the ATM-capable intermediate system or end system, while network interworking utilizes another IWF to convert the cells back to frames again. Network interworking simply uses ATM transport for moving frames through the switching fabric, usually either at very high speeds or mixed with other, non-frame-relay traffic, or both. Network interworking is fundamentally what is being done today by systems that provide frame relay interfaces to ATM switching fabrics: the IWF is implemented on the frame relay interface cards and performs frame/cell conversion and header function mapping.

3.8.2 Frame/Cell Conversion

In order to maintain the integrity of control information being transmitted within the header of a frame relay frame across a frame relay network to an ATM network interworking connection, or to properly communicate control information from frame relay to ATM in a service interworking situation, it is necessary to convert the variable-length frame relay frames to the fixed-length cells of ATM and, in the case of network interworking, back again. In addition to a fairly straightforward frame segmentation and reassembly process, all header information must be passed along as well.

The frame segmentation process is detailed in Figure 3.12. One thing implied in Figure 3.12, but not stated explicitly, is that ATM inherently has more overhead than frame relay. A Q.922 frame relay frame is put through the frame relay service-specific convergence sublayer, where it loses its two-byte frame check sequence, but keeps its three-byte header, and is then passed to the ATM Adaptation Layer 5 (AAL5) common part convergence sublayer, where some control information is added and the frame is padded out so that it is evenly divisible by 48, the payload size of the ATM cell. The unit is then passed to the AAL5 segmentation and reassembly process, where the 48-byte payloads are parsed and passed to the ATM layer, where five-byte headers are pre-pended to the 48-byte payload prior to being switched on their way to their destinations.

In this process, additional overhead for the ATM cells is added at the rate of 5 bytes per 48 bytes of frame size. This process can add a substantial amount of overhead in systems where frames are short and are not evenly divisible by 48.

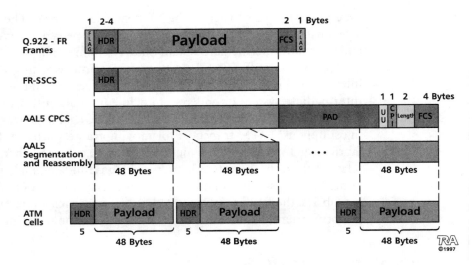

Figure 3.12   Frame Segmentation into ATM Cells. Source: *Frame Relay Forum White Paper: "Frame Relay and Frame-Based ATM: A Comparison of Technologies,"* June 1995.

3.8.3   Header Function Mapping

Some functions of frame relay and ATM are identical and can be mapped directly while others are a bit different and must be interpreted. Figure 3.13 shows the header function mapping process graphically. Information that is translated, or mapped, as a part of this process includes address information, congestion signaling, and eligibility for discard during congestion.

DLCI to VPI/VCI Mapping

Traditional protocols such as X.25, SDLC, IP, Ethernet, and Token Ring utilize "from" and "to" addressing in their header. Frame relay and ATM both utilize connection identifiers that identify the path of information with a single number (the frame relay DLCI) or pair of numbers—the ATM virtual path identifier (VPI) and virtual connection identifier (VCI). Mapping to and from DLCI and VPI/VCI involves translation of the DLCI and VPI/VCI.

DE to CLP Mapping

The ATM equivalent of the discard eligibility bit is the cell loss priority (CLP) bit. A direct mapping, one to the other, is possible, giving each of

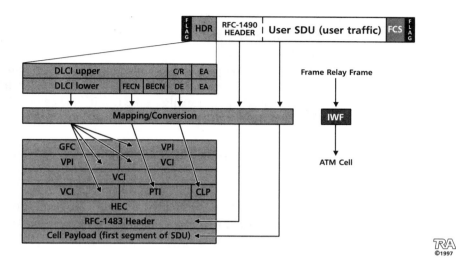

Figure 3.13 Frame-Relay-to-ATM Header Function Mapping. Source: *Frame Relay Forum White Paper: "Frame Relay and Frame-Based ATM: A Comparison of Technologies," June 1995.*

the individual cells carrying their respective 48 bytes of the frame the same chance of being discarded in case of failure. This actually has the effect of increasing the probability that a frame will be discarded because a single DE bit will cause the frame to be discarded or not discarded, while the dropping of a single cell will cause the frame's frame check sequence to be incorrect and cause the dropping of the entire frame.

FECN to EFCI Mapping

The ATM equivalent of the forward explicit congestion notification (FECN) bit is the explicit forward congestion indicator (EFCI) bit, which is the middle of the three bits that make up the payload type indication (PTI) field of the ATM cell's header. A one-to-one mapping of these bits is also possible, with the cell's being more accurate in terms of conveying congestion information because there will be more cells for any frame greater than 48 bytes than there are frames, and more occurrences of EFCI bits than FECN bits during a certain period of time. Because more EFCI bits will occur during the same period of time, congestion mechanisms that are cell based will "converge" more quickly—that is, indicate congestion sooner—because congestion indication and reaction are statistical, relying on the last *n* bits and what percentage of them are a one or a zero rather than reacting to congestion on a one-to-one basis.

The basic five-byte ATM header format, while it does support forward congestion indication, does not support a BECN-type bit to provide for a closed feedback congestion loop. The ATM Forum has adopted a closed-loop congestion mechanism, which may be implemented either on an end-to-end basis or on a hop-by-hop basis that utilizes a bit in an optional additional overhead bit appearing in the traditional cell payload.

FCS versus HEC

The frame check sequence (FCS) of frame relay is intended to check the validity of the entire frame, including the header and payload, while the header error check (HEC) of ATM only verifies the integrity of the ATM header. This does not present a problem operationally, however, because the higher-layer protocols encapsulated in frame relay, and then into ATM, ordinarily have their own equivalent of FCS, which is used to check the integrity of information being transmitted and to take appropriate steps to assure validity.

3.9 Conclusion

Frame relay is a standardized interface that provides multiplexed access to bandwidth-on-demand backbone networks and delivers LAN-like performance over the wide area. Frame relay can enable reduction of direct and indirect costs, can simplify network design and operation, and is applicable to local area network interconnection, host-to-host communications, and traditional terminal environments. Frame relay can provide a common interface method for many traditional and emerging data communications requirements and complements cell relay backbones.

In Part 3, we will begin to look at actual frame relay applications. We will take a look at representative case studies covering four diverse areas of frame relay applications. We will look at traditional terminal traffic, migration to distributed computing, LAN-to-LAN, and LAN interworking applications. Unlike the real-world case studies in Part 4, the conceptual case studies represent a composite of common requirements from several different companies in each case study, as opposed to the requirements of a single company. In many ways the conceptual case studies are a better learning tool because they are more representative of a group than any one case study from a single company could be, and they will definitely prepare you to fully appreciate the customer-specific case studies that follow.

PART THREE

Conceptual Case Studies

CHAPTER FOUR

Traditional Terminal Traffic

Traditional terminal applications, such as IBM 3270 and DEC VT-100, do not get much press anymore: they are well known, widely deployed technologies in their declining years. Even so, traditional terminal applications still represent a very large part of the information carried on corporate networks and are still the most common devices found on networks today. This fact is obscured somewhat because many "traditional terminal" applications are now operated from personal computers running emulation programs, connecting to their host computer either through dial-up modems, direct connections using emulator hardware, through local area networks, or via the Internet or intranets using TN3270 or Telnet packages. It is because of the predominance of traditional terminal applications that we begin our conceptual case studies with this type of application.

4.1 Case Study Background

Our first of four composite case studies is a manufacturer with 131 remote sales offices and warehouses located throughout the United States. Through acquisition, the manufacturer has two data centers and a highly

Table 4.1   **Terminal/Host Combinations**

	Hosts	
	IBM	DEC VAX
Terminals		
3270/SNA	native mode	SNA to X.25 (STX)
3270/BSC	BSC/SNA protocol converter	BSC to SNA+STX
VT-100	VT-100/SNA protocol converter	native mode

heterogeneous terminal population. One data center, located in Los Angeles, California, operates a group of Digital Equipment Corporation VAX computers. The second data center, located in Atlanta, Georgia, houses IBM mainframes.

The present remote terminal population is 28 off-brand IBM 3270 BSC look-alike terminals, 45 DEC VT-100 terminals, 57 IBM 3270/SNA terminals, and one Novell LAN with several PC workstations and an SNA/3270 gateway that allows LAN-connected PCs to access the IBM host as though they are SNA/3270-type terminals. In order to provide connectivity from any terminal to any host, the manufacturer has carefully assembled a patchwork quilt of emulators and protocol converters, but they do not operate very well.

All terminals are connected via terminal packet assembler/disassemblers (PADs) to a private X.25 backbone. The terminals access the desired hosts across the X.25 backbone.

Table 4.1 describes the possible combinations of terminals and hosts that are accommodated in this network as well as their method of connection. The PCs on the LAN are treated as 3270 terminals because that is how they appear to the host.

4.2 Problem Statement: Slow Response Times

The manufacturer has become concerned with abysmally slow terminal response times. Poor response times at terminals translate into poor customer service. Poor customer service, in turn, translates into revenues lost to competitors with faster, more responsive systems. High overtime costs are also attributed to slow terminal response and poor performance by the protocol converters: employees have to work evening and weekend hours entering payroll, sales order, and inventory data that could not be entered during normal working hours.

Another side effect of the slow response times was that the network was virtually frozen. No new applications could be added because there was no more time to use them. For example, the manufacturer wanted to add companywide electronic mail to their network. They knew electronic mail would allow faster distribution of important price and policy updates, customer special-order information, and other documents that are usually sent by expensive Federal Express or slow U.S. mail.

The slow, overburdened network could not accommodate this (or any other) new application, and therefore it was a barrier to the company's being competitive in their market.

4.3 Response Time Analysis

An analysis of network response times showed an average response time of 7–10 seconds when accessing IBM-based applications and 5–7 seconds when accessing DEC-based applications (see Table 4.2).

The manufacturer performed several steps to reduce response times. Beginning response times were 7–10 seconds for IBM and 5–7 seconds for DEC. By the end of the first optimization steps, the average response times were $4\frac{3}{4}$ seconds on the IBM mainframe and $4\frac{1}{4}$ seconds on the DEC computers.

Table 4.2   **Response Time Analysis**

Description	Host Response (seconds)		Terminal Response (seconds)	
	IBM	DEC	IBM	DEC
Beginning response times	7–10	5–7	Immediate	$1\frac{1}{2}$–2
Optimize host applications and file organization	6–8	5–6	—	—
3270 spoofing	5–7	—	—	—
Local echo for VT-100	—	—	Immediate	Immediate
Upgrade to NACs and 19.2	$4\frac{3}{4}$	$4\frac{1}{4}$	Immediate	Immediate
Average response times after first optimization steps	$4\frac{3}{4}$	$4\frac{1}{4}$	Immediate	Immediate

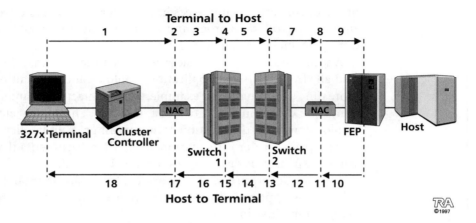

Figure 4.1   End-to-End Connectivity and Delay Elements

The manufacturer felt response times of 4+ seconds were still poor and set a sub-3-second response time objective. The manufacturer revisited the X.25 backbone and reviewed the X.25 network more closely. A sample case involving a 3270 terminal requesting a full screen of information was developed. The X.25 network was diagrammed, Figure 4.1, and all known components of latency were added to it.

The request from the terminal is 9 bytes long. An additional 37 bytes of SDLC overhead (such as source and destination addresses and other information) are added to the 9-byte request, for a total of 46 bytes of SDLC framed information to be transferred. At 8 bits to the byte, there are 368 bits to be transferred. From this point forward, to insure the most accuracy we can possibly use, latencies will not be measured in seconds, or fractions of seconds, but rather in milliseconds (ms).

Thousandths of a second may seem to be a pretty fine granularity, but in calculating network latencies, thousandths of a second add up pretty quickly: only 200 ms make ⅕ second, 250 ms make ¼ second, and 500 ms make ½ second.

The terminals are attached to the network access controllers (NACs) at 19.2 Kbits/second; therefore, it takes 19 milliseconds to transfer the 368 bits of our message from the 3270 terminal to the NAC. The 19 ms required to transfer the 368 bits from the terminal to the NAC is called *serialization delay.* Serialization delay is calculated by dividing the number of bits to be

Table 4.3 **Bits/Transfer Calculation**

Calculation of number of bits to transfer:	
Request size	9 bytes
Plus SDLC overhead	+ 37 bytes
	46 bytes to transfer
46 bytes	46 bytes
Times 8 bits/byte	× 8 bits/byte
	368 bits to transfer

transmitted (in our case 368) by the speed with which the medium will transmit the bits (in our case 19.2 Kbits/second).

The NAC takes an average of 200 ms ($\frac{1}{5}$ second) to process the request message, which also includes adding X.25 overhead (packet layer, ISO Layer 3) source and destination addresses and control information to create a full-fledged X.25 information packet and data link layer (ISO Layer 2) addressing and control information. The new overhead adds 19 bytes, bringing our transmission total to 520 bits. Serialization delay encountered when transmitting from the terminal NAC to X.25 Switch 1 is 9 ms.

X.25 Switch 1 requires 250 ms ($\frac{1}{4}$ second) on average to process and begin retransmitting our X.25 packet to Switch 2. The serialization delay at the port where our data leaves Switch 1 for Switch 2 also requires 250 ms on average to process our X.25 packet and begin retransmitting it on to the host NAC. The host NAC takes about 200 ms to process our X.25 packet, which includes removing our 19 bytes of X.25 overhead and forwarding only an SDLC frame to the FEP.

Transmission of the SDLC frame from the NAC to the FEP takes 6 ms. The total time from our 3270 terminal to the host is 952 ms, or almost 1 second.

Tables 4.3 and 4.4 review what we have figured out so far.

After approximately 1 second of host processing, the transfer steps are repeated in reverse order. The only real difference is that the host does not actually send a full 80-column-by-24-row screen image. What is transmitted is a message that is compressed by an average of 15% in this scenario. This gives us a 1,632-byte transmission from the host to the terminal. Our new host-to-terminal calculations are shown in Tables 4.5 and 4.6.

Table 4.4   **Terminal-to-Host Latency Calculation**

Calculation of terminal-to-host latency:

(1) Serialization (terminal to NAC @ 19.2K)	19 ms
(2) NAC processing (plus X.25 overhead = 520 total bits)	200 ms
(3) Serialization (NAC to Switch 1 @ 56K)	9 ms
(4) Switch 1 processing	250 ms
(5) Serialization (Switch 1 to Switch 2 @ 56K)	9 ms
(6) Switch 2 processing	250 ms
(7) Serialization (Switch 2 to NAC @ 56K)	9 ms
(8) NAC processing (minus X.25 overhead = 368 total bits)	200 ms
(9) Serialization (NAC to FEP @ 56K)	6 ms
Total terminal-to-host latency	952 ms

* Numbers on left side are keyed to Figure 4.1.

Table 4.5   **Bits to Transfer Calculation for Compressed Screen**

Calculation of number of bits to transfer:

Screen size (80 bytes x 24 bytes)		1,920 bytes
Apply compression of 15% to get		1,632 bytes
Add SDLC overhead of	+	37 bytes
		1,669 bytes to transfer
Bytes to transfer		1,669 bytes
Times 8 bits/byte	×	8 bits/byte
		13,352 bits to transfer

Table 4.6   **Host-to-Terminal Latency for Compressed Screen**

Calculation of host-to-terminal latency:

(10) Serialization (FEP to NAC @ 56K)	233 ms
(11) NAC processing (plus X.25 overhead = 13,504 total bits)	200 ms
(12) Serialization (NAC to Switch 1 @ 56K)	235 ms
(13) Switch 1 processing	250 ms
(14) Serialization (Switch 1 to Switch 2)	235 ms
(15) Switch 2 processing	250 ms
(16) Serialization (Switch 2 to NAC @ 56K)	235 ms
(17) NAC processing (minus X.25 overhead = 13,352 total bytes)	200 ms
(18) Serialization (NAC to terminal @ 19.2K)	679 ms
Total host-to-terminal latency	2,518 ms

Table 4.7   **Total Interactive Response Time**

Total terminal-to-host latency	952 ms
Plus host processing	1,000 ms
Plus total host-to-terminal latency	2,518 ms
Total interactive response time	4,470 ms

Table 4.8   **Latency Contribution by Component**

Item	Total Latency	Percent Contribution
Host processing latency contribution	1,000 ms	22.4%
NAC processing latency contribution	800 ms	17.9%
Serialization latency contribution	1,669 ms	37.3%
Switch processing latency contribution	1,000 ms	22.4%
Total latency	4,470 ms	100.0%

In order to calculate the total elapsed time experienced by the 3270 terminal user in our sample case, we must perform one more calculation, total interactive response time, shown in Table 4.7.

The total interactive response time calculation shows our total response time to be about 4½ seconds, which tracks pretty well with our observed average of 4¾ seconds. Minor variations in processing times by the NACs (and/or X.25 switches and/or host) could easily account for 250 ms (¼ second).

The next step performed was the calculation of which components of delay contribute the most latency to overall interactive response time (Table 4.8). This is done by adding up all of the latencies in each category and determining their contribution to the total. Table 4.8 and Figure 4.2 show that 22.4% of the total latency is attributable to the X.25 switches, another 22.4% is contributed by the host, 17.9% is a result of NAC processing, and 37.3% is attributable to serialization delay.

The host processing times have already been reduced about as much as they are going to be right now, so they are considered fixed. The NACs are brand-new and solve some very serious connectivity problems, so the 800 ms of latency that the NAC processing contributes will be considered fixed as well.

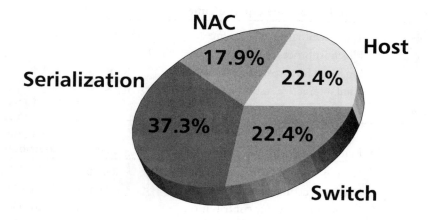

Figure 4.2   Latency Contributions

4.3.1 Network Latency Reduction

The two areas that are left are switch processing and serialization delay. Let's review switch processing first. The X.25 switches used are based on older microprocessor technology. The older technology adds an average processing delay of about 250 ms each way. The network design is already optimized in terms of minimum number of switches (3) required to maximize performance and minimize communications line costs. In order to obtain faster processing, the manufacturer will have to upgrade to a new technology. In parallel with this study, they have investigated frame relay interface offerings more carefully. They have learned that cell relay technology is an optimum backbone switching mechanism for use with frame relay.

A cell relay backbone would use switches that do not interpret the entire frame at each node. Fixed-length pieces of the frames (cells) are routed over the cell relay backbone at high speed. Cell relay switches introduce an average latency of only .5 ms per node. If latency is recalculated based upon the new switch processing latency of .5 ms per switch, our results would be as shown in Table 4.9.

By simply replacing the X.25 switches with frame relay interfaces to cell relay switches, the manufacturer could shave almost another full second from the latency. It must be pointed out here that the X.25 switches in question are very old switches that had been in place since the 1980s and

Table 4.9   **Latency after Frame Relay**

Item	Total Latency	Percent Contribution
Host processing latency contribution	1,000 ms	28.8%
NAC processing latency contribution	800 ms	23.0%
Serialization latency contribution	1,669 ms	48.1%
Switch processing latency contribution	2 ms	.1%
Total latency	3,471 ms	100.0%

that the X.25 switches available today are only slightly slower than routers. It is because older X.25 switching technology is being replaced that the differences in this case study when going from X.25 to frame relay are as good as they are.

At this point the manufacturer has yet to achieve their sub-3-second response time objective. The good news is that serialization delay has not yet been addressed. Next, we must assess the impact that frame relay might have on serialization delay. All data communications links in the network could theoretically be increased to T1 speeds of 1.544 Mbits/second, but we will soon see that the actual implementation of specific pieces of hardware would not allow us to do so in the real world.

T1 provides the largest bandwidth readily available from North American telecommunications carriers. T1's transfer rate is below frame relay's maximum interface rate of 2.048 Mbits/second. The maximum 2.048-Mbit/second interface rate is the same as European E1, which is mandated by frame relay's standing as an international standard. T1 would, exclusive of NAC and host processing times, provide near instantaneous response times in this scenario, but T1 everywhere is not a practical solution.

The connection from the 3270 terminal controller to the NAC will not handle T1, but could be increased from 19.2 Kbits/second to 56 Kbits/second. The IBM 3270 terminal controller will not support connection at speeds greater than 56 Kbits/second. The manufacturer decides that this upgrade would be too expensive for all 131 sites (over $280,000) and the monthly leased line costs would be exorbitant as well. This connection will, therefore, stay at 19.2 Kbits/second.

The $280,000 figure and all prices that follow in this case study are provided for rough order-of-magnitude estimation only. While these costs will be representative of actual costs at the time of this writing, you should consult your own vendor for prices specific to your company.

The terminal NAC-to-switch connections are presently operating at 56 Kbits/second. If the X.25 switches are retained, 56 Kbits/second is the highest rate that can be supported because the X.25 standard limits interface speeds to 64 Kbits/second. In fact, 56 Kbits/second is the highest speed supported by the manufacturer of the X.25 switch; frame relay would allow us to go to 2.048 Mbits/second.

Another important consideration, however, is the NAC. The NAC can only support a maximum 128-Kbit/second frame relay trunk, which seems a gracious plenty for 19.2-Kbit/second terminal connections. The company will, therefore, increase the NAC-to-switch connections to 128 Kbits/second if the X.25 switches are replaced with cell relay switches. Trunks between switches presently operate at 56 Kbits/second. The maximum speed provided for in the X.25 standards is 64 Kbits/second, but 56-Kbit/second DDS circuits are being used in this network, making 56 Kbits/second the effective X.25 maximum. A shift to a frame relay interface with a cell relay backbone would allow replacement of the 56-Kbit/second trunks with T1 trunks. While the cost would seem much higher for T1, only three 56-Kbit/second trunks would be replaced with three T1 trunks in the current design. The cost difference would be spread over 131 sites.

4.3.2   Cost Assessment

Replacement of all three 56-Kbit/second trunks with T1 trunks would increase monthly costs from $12,260 to $43,078 and would require one-time installation costs (nonrecurring charges, or NRCs) of $11,764.

The difference of $30,818 per month seems significant, but management is willing to spend $235 per month per site for the performance increases that have been calculated. Payroll costs for overtime are in the range of $1,200 per site per month, and the net effect of this upgrade would be a savings of about $1,000 per site per month (over $1.5 million annually).

The replacement of the X.25 switches would also require an investment in three cell relay switches with frame relay interface, which would cost approximately $50,000 each, or $150,000. The three cell relay switches could be leased at a monthly cost of approximately $3,900.

The proposed network would yield cost savings of $1.5 million per year and provide a strong platform for expanding applications. New applications could make the manufacturer more competitive in their marketplace and make an even larger contribution to the bottom line than the $1.5 million-per-year savings.

Based upon these calculations, the manufacturer decides to replace the X.25 switches with cell relay switches equipped with frame relay interfaces. The 56-Kbit/second DDS lines will be upgraded to T1 lines. Because of cost considerations, NAC to FEP links will not be upgraded at this time.

4.3.3 Latency Improvement after Upgrade

Based upon the decisions about upgrades to the communications facilities and switches, total latency was recalculated (Table 4.10).

How has the use of frame relay on a cell relay backbone affected latencies? Table 4.11 shows that the results are impressive.

The new configuration, utilizing a frame relay interface with cell relay switches interconnected at T1 speeds, would meet the manufacturer's sub-3-second response time objectives. The monthly T1 costs and additional hardware costs are well justified. Based on the tangible cost savings in payroll (over $1.5 million per year) and intangible benefits of better morale and better customer service, the decision was made to move forward with a new frame relay network.

Table 4.10   **Latency after Upgrade**

Item	Total Latency	Percent Contribution
Host processing latency contribution	1,000 ms	34.9%
NAC processing latency contribution	800 ms	27.8%
Serialization latency contribution	1,066 ms	37.2%
Switch processing latency contribution	2 ms	.1%
Total latency	2,868 ms	100.0%

Table 4.11   **Latency Improvement Comparison**

Item	Original Latency	New Latency	Difference
Host processing latency	1,000 ms	1,000 ms	—
NAC processing latency	800 ms	800 ms	—
Serialization latency	1,669 ms	1,066 ms	603 ms
Switch processing latency	1,000 ms	2 ms	998 ms
Total latency	4,469 ms	2,868 ms	1,601 ms

4.3.4 Private versus Public Frame Relay Network Option

Before committing to build a private frame relay network, the manufacturer reviewed the possibility of using a public frame relay network. The manufacturer found several benefits in using the public network: There is no need to invest in the cell relay switches because they are imbedded in the public network and the hardware cost is built into the cost of the service. The public network provider offers 24-hour-per-day, seven-day-per-week network management with no increase in head count, as compared to the 6 AM EST to 6 PM PST, five-day-per-week coverage that the manufacturer presently provides internally. The public network allows many more alternate paths for rerouting than the manufacturer could reasonably afford, so the public network will provide a more reliable solution. The public frame relay network offers accurate budgeting of costs because of fixed monthly fees. And when operations are once again expanded, the manufacturer will be able to connect their new acquisitions quickly and cost-effectively to the public network anywhere in the United States.

The only question that remains is what services to purchase on the public network. This question must be answered before pricing can be developed. The connection to the public network will supply 128 Kbits/second of bandwidth between the NACs and the public network's frame relay interfaces/cell relay switches. The public network's cell relay switches would move information at T3 speeds inside the network, thus giving the full reductions in response time the manufacturer has calculated.

Table 4.12 shows that price was also a compelling argument for using a public network because it was a fraction of the cost of the private offering, is more flexible, and provides 24-hour-per-day, seven-day-per-week network management at no additional cost.

Based upon the pricing and several excellent customer references, the decision was made to use the public frame relay service. The public frame relay approach yields sub-3-second response times, enhanced network management, configuration flexibility, rerouting, and the lowest possible cost.

Table 4.12   **Public vs. Private Cost Comparison**

From	To	Circuit Miles	Present 56K	T1 Monthly	Non-recurring	Public Net Monthly	Non-recurring
Atlanta 404–850	Seattle 206–433	2,196	4,700	17,661	4,150	1,420	700
Los Angeles 213–386	Atlanta 404–850	1,931	4,564	15,858	4,031	1,420	700
Seattle 206–433	Los Angeles 213–386	968	2,996	9,559	3,583	1,420	700
Monthly totals		5,095	12,260	43,078	11,764	4,260	2,100
Additional hardware			0	153,280		0	

4.4 Conclusion

In this conceptual case study, frame relay was used to replace an existing X.25 installation. Is this an ideal application? It certainly is. Did the customer use all of the features and capabilities of frame relay? No, not really, but the parts they used solved the problems they had. The replacement of X.25 networks was a big issue in the United States during the earlier part of the 1990s and is becoming less of an issue today. But there is a great deal of X.25 still working internationally, which may be migrated to frame relay over the next couple of decades, depending on the regulatory and pricing issues in a given country and the privatization of the country's postal, telephone, and telegraph authorities.

The next case study will focus more on architectural changes, specifically a decentralization of computer processing, and less on specific issues like latency. The next case study highlights one of the many ways in which frame relay is an enabling technology that can be used to create opportunities for businesses to implement new applications systems or architectures.

CHAPTER FIVE

Migration to Distributed Computing

In the early years of information processing, the computer was, by necessity, a single, centralized device that provided a centralized information repository and data processing capability for the entire corporation. The early computer was housed in a special, environmentally controlled facility and was tended to by small armies of specially trained technicians, often wearing white lab coats. More than any two other factors, it was the high cost and physical delicacy of the device that caused it to be centralized and shared.

The next evolutionary step was to provide local interactive terminals, which allowed the "simultaneous" sharing of the central computer by multiple users. The local interactive terminals were outside of the specially controlled environment but still within a short distance. The next step, obviously, was to allow the terminals to operate at a greater distance, across traditional analog telephone lines, via modems. And then came the personal computer revolution.

The personal computer revolution placed both computer and data on the desk of the users. The popularity of personally dedicated computing resources soared, even though data integrity could not be easily assured in the new environment. While the storage of local data on a personal

computer for personal use, and later on LAN file servers for shared depart-
mental use, was initially favored by the users, it was soon obvious that sharing of data among users, especially those located some distance apart, and
coordination of version control, updates, backups, and other critical functions were made difficult by the physical distances. Many organizations
solved this problem by centralizing information repositories, so that they
could be managed centrally, but distributing computer power on desktops.
This is the exact point at which we meet the company in our next case
study: they have decided to distribute access and processing of information from a central repository.

5.1 Case Study Background

Our second conceptual case study is a check authorization company based
in Memphis, Tennessee. The check authorizer employs approximately 9,000
people and has five regional check-clearing call centers located in Los
Angeles, Dallas, Chicago, New York, and Memphis. The corporate data
center is located in Memphis as well.

When a retail business is offered a check by a customer, the retailer dials
a toll-free 800 number that connects the caller to one of the regional call
centers. The call center operator keys the customer's driver's license number, checking account number, check amount, and the merchant's ID
number into an IBM 3278 or IBM 3178 display terminal, which is connected to an IBM 3274 or 3174 cluster controller.

The information is transmitted to IBM 3725 and IBM 3745 FEPs and
compared to a central database shared by several IBM 4381 host processors. The database contains bad-check information from all 50 U.S. states.
If no match is found in the database, an authorization number is transmitted to the operator, and the merchant's account is charged a service charge.
The call center operator then tells the merchant the authorization number,
and the transaction is completed.

As seen in the example above, all of the information is centrally stored
in Memphis. The present centralized approach introduces large amounts
of latency into the transaction process. Because network delay can be translated into terminal operator and customer waiting time, and because the
check authorizer pays their terminal operators a salary, it is possible to

translate network latency into lost money. For this reason, the check authorizer has reviewed alternatives and determined that the expense of installing LANs in the regional call centers is justified.

Any solution the check authorizer ultimately selects must be consistent with IBM's Systems Network Architecture. The check authorizer runs a traditional IBM shop.

5.2 Application Analysis

Let's take a closer look at a typical call center. Each center is approximately the same size, with the New York and Los Angeles centers being slightly larger. The typical call center has 1,300 call center operators at peak load. Each operator occupies a position with an IBM 3278 or newer IBM 3178 display terminal, as shown in Figure 5.1.

There is one supervisor per 25 call center operators, each with their own IBM 3178 display terminal, and another 30 display terminals required for administrative purposes. That would bring our terminal count per call center to 1,300 + 52 + 30, or 1,382 terminals.

Each of the display terminals is connected to an IBM 3174 or older IBM 3274 control unit (CU). In order to optimize performance, no more than 16 display terminals are connected to a single control unit (or, as they are often referred to, "cluster controller").

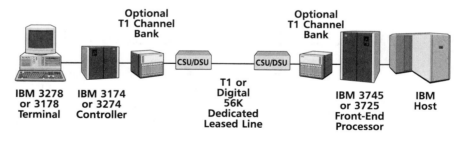

Figure 5.1 Typical Call Center Terminal Configuration

Table 5.1   Cluster Controller to FEP Connections

1,300 call center operators, at 16 per CU	82 CUs
52 supervisors, at 16 per CU	4 CUs
30 administrators, at 16 per CU	2 CUs
Total	88 CUs

The number of connections that need to be made from cluster controllers to FEPs is 88 (see Table 5.1). The connections from the 88 control units located in the remote call centers are accomplished through a combination of dedicated digital leased lines and T1 lines with time division multiplexed channel banks. The net effect, in either case, is a dedicated 64-Kbit/second connection from the remote cluster controller to the Memphis host site.

5.3   Solution: Remote Token Ring LANs

The check authorizer reviewed several different possibilities, including the option of decentralizing operations as well as using remote front-end processors to improve response times. The check authorizer finally determined that bridging remote token ring LANs into Memphis would be the best solution. Not only would a bridged token ring approach provide the lowest latencies, it would also position the check authorizer for future LAN-based applications.

5.3.1   Remote LANs with Dedicated T1 Lines

What would a bridged remote token ring configuration look like? Figure 5.2 shows that IBM 3178/3278 display terminals would be connected to IBM 3174/3274 CUs via coaxial cable. The 3174/3274 CUs would be connected to token ring LANs. The token ring LANs would be connected to token ring bridges. The token ring bridges would be connected to T1 lines. The T1 lines would be connected to token ring bridges in Memphis, which would be connected to one of several token ring LANs in Memphis, which would be connected to FEPs via Token Ring Interface Couplers (TICs).

Let's take a look at what this would cost for a representative site, say, from the Los Angeles data center to Memphis. Details are shown in Tables 5.2 and 5.3.

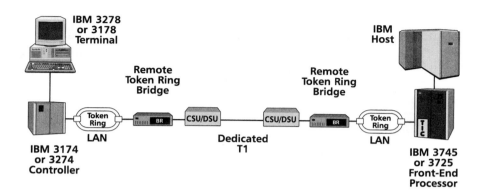

Figure 5.2 Bridged Remote Token Ring Solution

Table 5.2	**Sample One-Time Hardware Costs for Remote Token Rings with Dedicated T1: Los Angeles to Memphis**		

Item	Qty	Each	Total
Token ring LAN bridge/T1 (both ends) (9 LANs are required to support all terminal controllers)	18	$9,500	$171,000
T1 CSUs (both ends)	18	2,000	36,000
Total			$207,000

Table 5.3	**Sample Recurring Costs for Remote Token Rings with Dedicated T1: Los Angeles to Memphis**		

Item	Qty	Each	Total
T1 lines from Los Angeles to Memphis	9	$16,921	$152,289
Total			$152,289

Hardware/software costs for remote FEPs were calculated at $640,000 with monthly expenditures of $84,605. These figures were compared with the cost of bridged token ring LANs using dedicated, leased T1 facilities. While the hardware/software costs of the token ring LAN were reduced $433,000 (from $640,000 to $207,000) over the remote FEP approach, the monthly costs jumped from $84,605 to $152,289, an annual increase of over $800,000!

The present restriction of 16 IBM 3178/3278 terminals per cluster controller is imposed due only to the 19.2-Kbit/second communications circuits. Using LANs connected to Memphis via token ring bridges would allow a doubling (from a maximum of 16 to 32) of the number of display terminals per cluster controller, which would help offset the cost of the upgrade.

5.3.2   Remote LANs with Frame Relay

The next step was to look at ways to reduce costs further, if possible, on the T1 connection from LAN bridge to LAN bridge. The check authorizer had been reading a lot about public frame relay networks and wondered if a high-speed public frame relay connection via multiple public frame relay networks (for redundancy) could be more cost-effective.

The company was able to locate three different manufacturers of token ring bridges that offered frame relay connections at 1.024-Mbit/second speeds and was able to locate special T1 DSU/CSU equipment capable of providing a V.35 connection at 1.024 Mbits/second to allow connection to a public frame relay network.

The pricing shown in Table 5.4 and Table 5.5, based on an average of the costs of the three public frame relay networks reviewed by the check authorizer, makes frame relay look very favorable compared to the T1 lines.

Table 5.4   **Sample One-Time Hardware Costs for Remote Token Rings with Frame Relay: Los Angeles to Memphis**

Item	Qty	Each	Total
Token ring LAN bridge/FR (both ends) (there are 9 LANs per call center)	18	$9,500	$171,000
T1 DSU/CSUs (both ends)	18	2,500	90,000
Total			$261,000

Table 5.5   **Sample Recurring Costs for Remote Token Rings with Dedicated T1: Los Angeles to Memphis**

Item	Qty	Each	Total
Public frame relay connections @ 1.024 Mbits/second	18	$2,320	$41,760
Total			$41,760

The token ring bridges with V.35 frame relay interfaces that operate at 1.024 Mbits/second are available for approximately the same cost as the T1 frame relay bridges. The special T1 DSU/CSU units are approximately $500 more each (or $9,000 more for our 18). The special T1 DSU/CSU is required to convert the channelized T1 provided by the LEC to a V.35 serial data stream required by the frame relay LAN bridges. The 1.024-Mbit/second frame relay connections cost $2,320 per month. Each end of the connection must be attached to the public network, which is the reason for the 18 connections.

Note that our private T1 example assumed the check authorizer is connecting their Los Angeles call center to Memphis. The monthly T1 costs for this example would vary by location. The connection from Chicago to Memphis via T1 would cost less (because it is only 504 circuit miles) than Los Angeles to Memphis (which is 1,704 circuit miles). In our public frame relay network example, the connection cost is the same, regardless of where we connect to the network. The public frame relay network providers are tending toward fixed, distance-insensitive pricing.

The check authorizer has only slightly increased the initial cost (from $207,000 to $261,000), while reducing monthly costs from $152,000 to $42,000 per month. The $90,000-per-month reduction in communications costs will pay for the $54,000 in hardware in about two weeks!

The check authorizer proceeded with the public frame relay option. By doing so, investment in terminal and controller equipment has been maintained. All regional sites are now upgraded to LANs, which provides a platform for migration to PCs, if desired, and migration for peer-to-peer and distributed applications, if desired. Terminal response times are improved, which has the benefit of better customer service (and revenues), and the decentralization of host operations was avoided.

5.4 Total Cost and Cost Justification

Table 5.6 shows the amount spent by the check authorizer when all work was completed and discounts were figured.

For the Los Angeles call center, for instance, monthly costs have been reduced from $225,632 (88 digital 19.2-Kbit/second point-to-point circuits, at $2,164 each) to $41,760. With no other considerations whatsoever, the financial payback on this frame relay installation would be 6.55 months ($1,205,000 cost/$183,872 per month savings)!

Table 5.6	Total Upgrade Costs	
Host upgrades ($2M/5 regions)	$400,000	
Host FEP upgrades	370,000	
TR/FR bridges	150,000	
CSU/DSUs, cabling, misc.	70,000	
CU upgrades to token ring	160,000	
Token ring LAN wiring/MAUs	55,000	
Total	$1,205,000	

Other important considerations, however, are the positive impact of providing better customer service and of being able to get more transactions done per hour. And one final important consideration: the check authorizer now has an infrastructure in place that will allow migration to LAN-based applications as the need arises.

5.5 Conclusion

Needless to say, the check authorizer is very pleased with their frame relay implementation. They have accomplished performance objectives, provided a platform for future developments, and they remain a true "IBM shop." In this case study, frame relay has been used to replace traditional data circuits. While there are some additional capabilities of frame relay, such as a multiplexed physical interface, which have not been used, the subset of frame relay functionality that this user focused on is fine for their environment. They have used many of the capabilities of frame relay to enhance and extend the life of their SNA network.

Our first two case studies have many similarities. Both companies have problems that were related directly to lack of performance in their wide area networks. Both companies have existing protocols on which they rely to operate their wide area networks (in one case, X.25, and in the other, SNA/SDLC). Both companies have cost concerns. Both companies looked for solutions to business problems, not ways to use new technologies. Both companies found solutions that use frame relay.

From the day the first pair of modems connected a terminal to a computer over telephone wires, the push has been on for higher and higher throughputs at lower and lower latencies. Frame relay is not a dramatic revolution in data communications, but rather, frame relay is an important evolutionary technology. The goal of these application case studies is not to imply frame relay is the only answer to the types of problems being studied, but instead to look at companies who have chosen to use frame relay and discover why they decided to do so. In this way, we may all be more educated and make better decisions for our own networks.

In order to put our applications in perspective, let's consider the big picture. The types of latency calculations performed in the first two case studies were not some new science. The exact same steps were taken to justify X.25 and SNA at 56 Kbits/second in networks based on 9.6-Kbit/second lines, and they are identical to the steps that will be performed to justify a move from 2-Mbit/second frame relay to high-speed 45-Mbit/second frame relay, and identical to the calculations that will justify the move from 45-Mbit/second high-speed frame relay to 155-Mbit/second and above SONET, and so on.

There are a number of important points about frame relay in the big picture. The increased bandwidth capacity offered by frame relay allows a way to traverse the gap between where networking is today and the next evolutionary step in network bandwidths. Frame relay provides a common, efficient transport of any type of framed data information (X.25, SNA, LAN protocols, encrypted information, etc.). Frame relay provides bandwidth-on-demand to applications with very bursty traffic characteristics, but may also be applicable to less bursty connections with low latency requirements.

Standards exist that allow frame relay products from many different manufacturers to interoperate. Public networks allow cost-effective implementations of frame relay for customers with small- to medium-sized networking requirements, and powerful nodal processors supporting the frame relay interface allow frame relay to make sense in very large private multimedia networks.

Our first two case studies dealt with instances in which more traditional data communications were desirable. Our first case study was of a company that has no present need for LANs—and may never actually move to LANs at all. They find their current terminal network to be cost-effective and sufficient for their needs. The X.25 piece of their network, and now frame relay, provide suitable addressing for their requirements, and conventional protocol conversion offers adequate connectivity.

Our second case study dealt with a company that is a pure IBM shop, in the tradition of many large DP environments. In the second case study, token ring LANs were installed more as a means of overcoming physical layer speed and cabling limitations than for delivering LAN-type services. Our second company installed frame relay primarily for the advantages of lower latencies and possible compatibility with announced IBM product direction. Our first company replaced X.25 with frame relay, while our second company supplemented SNA with frame relay.

As we will soon see, our third case study company found many of the same reasons to use frame relay: efficiency, low latencies, bandwidth-on-demand, good price performance, and (because of standards) a variety of interoperable frame-relay-equipped products from which to choose.

CHAPTER SIX

LAN-to-LAN Applications

Many applications are driving the need for large amounts of bandwidth. Two of the most common large-bandwidth applications are imaging (the storage, manipulation, transport, and display of a single image) and video (the real-time or near real-time transport of many single images per second to give the appearance of a moving picture). The most important characteristics of images, from a networking point of view, are that images require a large amount of bandwidth to transport within acceptable time frames and that images produce much larger files for storage of the same type of information than any other file format. That is to say, for instance, that a book page might use 12,000 bytes of storage space when it is stored as a text file, but may require 10 or 15 times that number of bytes, or even more, to store the page as an image, depending, of course, on the quality of the image.

The movement of larger and larger files in a timely fashion requires more bandwidth, and that is exactly why the subject company in this case study adopted frame relay, but not until they had exhausted other possible avenues.

6.1 Case Study Background

We will now take a look at a retailer of automotive parts and supplies based in Dallas. The retailer was losing market share to competitors. An in-depth report was compiled by an independent market research firm. The report indicated the retailer was consistently rated first or second in their markets for low price, first or second in their markets for customer service, and in the top of the group for location and hours of operation.

6.2 CARS Imaging Application

This report card was similar to many they had received over the years—consistently good—but they were still losing market share. Further studies showed that the number of competitors had practically doubled while the revenue base was only 74% more. This accounted for a loss of market share, with twice as many competitors vying for only 74% more revenue.

It was clear the retailer needed a way to distinguish themselves from competitors. To accomplish this goal the retailer devised CARS (Complete Automotive Reporting Service). CARS is an online system that performs three major functions:

1. CARS improves sales by distinguishing this retailer from others in their market (who have no such system).
2. CARS improves sales by providing written and graphical documentation to accompany a part (or parts) when needed, at no extra charge. This will reduce or eliminate nonproductive return trips to the retailer by the customer and allow the customer to perform the needed repair or service "like a pro."
3. CARS improves sales by increasing the number of people performing maintenance or service on their vehicles because CARS will provide rudimentary written troubleshooting assistance, specific to make, model, and year of vehicle, which will enable even the novice to purchase and install the proper part or correctly perform the needed maintenance (oil change, tune-up, etc.).

The initial release of CARS is an indexed online search and retrieval of manufacturers' and Chilton's automotive manuals. In order to build the initial information base, all manuals were scanned in their entirety, indexed, and placed on several CD-ROMs. In the CD-ROM products used in the CARS system, each CD-ROM is capable of holding about 680 MB of information (or about 2,200 scanned black-and-white pages). Even compressed, each page image is about 310 KB.

Even though 2200 pages may be stored on each CD-ROM, several dozen CD-ROMs are required to store complete data for all makes and models of cars and light trucks for a number of decades of year-models. The CD-ROMS are stored online in CD-ROM towers ("jukeboxes"), which are attached to three 486 40-MHz CD-ROM servers.

The retailer decided to use its existing LAN/WAN infrastructure to deliver the information. A special CARS terminal (a Pentium 200-MHz MMX personal computer with a 20-inch multiscan monitor and directly attached laser printer) is connected to existing 10-BASE-2 thin Ethernet LANs in each of 204 retail stores. An upgrade to 100-BASE-T twisted-pair Ethernet was considered but put off for budgetary reasons.

Because of the increased bandwidth demand from the new application, the existing 56-Kbit/second DDS point-to-point lines were upgraded to point-to-point T1 lines. While the 56-Kbit/second lines were more than sufficient to handle email and other miscellaneous applications, the new application demands much larger bandwidth capabilities.

Figure 6.1 shows the initial CARS LAN/WAN infrastructure. A 10-BASE-2 thin Ethernet LAN with generally no more than seven workstations (including the CARS workstation) was connected via a T1 LAN bridge to a point-to-point T1 circuit. At the Dallas end of the connection, the T1

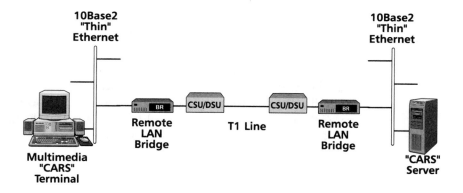

Figure 6.1   Initial CARS Application

circuit terminates into a second T1 LAN bridge, which connects the remote LAN to one of five 10-BASE-T Ethernet LANs in Dallas.

The 204 incoming T1 lines from retail stores are distributed across the five LANs based upon the sales region the store belongs to. There are approximately 40 incoming T1 lines per LAN. The customer is using Novell 386 Netware as a LAN NOS.

6.3   A Look at Possible Cost Reduction

At this point, performance of the LAN/WAN infrastructure seems to be very good, but the cost of the WAN portion of the infrastructure is extremely high. Although performance, and not cost, is the primary goal, the retailer decides to see if costs can be reduced while not negatively affecting service.

In order to understand the thought process of this company, it is important to understand their priorities. The retailer's priorities, in order, are high performance, low cost, and a combination of hardware, software, and communications technologies that will let them grow and expand their applications in the future. The company is willing to spend more for high performance if they must, but would ideally like to get the most performance while keeping costs down.

Let's take a much closer look at the costs involved in running this network. A monthly bill, after discount, of an average $12,732 per store, or $2,597,328, is justifiable based upon increased sales and customer satisfaction index data. However, the retailer would like to reduce costs, if possible, while keeping response times and other parameters the same. The retailer decides to focus attention on reducing the cost of the T1 facilities because all other equipment (LANs, CARS terminals, etc.) is owned and would be required regardless of the bandwidth between sites. The retailer originally decided to use T1 circuits between sites because T1 service offered the most bandwidth that could be purchased at the time from LECs and IXCs. The retailer decided to take a closer look at the T1 utilization to determine if other options existed.

6.3.1   Cost versus Performance Analysis

The first step was to measure the actual bandwidth utilization of the T1 line. The retailer rented some sophisticated performance-monitoring equipment and determined over a three-day period that the maximum bandwidth consumption from Dallas to a remote site was 614,400 bits/second, or 40% of the T1 line. The median busy-hour bandwidth utilization over the period was 484,620 bits/second, or 32% of a T1. This first measurement was most important because it measured the bandwidth used by the very large image transfers from Dallas to the retail stores.

The retailer had determined peak traffic during the three-day study period from remote sites to Dallas never exceeded 47 Kbits/second, or less than one 64 Kbit/second DS0 channel. This statistic measured the small requests that traveled from the retail stores to Dallas to request the large image transfers measured above. While this statistic was interesting, it was never considered to have much value. Because circuits are bidirectional, if a customer buys 614,400 bits/second in one direction, they must buy 614,400 bits/second in both directions.

Traffic from remote sites to Dallas, which contained queries only, required much less bandwidth. Therefore, the 614,400-bit/second maximum figure will be used for purposes of planning. A little more research turned up the fact that the T1 LAN bridges were rated by the manufacturer of the bridges at a forwarding rate of 1,200 packets per second. This means the LAN bridge can send up to 1,200 packets per second over the T1 line. Had the bridge manufacturer used 128-byte packets, the performance would have approached the ability of the T1 line to carry information, while an even larger packet size would have overrun the T1 capacity. The manufacturer had, in fact, used 64-byte packets. At 614,400 bits/second, even with allowances for bridge-to-bridge protocol overhead, the bridges were performing at 100% of rated capacity, or 1,200 packets per second.

Even though the slowest point in the connection is the bridges, this did not create a problem for the retailer. Performance of the applications was quite good, so the throughput of the bridges was not a problem.

6.3.2 Fractional T1 Considered

What the slow bridge situation did create was an opportunity—the opportunity to reduce costs. Not all of the T1 bandwidth was being used, nor would it ever be used with the current LAN bridges. This created an opportunity to save money by simply buying less bandwidth. The first consideration was fractional T1. A T1 circuit is divided into 24 identical channels, or DS0s as they are often referred to. Each DS0 can carry 56 Kbits/second plus signaling information, or a total of 64 Kbits/second of user data. A full T1 circuit is expensive and not required by the retailer. The retailer only requires 10.97 DS0s (614,400 bits/second, 56 Kbits/second per DS0). Because DS0s can only be purchased in discreet units, the retailer needs 11 DS0s, or less than half a T1.

When pricing the fractional T1 service, the retailer learned several important things about the practical aspects of fractional T1 and fractional T1 tariffs. The retailer wished to investigate frame relay as well. The long-haul carrier with whom the retailer had been dealing also offers a public frame relay service and offered to help the retailer learn more about the public frame relay network as an alternative.

6.3.3   Frame Relay as an Alternative

The retailer learned some important terms and concepts and also discovered some very important things about public frame relay network pricing. The retailer learned about simplex connections, committed information rate, port speed, and burst handling. In order to really understand the frame relay options, the retailer (with the help of their carrier) compared frame relay (which they did not understand) with the fractional T1 solution (which they did understand).

6.3.4   Frame Relay and Fractional T1 Compared

With fractional T1, a full 768-Kbit/second circuit (12 DS0s, or one-half T1 bandwidth) is required from end to end. (The carriers do not offer 10 or 11 DS0 FT1 service from end to end.) It is also possible to combine more than one FT1 circuit for delivery to the premises using a digital cross-connect system (DCS). This lowers access charges on the local loop portion of the service.

Frame relay uses a higher-layer protocol that allows it to take advantage of bandwidth-on-demand and allocate bandwidth in the backbone as needed. FT1, on the other hand, is not intelligent: it does not interpret the FT1 information; it merely transports it from one end to the other, bit for bit, over a fixed communications path. FT1 does no protocol interpretation and provides no special handling. FT1 service is an example of a simple circuit.

With frame relay, the bandwidth requirements of the endpoints can be accommodated separately from each other because the network is intelligent and interprets the content of the frame relay messages. For instance, a host that supports several remote sites might be connected to the backbone network via a very high-capacity (up to 2.048-Mbit/second) frame relay interface connection. The sum of all of the several connections to the remote sites might be 2.048 Mbits/second, while the individual connection from a single remote site to the network might be accommodated by a low-speed connection to the backbone (commonly as low as 64-Kbit/second, though the lower limit is not defined by standards).

6.4 Configuring Frame Relay

Now that the parameters are well understood and a move to frame relay looks feasible, the retailer will perform an initial frame relay configuration and put the interim configuration out for bids to public network providers. The retailer may do this in two steps: first, a less formal "request for information" step, in which they solicit comments on their design and allow the public network providers to recommend changes and alternatives, followed by the formal "request for proposal" step.

6.4.1 Remote Site Configuration

In the retailer's frame relay network, for instance, remote site connections to the public frame relay network will be different than Dallas connections. The network only has to guarantee a maximum input to the network from the remote site of 47 Kbits/second, while it is possible higher-rate bursts may have to be accommodated. This is done in frame relay by specifying an access rate that is as large as the largest burst that must be accommodated and a committed information rate (CIR) greater than or equal to the rate that must be guaranteed. Proper engineering of the backbone will assure the CIR can always get through, and shared excess backbone capacity will allow short bursts in excess of the CIR to be accommodated as well.

Excess capacity in the backbone is a function of bandwidth that is not being utilized by other connections operating below their CIR plus excess capacity engineered into the network to accommodate bursts. The carrier offers a CIR of 64 Kbits/second with two possible burst rates: 256 Kbits/second and 1Mbit/second. A committed information rate is the amount of information a frame relay network guarantees it will transport, even under heavy-use conditions. A burst rate is the largest burst of information a frame relay network will accommodate for a short amount of time, network conditions permitting.

A CIR is guaranteed, while a burst rate is not. Because of the fine granularity in which bandwidth is managed within the carrier's T1 cell relay backbone, however, some amount of bandwidth in excess of the CIR is almost always available.

The retailer will choose a CIR of 64 Kbits/second and a burst rate of 1 Mbit/second. The retailer chooses a burst rate of 1 Mbit/second because the T1 circuit that connects the customer site to the frame relay network is a traditional circuit and provides bandwidth in fixed increments, and 1 Mbit/second is one of the fixed increments offered. A maximum of 614,400 bits/second is required between Dallas and the network to provide connectivity to the remote sites, and a 1-Mbit/second connection will, because of the statistical nature of the traffic, provide connectivity to more than one remote site.

6.4.2   Host Site Requirements

At the Dallas site, a maximum of 615 Kbits/second is required, but the median busy-hour requirement is 485 Kbits/second per connection. This means that one 1-Mbit/second frame relay port in Dallas can very safely accommodate connections to two remote sites. This is true because the 615-Kbit/second peak was a measured peak during the study period and not a steady requirement. It is unlikely that demand from both logical frame relay PVCs connecting Dallas to the backbone will be 615 Kbits/ second simultaneously, and because the median requirement of 485 Kbits/second times two is less than 1 Mbit/second, then 1-Mbit/second access rate should accommodate both.

Multiplexing via Frame Relay DLCIs

Because of the multiplexed nature of frame relay, connections to one or more other sites can be accomplished over a single physical connection to the frame relay network. Multiplexing in frame relay is made possible by frame addresses, called data link connection identifiers (DLCIs), similar in purpose to X.25 source and destination X.121 addresses or SDLC frame addresses.

The retailer was very pleased with the ability to multiplex more than one logical connection over a single physical connection and wished to capitalize on this capability. The question was, "Can more than two logical frame relay connections be accommodated over a single physical connection to the backbone network, without sacrificing throughput?"

Time Zone Effect

A review of the traffic study data revealed the 485-Kbit/second median busy-hour utilization is accurate, but is shifted in time by one hour for each time zone. Incoming circuits from the remote sites are terminated on five LANs based on the region they belong to: the regional organization of site connections logically groups the sites (and connections) by time zone. This means demand is greatest on one or two of the five LANs at different hours of the day. Put another way, the amount of information transmitted from Dallas to the remote sites would be greatest on different frame relay connections at different times of the day; at any time of day the load across all frame relay connections would not be evenly distributed.

By redistributing connections based on time zone, instead of by region, it was determined that 615-Kbit/second peaks are still possible occasionally, and the median busy-hour utilization is still 485 Kbits/second per connection, but the likelihood of having simultaneous 485-Kbit/second median busy-hour connections occurring simultaneously has been greatly reduced.

For example, prior to taking the effects of the time zones into account, let's say two logical connections to remote sites from Dallas were handled on a single 1-Mbit/second frame relay connection. If the two remote sites were in New York City and Newark, New Jersey (the same time zone), it is likely they would both experience busy hours at the same time. The median busy-hour demand is 485 Kbits/second; therefore, both would almost assuredly be serviced without delay. If there are four sites that share a single 1-Mbit/second connection, and they are in New York, Chicago, Denver, and Los Angeles, they are all very likely to get the bandwidth required during their busy hour with no delay. An approach such as this would cut the number of connections from Dallas to the frame relay network in half. Please note that this example is making very good use of frame relay's ability to multiplex connections but is very "safe" and is not taking advantage of frame relay's oversubscription capability.

Final Host Site Configuration

A quick mathematical modeling effort shows four logical frame relay connections can be supported on a single physical connection to the public frame relay network with a 512-Kbit/second CIR over a 1-Mbit/second network connection. It is possible to support even more connections simultaneously, but with a diminishing likelihood that the bandwidth will always be available. These calculations are very conservative. A less conservative view might allow a dozen or more logical connections per physical port. The congestion mechanisms in frame relay (as we will discuss in depth in a later chapter) will handle fairly dramatic oversubscription of bandwidth.

The idea of distributing traffic to maximize shared connections is a concept that made no sense at all in the FT1 scenario. The FT1 circuits are traditional fixed circuits: they provide a fixed bandwidth from end to end. The frame relay connections, on the other hand, provide a multiplexed physical connection to a bandwidth-on-demand cell relay switching fabric that manages all network bandwidth as a common pool.

6.5   Frame Relay Pricing

Table 6.1 shows recurring pricing for the frame relay solution. And, because frame relay will require installation and special DSU/CSU equipment, the retailer calculated these costs, as shown in Table 6.2.

Table 6.1	Remote and Host Site Monthly Frame Relay Pricing	
Remote sites:		
	1-Mbit/second FR connection with 64-Kbit/second CIR	$2,735/month
	for 204 remote sites	× 204
	Monthly remote site cost	$557,940
Dallas site:		
	1-Mbit/second FR connection with 512-Kbit/second CIR	$4,730/month
	for 204 remote sites at 4 sites/connection	× 51*
	Monthly Dallas site cost	$241,230

*Could be made more efficient and costs further reduced with oversubscription of frame relay bandwidth

Table 6.2	**One-Time Cost for Frame Relay**	
	Frame relay installation costs (average)	$3,500
	Cost of new DSU/CSU (2 ends)	5,000
	Salvage cost/present T1 CSUs (2 ends)	2,000
	Cost of change to frame relay	$10,500
	Divided by 12-month payback period	÷ 12
	Initial cost/site for 12 months	$ 875
	Total installation cost (204 sites)	$178,500/month for 12 months
Table 6.3	**Frame Relay Cost Savings**	
	Remote site monthly cost	$ 557,940
	Dallas site monthly cost	241,230
	Install spread over first year	178,500
	Frame relay monthly cost	$ 977,670
	Present monthly cost	$2,597,328
	Monthly savings with frame relay	$1,619,658

The retailer also calculated the cost savings possible with a public frame relay network-based solution, as shown in Table 6.3.

The savings are phenomenal, with no increase in latency or reductions in reliability. These savings represent over half a million more dollars saved per month than the very attractive fractional T1 alternative the retailer also researched. The retailer was very pleased with the frame relay option and began implementation immediately.

6.6 Conclusion

This case study company has taken advantage of more of the capabilities of frame relay than the first two case studies. A bidirectional traffic study allowed network connections to be purchased based upon actual usage. A committed information rate (CIR) allows the customer to be guaranteed a certain amount of bandwidth in the network. A burst rate, which is also the speed of the port that the retailer is connected to in the public network, allows the retailer to burst to a higher bandwidth, if needed, for short periods of time. In this way the retailer can contend for some or all of the surplus bandwidth in the shared bandwidth pool. The multiplexed physical interface provided by frame relay allows the retailer to achieve an overall reduction of the number of public network connections, which lowers costs and makes the network more manageable.

And, most importantly, all of these steps are taken with no impact on their application. The retailer is greatly pleased with their frame relay network. They have reduced costs by over $1.5 million per month, maintained response times and service levels, and now take advantage of seven-day-per-week, 24-hour-per-day network management from their carrier without having added head count. Interestingly, this retailer has realized substantial benefit without having taken advantage of all of the capabilities of frame relay. In the next case study, the subject company pushes frame relay to its limits.

LAN Internetworking

This company is using all of the capabilities of frame relay to their fullest extent, and, unlike the previous case studies, which were domestic U.S. centric, this case study represents an international application of frame relay. This application, LAN internetworking, represents frame relay implemented in an Internetlike fashion; in fact, the only reasons why the actual global Internet is not used for this application are security and performance. The case study subject company is a financial institution and must maintain strict control of the movement of financial information with minimum risk of compromise or loss, as well as assuring the timely and accurate delivery of information—something not guaranteed by the Internet.

7.1 Case Study Background

Our final conceptual case study is a London-based financial institution with operations in the major developed countries around the world and branches in major cities within those countries. As we begin the case study, the financial institution, we'll call them GlobalBanc, Inc., has 968 remote offices and totally centralized automation. Under the present system, personal and corporate financial information is collected at the 968 remote offices and entered into a PC-based transaction system. The PC-based system uses a local LAN file server for local transactions and a dial-up system to the appropriate other branch for remote transactions. The dial-up system may either be from one PC to another or, very often, a phone call, fax, or telex from branch to branch in cases where equipment incompatibilities or unavailability of local dial-out facilities dictate. A diskette for each client is then sent via overnight courier to London for processing.

GlobalBanc is at a major crossroads. They would gladly have continued with the present methods on into the future: the present methods are simple, the equipment is paid for, and it works. Competition, however, is forcing GlobalBanc to be able to access financial information from other financial centers more quickly, complete transactions faster, and reduce the effects of differences in time zones on their customers' financial situations. GlobalBanc must move from completely centralized traditional data processing to a LAN server-based distributed arrangement.

7.2 New Applications

The first step was for GlobalBanc to review their present application situation. They had fairly consistent configurations of personal computers and LAN servers in their various offices as well as in their London headquarters facility. All equipment had been recently purchased, and, even though the colors of the cases and trademarks on the front were different, they all had "Intel Inside™"—mostly 486s, and some Pentium machines.

The two areas requiring a major overhaul were the telecommunications systems interconnecting the offices with each other and the applications themselves, which were based upon remote preparation of information that was sent on diskette via overnight courier, at very high annual expense, to London for incorporation into central databases. The applications were redesigned around a fully distributed approach, with each office maintaining several databases, all of which would be accessible over a private wide area network.

The financial institution leveraged its international presence very well by having the software development divided into two large projects and done in parallel in two different countries. The development of client financial databases and migration methodology was done in India, where programmers are inexpensive and the quality of their product is very high. The Indian firm retained for the development is widely known for their distributed database innovations and was more than happy to respond to GlobalBanc's request with a cost-effective proposal. The development of the client financial databases would be done using the Windows 95 graphical user interface (GUI). All development would be done in three language variations: in English, the official global language of GlobalBanc; in French, which is a requirement to operate in France; and in Canadian French, which is a requirement to operate in French Canada.

The development of new server applications that would leverage in-country financial information for the benefit of GlobalBanc's worldwide audience would be done in Russia. The bid for this development was let to a large programming firm with offices in Moscow and St. Petersburg and would leverage the strong Web development capabilities of the Russian firm. The Russian firm would develop World Wide Web servers that would be positioned at the head office in each country and would provide current financial information gathered from several in-country sources and the financial institution's own analysts in a well-known, easy-to-learn, and easy-to-use format: Web pages. This would, in effect, create an internal company Internet, or GlobalBanc intranet, which would leverage the popular tools of the Internet but on a network that would not, for security reasons, be connected to the Internet at all. Access to the GlobalBanc intranet would be via Netscape Navigator browsers, which would operate in one of the Windows 95 windows on the client personal computer.

GlobalBanc has designed the application and written custom application software. The application is fully distributed in its operation to reduce the impact of a catastrophic event in a single centralized operation. They are now at a point of determining the proper network design upon which to implement their application.

7.2.1 Logical Application Flow Analysis

Let's review the financial institution's logical application flow and see what this means in terms of network design. Client financial information and other transaction data, such as deposits and withdrawals, buy and sell orders for stocks on many world markets, or country-to-country fund transfers received from the client, are entered via the Windows 95–based application on a PC. The PC is the same PC that has been used to prepare the disks to send to London. The only differences are that the PC will now be connected to other locations than just the local server via the thin-wire Ethernet LAN and it is now running a new application program. The PC is now called a Transaction Management Station (TMS), largely out of GlobalBanc's desire to highlight the fact that the same equipment is running their new application. The new transaction application has two parts, a foreground component and a background component. The foreground component allows entry of client financial information and final validation prior to processing; the background component takes finished client transactions and transmits them for processing. The background component also creates an entry in a Master Tracking Database, centrally located in London, when a transaction is transmitted from the TMS. This is, of course, independent of the Intranet-based Web server application, which may be used as the basis for the decisions that the transactions being generated represent.

Let's track a client file through the system in order to get a clear understanding of the communications requirements. We will consider the case of a client who lives in Bermuda, but has major holdings and financial dealings in the Netherlands, Germany, and Japan. The client needs access to local financial information in these three countries as well as, from time to time, other world markets, via the local GlobalBanc office in Hamilton, Bermuda.

The client's transaction information is entered via the TMS's foreground application and validated, as appropriate to the transaction. The background application determines that the transaction(s) have been marked as acceptable for processing. The background application logs the transaction(s) in the Master Tracking Database in London. In the case of a telecommunications outage, all Master Tracking Database updates are logged in a sequential transaction holding file and processed immediately upon return of telecommunications services. The background application transmits the transactions to the correspondent offices, as appropriate.

The Master Tracking Database in London is updated after the transfer is complete and for each step in the processing cycle until the final transaction has been completed.

It is also noteworthy that the Web-based application utilizes software agents that operate on the personal computer of the client's representative in the local office and are programmed to notify the client's representative if certain parameters change. The representative may then act on the client's behalf or call the client for a decision. In the case of the client based in Bermuda, a software agent is constantly monitoring the value of the Japanese yen, the German deutsche mark, the British pound, and other important world currencies as well as stock prices of key stocks and other leading economic indicators. A change of more than the amount programmed will notify the GlobalBanc representative, who will make a decision on the action to take.

7.3 Networking Requirements

What are the communications requirements for this application? Immediate response times are absolutely critical, as is connectivity: any office must be able to communicate directly, immediately, and reliably with any correspondent office, as required, and there is absolutely no way to anticipate needs in advance because they are dictated by changes in the world financial markets. Also, any GlobalBanc office must be able to communicate with London Centre in order to keep the Master Tracking Database updated and synchronized.

7.3.1 Reliability

Reliability is extremely critical to GlobalBanc, especially during the very busy periods that occur when major world currencies fluctuate widely. In order to reduce the impact of communications outages, each TMS can store client financial information for up to 500 clients on the local 1.2-GB disks. In this offline mode, a communications outage of up to several hours can be accommodated with no interruption of work, though an outage still represents a significant amount of exposure in international transactions when changes are occurring rapidly, and these transactions will be sent by fax, telex, or voice call, if possible, during network outages. One spare TMS is also configured and attached to the LAN for every 10 active TMSs to provide TMS redundancy. The 968 offices average 50 active TMSs and 5 spare TMSs. Based upon an average of 55 TMSs at each office, there are 53,240 TMSs in the network.

7.3.2   Network Logical Architecture

GlobalBanc defined a hierarchical access network with a mesh inner core network. A small, single trunk router on the LAN at each remote office would be connected to a single large router located at a physically centralized office within a geographical area (Figure 7.1). For instance, in Canada, remote offices in Vancouver, Montreal, and Ottawa would be connected to a large central router located in Toronto. Up to 9 offices, plus the office serving the geographical area (also the location of the large router), for a total of 10 offices, would be concentrated by the large router.

Connections from the remote offices to the concentration point would be single point-to-point connections. Where possible, ISDN or analog dial backup would be provided for the router trunk. For reliability and capacity purposes, the concentration point is connected to two other router concentrator sites in adjacent countries. A connection also exists from each remote office to London Centre. This design reduces costs as much as possible and allows global connectivity and alternate routes from each concentration site.

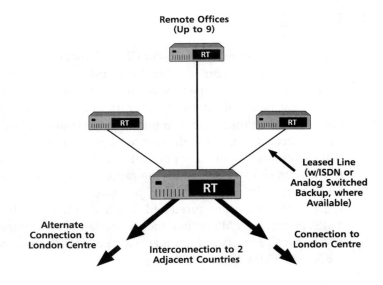

Figure 7.1   GlobalBanc Architectural Example

7.3.3 Two Physical Architecture Choices

GlobalBanc looked at two scenarios: a router internetwork and a frame relay network based on routers. The 968 remote offices would be concentrated into an outer ring of 97 routers, smaller countries having a single concentrator router and larger countries having more than one concentrator router. This would be true for either the router internetwork or frame relay scenario. The difference would be the way the routers are interconnected. For a router network, a mesh of leased lines would interconnect the routers. For frame relay, each router would be connected by two or more physical connections to the cell relay backbone, and those connections would provide connectivity to all 967 other routers.

Leased-Line Options

Each of the 97 concentrator routers would be connected to two adjacent countries' concentrator routers. This would require 194 circuits/connections and is exactly the same for both scenarios. The entire idea of a fully router-based internetwork was discarded for several reasons: line costs for full mesh interconnection of concentrator routers were too high, router configurations were unrealistic to allow full interconnection, and leased lines were not available to all countries where connectivity is required.

An interim step was evaluated that would use a further tiering of routers by continent, but this was unworkable as well. As a tiered alternative to a full mesh, GlobalBanc considered a ring topology to interconnect routers with fewer leased lines, but the several variations of ring topology studied lowered costs but introduced too much delay. The delay in the ring design is a function of the protocol processing at each intermediate router in a path from source to destination. Star topologies are not considered sufficiently reliable and are very expensive in terms of line costs, so they were also discarded as an alternative to full physical interconnection of routers. The final option for a fully leased-line router-based internetwork was a hybrid ring/mesh network, but hybrid ring/mesh networks are considered too complicated to manage and, like the tiered approach, also introduce higher equipment costs and latency.

Frame Relay Option

GlobalBanc now considered the second alternative technology: frame relay. Recall each remote site is connected to a concentration site, and each concentration site is connected to concentrator sites in two adjacent countries.

With this in mind, let's look at how frame relay can provide the infrastructure for this network. Routers at each of the 968 sites need to be logically interconnected to all concentrator routers plus London Centre, ideally, without using any bandwidth until bandwidth is required.

Frame relay has a mechanism that provides logical connections with bandwidth-on-demand. Frame relay uses an addressing mechanism based upon data link connection identifiers (DLCIs). The number of possible DLCIs allowed for by frame relay standards is virtually limitless, but in present frame relay implementations, there are 1,024 possible DLCIs, and of the 1,024 possible DLCIs, 32 DLCIs are reserved for other uses, leaving 992 DLCI addresses for user assignment. This means a single frame relay device may logically address up to 992 other devices. This is well above the 101 logical addresses (100 concentration sites plus London Centre) required for GlobalBanc's application. The reason a DLCI is not required for each remote office is that DLCIs only identify a connection to the frame relay network and do not take into account any networks or devices that might reside beyond the router being attached to the frame relay network. The addressing and routing functions for those devices are handled by the router.

Each interface to the network may be sized according to their own particular requirements, and several logical connections may be combined from several remote sites into a single physical connection. GlobalBanc has 74 sites in Japan, for instance. Each of the 74 sites is connected to a concentration site. There are, therefore, eight concentration routers, at eight different sites, in Japan alone.

Each concentration site is physically connected to two adjacent countries' concentration sites. This means there are two physical frame relay connections from each concentration site to the frame relay backbone network. Each concentration site, however, is logically connected to all 99 other concentrator sites and London Centre through the network. While only one or two of the logical connections are likely to be requiring bandwidth at any moment in time, all 101 connections are set up and can carry information if needed. This is an example of *oversubscription*—providing more connections over a physical circuit than the physical circuit should carry. Oversubscription takes advantage of the quiet times in communications protocols to multiplex information. Oversubscription can save costs but can also produce congestion and delays if not properly applied.

An example of oversubscription that works well is when many members of the same family share a single telephone. There is generally some protocol for determining which of many subscribers (family members) use the single resource. An example of oversubscription that does not always work well is when an airplane is overbooked. If all passengers show up to claim seats, then congestion and delays occur. If not all passengers show up, however, then the oversubscription has brought a financial benefit to the airline because all, or most, seats are filled with revenue-generating customers.

Oversubscription, when used correctly, can lead to profound efficiencies in frame relay networks. Oversubscription, when used improperly, can lead to inefficient bandwidth utilization because of undersubscription (when too few PVCs are configured per frame relay connection) or network congestion (when far too many PVCs are configured per frame relay connection).

GlobalBanc needs a full mesh network, without the associated costs and latencies. What GlobalBanc has is logical full mesh interconnection, without the delay and dollar costs of a physical full mesh network; every site is connected to all 100 required possible destinations. This configuration is much like a wide area LAN. It is also noteworthy that the end-to-end latency is minimized.

7.3.4 Non-Frame-Relay Sites

One of the reasons for elimination of the all leased-line network was that leased-line connections were not available to all desired locations. The truth is, in a global perspective, frame relay is not truly ubiquitous either. In some cases, GlobalBanc was required to integrate some older, lower-speed technologies with frame relay in certain countries to accommodate end-to-end connectivity. A case in point is Ho Chi Minh City, Vietnam. Frame relay is not available in Ho Chi Minh City, but X.25 is available. In this case, for example, GlobalBanc provisioned an X.25 connection from Ho Chi Minh City to Singapore, and in Singapore used an X.25-to-frame-relay gateway protocol conversion service provided by the carrier to join the global frame relay network.

7.3.5 Network Management

There is still one other important issue that has not been addressed: network management. A network of this type is extremely complex and has its own management issues. The first area of difficulty is encountered when attempting to keep the configuration and address tables of a frame relay access device (router in this case) and frame relay network device (cell relay switch with frame relay interface) synchronized. The second problem area is the amount of bandwidth required to perform configuration synchronization updates and other management functions.

An optional extension to the frame relay standards (known as Annex D of the ANSI frame relay specifications and as Annex A of the ITU-T standards) provides a synchronization methodology: the local management interface (LMI). Frame relay networks whose access devices and network devices support LMI avoid configuration inconsistencies: additions, changes, and deletions of PVCs are made via commands to the network device, and the access device is automatically synchronized via LMI message exchanges. LMI messages also allow the status of the remote portion of PVCs to be sent to the frame relay access device. This allows frame relay access devices to be aware of the status of remote access devices and perform their routing algorithms or other necessary functions more efficiently. Let's assume a local frame relay access device is a terminal packet assembler-disassembler (PAD), for instance, and the remote frame relay access device is a host computer. If the local frame relay access device is notified that the host is down, it can send an appropriate message immediately to terminal users without having to wait for a time-out period to occur in order to ascertain the same information. Additionally, this mechanism allows the source of problems to be pinpointed more specifically.

Another concern of GlobalBanc was the amount of network bandwidth that would be used by network synchronization and status messages. Status messages and broadcasts often represent a large portion of WAN bandwidth utilized when interconnecting LANs. In a frame relay network without LMI, all status messages from access devices (in this instance, routers) to other access devices would have to be sent one time for each destination.

In our case, a single router update message would have to be sent 1069 times to update all routers. There are 100 routers in the main internetwork and 968 routers in the remote offices. Even a very small message, sent frequently enough, could bottleneck the entire network, and it is very likely status changes will occur pretty regularly in a network of this size. We are not, at this time, referring to LMI-specific status messages, but rather we are referring to router status and management messages that are used between routers for information exchange and overall network configuration synchronization. The chosen topology and choice of the "open shortest path first" (OSPF) routing protocol has greatly reduced the total bandwidth used for updates because, unlike older, less sophisticated routing protocols such as RIP (router information protocol), OSPF only updates neighboring routers when a topology change event occurs in the network.

7.4 Conclusion

While this case study has not covered all aspects of operating such a complex frame relay internetwork, it has covered all of the practical considerations that are related directly to frame relay. GlobalBanc is taking advantage of all of the presently available frame relay capabilities: large addressing capability (using DLCIs), multiplexing of many logical connections over a single physical port, bandwidth-on-demand and oversubscription, intrinsic low latency when used with well-designed private network or carrier backbone, and LMI for synchronization of configurations and status of attached frame relay access devices (routers). In choosing frame relay, GlobalBanc has chosen a networking methodology that provides all needed functionality for present requirements and a platform for future growth and new applications.

In ending the GlobalBanc case study, we are also ending our conceptual case studies—case studies that were perfect examples of frame relay applications, that were without major problems, and that fit their intended function perfectly. We will now move to the real-world case studies, those that have real company names and real issues. The conceptual composite requirements case studies have allowed us to focus on frame relay and ignore other issues. We will now move to the real world, where other issues are as important as, and in many cases more important than, frame relay.

PART FOUR

Real-Life Case Studies

CHAPTER EIGHT

Traditional IBM Environment

This chapter explains how one company uses frame relay in a traditional IBM environment. Their size, issues, and answers are representative of the single most prevalent telecommunications and computing environment.

8.1 Case Study Background

Caliber Technology, Inc. (CTI) is the technology arm of Caliber System, Inc., formerly Roadway Services, Inc. CTI provides a common, unified telecommunications infrastructure and computer services support to the many operating divisions of Caliber System, Inc. Among the operating divisions of Caliber System, Inc., supported by CTI are RPS; Roberts Transportation Services, Inc.; Viking Freight, Inc.; and Caliber Logistics Systems, Inc. Caliber has been working since 1994 to move its 1,400 locations to a common frame relay infrastructure in response to competitive pressures in the transportation marketplace and the attendant need to better leverage key information resources.

Caliber also provides contract services for management of Roadway Express's network. This contract extends to the end of 1998.

Headquartered in Akron, Ohio, and founded in 1930, Roadway Express, Inc., is one of the nation's largest less-than-truckload (LTL) freight carriers and provides service in two-day and farther regional, national, and international markets. Roadway Express offers reliable, responsive, and efficient transportation services between all 50 states, Canada, Mexico, Puerto Rico, and Japan, plus export services to 62 countries on five continents. Roadway Express operates more than 400 facilities in North America, ranging in size from neighborhood terminals with half a dozen loading doors to a 460-door consolidation/distribution center in Chicago Heights, Illinois. More than 64% of the terminals are owned by the company. Roadway Express employs approximately 26,000 people and operates a fleet of more than 40,000 trucks, trailers, and tractors. In fiscal year 1995, Roadway Express handled a total of 13.9 million shipments, and total revenues were $2.29 billion.

CTI is presently consolidating a variety of their client's and their own operating company's networks onto the unified frame relay network infrastructure. Traditional IBM SNA traffic, TCP/IP, IPX, and Tandem asynchronous EXPAND protocols all coexist on the new network infrastructure. CTI needs to continue to support mainframe applications for many years into the future and is not willing to rewrite working host-based applications to accommodate changes in the network infrastructure. CTI's network uses the AT&T InterSpan public frame relay network service to replace a nationwide network of 9.6-Kbit/second analog and 19.2-Kbit/second digital leased lines.

CTI is representative of many large, traditional SNA shops who are just now starting to make the move away from the traditional analog and digital point-to-point and multidrop leased-line environment to frame relay and eventually, in many cases, to ATM. And, like many similar large shops, CTI must support the legacy SNA for the time being while introducing new services and capabilities (such as imaging) and maintaining or improving levels of reliability and availability.

While CTI is representative of large commercial, institutional, and governmental SNA shops who are making—or planning to make—the move to frame relay, they are not too representative, in terms of number of sites, of organizations who have already adopted frame relay as their primary information transport and are using frame relay, as CTI is, on a daily basis. In fact, with over 1,400 sites in the network, CTI dwarfs the "average of less than 9 ports per customer with only 2% of frame relay customers having over 151 sites" (Taylor 1995). In this regard, CTI is a leader among SNA shops in their early use of frame relay technology on such a wide scale.

Recently, CTI has gone through an even more aggressive step as they try to focus their efforts on maximizing profits in their core business. CTI has outsourced some of the management of their frame relay network.

To compress the learning curve of its organization, Caliber Technology contracted with Paradyne to provide two frame relay technicians for on-site support and technology transfer. In addition to providing technical guidance and problem resolution skills, the technicians also helped to develop the architecture master plan. To address the logistical and technical issues associated with the installation of medium- and large-capacity sites, a standard configuration and cabinet were developed, with all components installed and tested prior to being shipped to each site. Although the initial installs were handled by the outsourced technicians, this process was quickly transferred to Caliber's people and was a considerable help in their learning process. The success of this approach can be judged by the fact that contracted on-site support was canceled 18 months into the project.

Providing maintenance for a frame relay network of this size provided additional challenges that were best solved by outsourcing. After carefully analyzing the financial ramifications and the service-level needs of the company, Caliber Technology contracted with Cisco Systems for maintenance. A benefit of this arrangement is that it provides access to the latest Cisco expertise and technologies at a considerable savings over an in-house approach. Further, the size of the Cisco organization ensures that critical service levels are sustained on a consistent basis, a factor especially important in Caliber's largest locations.

In many ways the challenges presented to such an organization seem daunting. But, as we will see in this case study, the job is made substantially easier by developing a master architecture, by defining templates to match the needs of various sizes of offices, and by working carefully and methodically, step by step over a period of time, toward the eventual goal. Another key element of success of CTI's endeavor came in the partnerships forged with vendors and suppliers and the key role cooperative partners play in the success of an undertaking this vast and pioneering.

8.2 Before Frame Relay

Before the move to frame relay, CTI's network was comprised primarily of SNA/SDLC (synchronous data link control) operating over 9.6-Kbit/second analog leased lines, and some 19.2-Kbit/second digital lines, from remote terminals and cluster controllers to large IBM mainframes and IBM AS/400s. In some cases, bandwidth requirements necessitated dedicated 56-Kbit/second or T1 capacity. The balance of connections represented Novell IPX, Tandem's EXPAND asynchronous terminal protocol, and TCP/IP traffic. In 1994, CTI completed work on a unified architecture document, which supported the corporate vision of improved information sharing between operating companies and a greatly enhanced flow of information within the company in general. The unified architecture included a move away from traditional leased lines to a more flexible, dynamic, cost-effective, and easily modified frame relay infrastructure that includes standardization on TCP/IP and support for legacy SNA as well as emerging requirements. CTI envisions supporting legacy SNA for at least three to four more years before it is phased out altogether by client-server applications, open architectures, and a frame relay/ATM transport environment.

8.2.1 Business Aspects

CTI is moving from a highly autonomous, decentralized holding company environment with nine diverse networks to a new environment with centralized control of information resources and network management. In the former environment, each independent operating company had a great deal of control over their network and computing environments: which platform was used, how applications were designed, and what type of network structure and protocols were used. In the new structure, each operating company's networking environment will be brought in line, slowly and methodically, with the company's unified architecture vision and accompanying set of standard products, protocols, and services.

The unified architecture not only specifies the use of the AT&T Inter-Span frame relay service for information transport but also identifies all Layer 1, 2, and 3 networking components and how they will work together. Among other key networking components specified in the unified architecture are Cisco routers, Paradyne CSU/DSUs, Bay Network's Synoptics Hubs, and other devices. Key selection criteria for networking components are remote manageability and ATM readiness, where applicable. Part of the return-on-investment analysis performed by CTI involved staff reductions as a result of fewer different types and flavors of network elements and greater manageability of those devices by the use of network software.

Requirements

The main requirements for CTI were

- flexibility
- greater network control
- staff reduction
- no loss of availability or reliability

CTI sees flexibility as the ability to add new sites to, delete old sites from, or move sites around the network in much less time than with the leased-line network, as well as the ability to provide more or less network capacity at those sites, as needed. Greater control of the network comes as a result of staff centralization as well as implementation of a standard set of networking components and software that are remotely monitored, configured, and managed. Staff reduction is anticipated to be achieved after network consolidation by elimination of redundant human functions when the nine different network control centers that existed in the older distributed model are brought together.

Flexibility   CTI is taking advantage of the flexibility of a virtual network with frame relay today and intends to extend that virtual network model in the future to include a hybrid frame relay/ATM infrastructure that uses frame relay UNIs to connect smaller, lower-speed sites to the corporate backbone and ATM UNIs to connect larger facilities and two host sites to the network.

The type of flexibility that CTI has already achieved has had tangible business benefits. In late 1995, there was a major reorganization of Roadway Services, Inc. Roadway Express, the original less-than-truckload (LTL) arm of Roadway Services was spun off as a separate company, with Caliber Technology providing network management services under an outsourcing contract through at least 1998. Caliber System, Inc., was then created and included RPS for small package delivery, Caliber Logistics for integrated logistics services, Roberts for time-sensitive delivery, and Caliber Technology as the technology arm. All of Caliber's LTL operations were consolidated under the Viking Freight operating company. As in any reorganization, many aspects of a company's operation can be paralyzed during the migration/transition period. The business impacts of this paralysis are lost revenues; customer dissatisfaction; employee confusion, retraining, and concern over their role in the newly reorganized company;

and diminished functionality of computing services while the transition is taking place. There are also numerous problems that can arise simply as a result of the length of time a system is in transition, and they are aggravated by longer transitions. It is, therefore, advantageous to limit this period of flux as much as possible.

In the case of CTI, the flexibility of the virtual network provided by frame relay was instrumental in cutting four to six months off of the planned transition period. This reduced migration period is largely a function of being able to turn up service more quickly than with traditional leased lines, as well as being able to modify bandwidth and other performance parameters more quickly.

Greater network control   As a part of the unified architecture and concurrent with the move to frame relay, CTI has implemented a set of specific, manageable networking components in the network. Though this could have been accomplished independently of a move to frame relay, it is noteworthy that the new unified architecture was so sweeping as to include new transport services as well as new networking devices. There are many benefits to making many changes simultaneously, just as there are many risks. The benefits are that disruptions to network services occur all at the same time, rather than in stages or phases, and once finished with the single migration, users can put the memories behind them and move on, rather than being besieged by wave after wave of disruption as the network moves through multiple upgrade phases. The risks, on the other hand, are that it may be virtually impossible to isolate and fix problems introduced by multiple simultaneous changes in the network. This tends to increase the severity of the impact of the single (cataclysmic) outage.

The business impacts of replacing a wide spectrum of different networking products with a small, carefully chosen, and consistent group of products are numerous. In terms of cost reduction, purchasing power and discount levels are enhanced by being a larger customer of fewer suppliers. By concentrating the buying power with a few vendors, it is possible to ask for, and get, important concessions as wide ranging as the very traditional bigger discount and as important as reprioritization of the vendor's planned introduction of new features. In CTI's case, the latter, reprioritization of the vendor's planned introduction of new features, was key to their success in network implementation because they were pushing SNA-TCP/IP integration to the limits of existing technology and needed control over the manufacturer's feature set prioritization. A smaller organization with less buying power, and therefore with less impact, would have either had to be less aggressive in their technical plans or simply waited.

Staff reduction   Another benefit of implementing manageable devices from a small group of well-regarded manufacturers is that CTI not only has enhanced their ability to manage the network from a single central site, it has also positioned itself for future staff reductions. Staff reductions occurred after the migration through requirements for fewer staff members because of less diversity in the managed devices, through consolidation of the prior nine centers of competency associated with the nine previously diverse network operations centers, and again through the outsourcing of the operation of the frame relay network after the postconsolidation network settled down. Staff reductions to date represent about 25% of the prior decentralized model and are anticipated to reach in the 35–40% range when fully implemented. The rate of staff reduction is largely related to the speed with which legacy applications are moved to the new TCP/IP protocol established as the company's standard.

No loss of availability or reliability   A final key requirement of the move to frame relay was no loss of availability or reliability of the network. Caliber's upper management and the network's users alike were cautious about trading a stable, reliable, and highly available network for something new and unproven at the proposed scale. An important aspect of the acceptance of the new network initiative, therefore, was the socialization of the idea that the new network would be at least as reliable and available as the existing leased-line infrastructure. A key to the acceptance was the virtual nature and self-healing aspects of the new network (versus the leased-line environment), as well as the use of switched access to provide alternatives to the dedicated LEC facilities in case of local loop failures.

8.2.2   Technical Aspects

We will now take a look at the technical aspects of CTI's environment. Both applications and communications will be discussed.

Applications

CTI's unified architecture addresses the support for different types of terminal systems across the network backbone. This architectural approach allows CTI to support the transport of many different transactions generated by different terminals, regardless of actual content of information packets. CTI's applications divisions are Mainframe SNA, AS/400 SNA, TCP/IP, and imaging.

Mainframe SNA   Mainframe SNA includes the support of traditional IBM 3270 terminals and personal computers and RISC 6000 workstations performing emulation of traditional IBM 3270 terminals in interactive, block-mode operation. The terminals are brought directly over from the leased-line environment with no modification to their operation. In the traditional Mainframe SNA environment, a 3270-type terminal is attached to a control unit (often called a *cluster controller*). The cluster controller is responsible for coordinating communications activities between the attached 3270-type terminal and a communications controller between the cluster controller and the host computer. The intermediate communications controller is called a front-end processor (FEP) and off-loads many of the tedious, repetitive, and capability-draining functions of communications from the host computer/mainframe.

The communications process of traditional SNA uses a method called *polling* to ask each cluster controller in turn if their attached terminals have anything to send. Each cluster controller is polled in a round-robin fashion based upon its numeric control unit address, and thereby given a fair chance to send information to the host for processing. This method, while antiquated by modern standards, is still in use in traditional IBM systems worldwide.

AS/400 SNA   IBM AS/400 communications are very similar to the operation of the Mainframe SNA with the exception of the occurrence of the FEP and some different model numbers. The AS/400 uses 5250/5394-type terminals and control units in lieu of the 3270 types, and there is no distinct and separate FEP function. In the case of the AS/400s, the front-end processor function is built into the AS/400 computer on a single card, and it is not an outboard function.

TCP/IP   As CTI moves to the client-server, open architecture environment, LANs are appearing more and more within the CTI environment. While LANs have been very common in many environments for 10 years or more, CTI was very disciplined in justifying their use and is just now introducing LANs into many aspects of their operation. IBM terminals have been the traditional mainstay of CTI's MIS function and have proven adequate for CTI's use up until the present day. Therefore, there were only widely dispersed pockets of Novell IPX/SPX and TCP/IP in the pre-frame-relay/preconsolidation environment.

This lack of existing LAN technology made the migration into the present environment far easier. Initiatives in the present network that are part of the unified architecture are a standardized network numbering plan used companywide to allow interoperation of systems to be accomplished far more easily and a shift to TCP/IP networking, which will provide a platform for future adoption of intranet technology.

Imaging   Caliber's plans included the need to support a legacy Viking Freight System imaging application running on the EXPAND protocol on Tandem. The application is key in that it is used to scan driver delivery records at selected sites and to transmit the signature of the recipient as well as the date and time of delivery to a central database. The information may then be retrieved online for customer or service representative requests for proof of delivery. The bandwidth used for this application is from 128 Kbits/second to 512 Kbits/second, depending on transaction volumes. There is also a possibility that a similar imaging application in place at RPS will eventually be moved from the RPS headquarters to field locations. If the business need drives this move, it cannot be supported by the present RPS network but could easily be accommodated as frame relay is extended to RPS.

Communications Environment

The pre-frame-relay communications environment was a very simple one: traditional leased lines connected a cluster controller—and, where appropriate, LAN bridges or routers—to a central site (Figure 8.1). In most cases, leased lines were older-technology 9.6-Kbit/second analog lines that had remained unchanged since their installation in the 1970s. The only reasons why a line might be upgraded to 19.2-Kbit/second digital is as a result of user complaints about performance or, more commonly, the relocation of a site or the opening of a new site. At some point, the cost of a 9.6-Kbit/ second analog line closely approached the cost of a 56-Kbit/ second line, but the replacement of the 9.6-Kbit/second analog lines was only evaluated as a part of a total network overhaul and move to a new network infrastructure.

In many ways, CTI brought their communications architectures, in one fluid motion, from a late-1970s architecture, through the 1980s and into the 1990s, and then positioned their communications architectures at the very leading edge of the SNA-over-frame-relay environment. CTI found two keys to justify frame relay:

1. need to upgrade bandwidth
2. serve multiple protocols

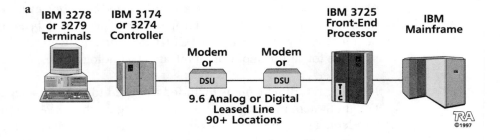

b

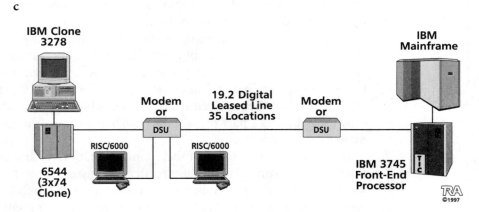

Figure 8.1   CTI Pre-Frame-Relay Physical Architecture: (a) IBM 327x Terminal Environment; (b) IBM 5250 Terminal Environment; (c) IBM Distributed Host Environment

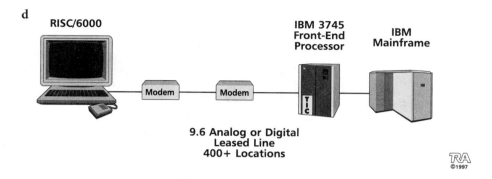

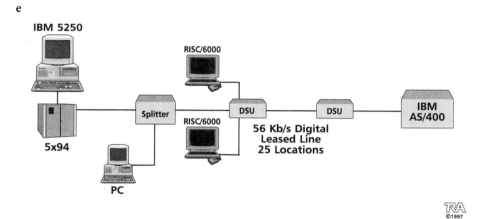

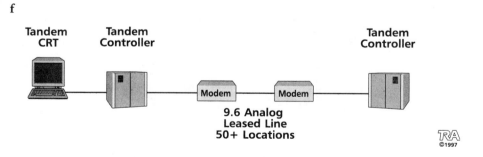

Figure 8.1 *continued:* (d) Remote Workstation Environment; (e) Remote Workstation and 5250 Environment; (f) Remote Tandem CRT Environment

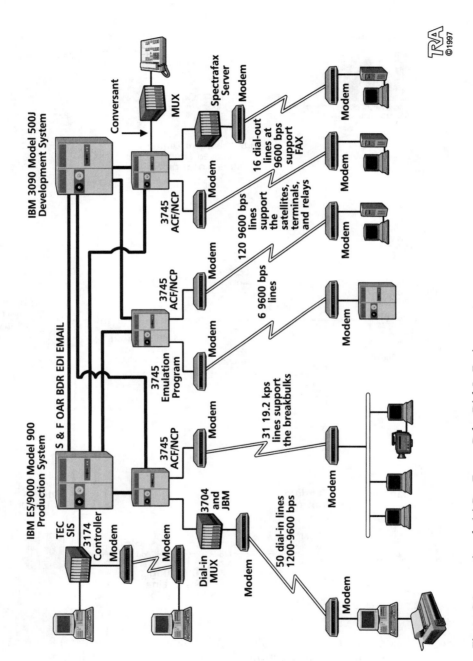

Figure 8.1 *continued:* (g) Pre-Frame-Relay Dial-In Environment

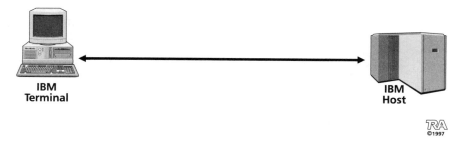

Figure 8.2 CTI Logical Architecture

Logical Architecture

The pre- and post-frame-relay logical architectures for traditional terminal users are identical (Figure 8.2), as a swap-out of the pre-frame-relay Layer 2 SDLC for the frame relay transport has no impact (beyond possible performance enhancements) on the upper-layer protocols or user applications. As we will see later, however, the presence of the larger bandwidths and other performance aspects of frame relay will enable new applications and network uses beyond that possible with traditional SNA/SDLC communications.

8.3 Frame Relay: Selection and Migration

Based upon the long time the old network had been in place (and simply grown by subsequent generations of network managers without architectural modification), CTI looked at the opportunity to rearchitect their corporate network as a chance to bring their network into the present day. They also realized that any decisions made about the direction of the network were decisions they were likely to have to live with for many years to come. For these reasons, primarily, CTI undertook an exhaustive evaluation process of networking alternatives as well as designing a future migration strategy into their plans. By looking not only at the present, but at how their present plans lead them down the path to the future, they sought to ensure the future health and growth of the network and ensure that the network would, after the initial migration, always be positioned slightly ahead of the demands placed on the network.

While the "master plan" covered the entire corporation, their unified architecture document formally addressed the needs and requirements of each operating company quite specifically. This was a wise approach, indeed, as CTI management realized that bringing together the previous islands of networking into a single networking infrastructure would only work, from both technical and human aspects, if every issue were evaluated and every situation were planned for.

8.3.1 Business Aspects

Caliber's upper management had set out a vision that would keep them "delivering exceptional service into the 21st century," and every operational area of the company was required to respond and do their share. One part of the initiative was a sweeping reorganization, which created Caliber System, Inc., from the former Roadway Services, Inc., and established CTI as the technology provider. CTI began by setting realistic expectations, performing an exhaustive study of alternatives, and choosing products and services to support the final choice of network architecture.

Expectations

In many ways CTI set very realistic expectations for their new frame relay network, and for this reason they were not disappointed. They expected a network that was more flexible than a nationwide leased-line network in terms of procurement, provisioning, and configuration. They expected more bandwidth than was available on their leased lines, and they expected to have a lot of problems, at least initially, in implementing SNA and mixed SNA-TCP/IP environments. CTI felt that most companies implementing SNA over TCP/IP did not do sufficiently careful analysis of the bandwidth required to avoid collisions and lost packets for specific applications. CTI felt that they could come to understand and manage this and feel that they've been successful. The only expectation that appeared realistic on the surface but later proved to be overly optimistic was the expectation that the carrier would take responsibility for comprehensive monitoring and support of the frame relay network and associated customer premise equipment.

In the early phases, CTI expected that their new frame relay network would

- provide more bandwidth than their existing analog leased lines and, realistically, even more than the 56-Kbit/second digital leased lines they could have used to replace the older analog technology

- position them for even higher bandwidths as requirements dictated in the future
- allow a great deal of configuration flexibility: reduce lead times on new orders, allow changes to be made in a period of days to existing sites, and allow sites to be moved with little impact on the operating environment
- support legacy SNA for the IBM mainframe and AS/400 environments separately from, and in conjunction with, the emerging TCP/IP environment
- reduce staff and free CTI to focus more on core business issues and less on hands-on operation of the network and its implementation and hour-by-hour management

Alternatives Considered

Because CTI runs a traditional IBM operation, they began by evaluating traditional alternatives and then moved through the more modern choices, finally moving through X.25, IBM's AnyNet options, frame relay, and ATM.

Leased lines   The first step was to look at leased-line alternatives. The leased-line alternative was to replace the existing analog leased lines with 56-Kbit/second digital leased lines, replace all modems at the sites with DSU/CSUs, and then to provide devices that allowed the emerging TCP/IP traffic to be transmitted within SNA/SDLC frames across the leased lines to the central site, at which time they would be separated again from the SDLC traffic and each traffic type would be sent its respective way: SDLC to the front-end processor, and TCP/IP to the LAN. The benefits of this approach were a fairly straightforward migration, support for TCP/IP, and enhanced manageability of the network through the use of intelligent and manageable DSU/CSUs. The drawbacks of this approach were high cost, the inability to accommodate future bandwidth demands greater than 56 Kbits/second, and the difficulty and long lead times for changing the network to meet emerging business needs.

X.25   The next step was to evaluate X.25. X.25 is a tried-and-true technology, has been around quite a while, is available in all of the (sometimes remote) geographical areas required by Caliber, and could provide larger bandwidths than 56 Kbits/second in many areas if needed, but not the very high bandwidth requirements that might be needed by some future applications. The feeling about X.25 was that it is, in the domestic U.S. sense, a dead-end technology: many other, better alternatives existed to this

20-plus-year-old telecommunications method, which are more efficient and take better advantage of the high-reliability/low-latency digital infrastructure of today. CTI also cited problems with the way in which SNA and Qualified Logical Link Control (QLLC) are supported on X.25 as reasons for not pursuing an X.25 option any further.

IBM's AnyNet   After discarding X.25, CTI spent some time reviewing the strategic and tactical benefits of IBM's AnyNet capabilities and products. IBM's

> AnyNet product family is a software approach to multiprotocol networking based on IBM's emerging Multiprotocol Transport Networking (MPTN) architecture. The objective of AnyNet is to allow a customer to
>
> - add new application types independent of the existing networks
> - extend the reach of an application over multiple networks
> - consolidate and simplify multiprotocol networks while preserving investment in existing applications
>
> This application and network independence is achieved by the implementation of the MPTN architecture, which separates the application support and the transport network.
>
> The AnyNet gateway allows customers to concatenate unlike networks into one logical network. The software gateways are currently implemented on OS/2 and MVS. Instead of having the conversion between different applications and different protocols reside on the desktop and in the operating system, the AnyNet gateway provides a single piece of equipment that can convert between TCP/IP and SNA. The gateway allows SNA applications to run over connected SNA and TCP/IP networks. An IPX-to-SNA gateway is a future direction for IBM. IPX is Novell's network layer protocol.
>
> These gateways operate at the transport layer (OSI Layer 4) and do not provide protocol conversion [simply encapsulation]. Native protocol data is put in an MPTN connection command and then sent across a new network type. The AnyNet access node on the second network receives the MPTN command and forwards the native data to the matching application. The native system can be any vendor's SNA or TCP system (Heckart 1994).

CTI decided not to use the AnyNet approach because the current state of development of the product was not satisfactory and there was a perceived lack of a good long-term vision. This view seems justified in that performance of the product was judged inferior (and still is!). Data Link Switching was more robust, especially with local acknowledgment.

Frame relay   Frame relay was then put under CTI's microscope. Even though they were beginning at an early stage in frame relay's history (the early adopter stage, during which many pioneers discover the differences between the reality of technologies and the hyperbole of marketing), CTI could see great merit in frame relay and how frame relay fit into the emerging world of virtual data networks—a model that meshed very nicely with their own vision of a highly flexible network. CTI saw how it could leverage the virtual "bandwidth pooling" aspects of frame relay by connecting very short UNI pipes to the edges of the bandwidth pool and using the high-speed backbone capability to transport their information over the long distance. CTI saw how the multiplexed physical interface could support several different information streams, if needed, to several different destinations; how this flexibility could give them remarkable agility in the future; and how the "intelligent leased line" aspects of the rerouting around failures that occur within the frame relay network could help sustain the high levels of availability and reliability that had become the trademarks of the existing network.

CTI evaluated three different scenarios using frame relay. One was a frame relay infrastructure utilizing IBM controllers and front-end processors with frame relay interfaces, one was a bridged network scenario, and one was a routed network scenario. The motivation behind the evaluation for all three was the same: to see how closely each met the demands of the unified network architecture in providing as close to a seamless transport as possible for all likely data types.

Even though the IBM devices with frame relay interfaces made the most sense at first, it became obvious that this approach was simply propagating the existing IBM SNA environment and not positioning CTI for future opportunities or utilizing the benefits and capabilities of frame relay beyond being a smart leased-line replacement. With this approach, CTI would simply replace the 9.6-Kbit/second analog port cards on the controllers and front-end processors with frame-relay-capable cards, and replace communications equipment in the middle, and it would be business as usual on the network. While least disruptive, it was also the least beneficial.

A similar alternative that was considered was the use of stand-alone SNA/frame relay adapters (FRADs) that would adapt the SNA for transport across the frame relay network and make the conversion back at the other end of the connection. Although more cost-effective than replacing older cluster controllers and upgrading newer models, this approach, too, only propagated the old SNA structure.

In terms of the routing versus bridging approach, CTI had wanted to keep the argument purely routing versus bridging, but the realities of SNA implementation did not allow this simplistic approach. While CTI attempts to utilize routing wherever possible (such as in support of TCP/IP), the SNA environment requires use of bridging in many instances, such as interconnecting token ring LANs. Therefore, CTI initially implemented source route bridging but has begun to implement Data Link Switching as that approach has matured.

ATM   And then came the evaluation of ATM. CTI determined that ATM was not yet ready for widespread commercial use because of technical development and cost. But because ATM follows the same virtual networking model as frame relay, offers bandwidth and flexibility beyond that of frame relay, and works in a philosophical partnership with frame relay as a logical next step in network evolution, CTI identified a migration strategy to a hybrid frame relay/ATM direction that would allow them to take advantage of frame relay today while not locking themselves out of participating in an ATM future.

CTI's final decision was to move forward with a frame relay infrastructure. The next step was the traditional "buy or build" decision. CTI evaluated vendors and looked at the complexity, capital cost, and ongoing operating costs of their own frame relay network versus what could be provided by major telecommunications carriers and service providers. CTI decided that a network from a carrier or service provider would be more cost-effective, less difficult to manage, and would allow them to focus more of their time and effort on using the network than on its day-to-day operation. The next step was to evaluate carriers and make a decision.

Carrier Selection Process

CTI limited their screening and selection process to three of the largest providers of frame relay services: Sprint, MCI, and AT&T. There were six major criteria upon which the carriers were judged:

- Domestic U.S. points-of-presence and service coverage
- International service coverage and philosophy (with emphasis on Canada and Mexico)
- Carriers' capability to provide turnkey operation
- Pricing, both nonrecurring start-up costs and recurring monthly costs
- Technical evaluation of network performance
- Ease of migration

Domestic points-of-presence and service coverage   One of the ways in which Caliber's requirements differ from those of other large corporations is that many of their largest facilities are in the most remote locations, far from city centers or other high-density population areas. This fact created a difficulty for two of the three carriers and left AT&T's InterSpan frame relay service out in front in the evaluation process at the end of the first evaluation phase.

Even though all major carriers provide coast-to-coast domestic coverage today through back-hauling of traffic (paid for by the carrier as part of the cost of a claim of comprehensive domestic U.S. coverage), this practice was not widespread at the time CTI made their evaluation and figured heavily into their selection process. Even today, though, the distance a carrier may back-haul traffic, while not significant from a cost standpoint because the larger carriers bear the back-haul cost from the nearest central office to the network point-of-presence, is significant from a network reliability standpoint: the longer the back-haul over a single leased line to the edge of the network "cloud," the greater risk of outages on the single thread connecting the site to the network.

International coverage   AT&T's InterSpan, in CTI's view, also provided superior coverage in the international arena. CTI specifically cited the AT&T Global Partners program and AT&T's approach of providing international coverage through a partnership with existing postal, telephone, and telegraph authorities or other national service providers, as opposed to spreading their resources too thin by trying to establish a service presence in every country or to buy a part of the local in-country carrier. CTI was also very pleased with AT&T's coverage in the areas of Mexico and Canada in which CTI operates.

Turnkey operation   While all carriers made claims to provide comprehensive network installation and ongoing support, AT&T had the most convincing story and, coupled with other aspects of the service offering, made AT&T a clear favorite by this step. As we will see, however, later in this chapter, this was to be a major problem area and the one area where expectations set during the selection process were not met.

Costs   In the final analysis, the selection of AT&T as a frame relay service provider was not determined by cost: other carriers seemed to be more cost competitive, ranging from 5–10% less expensive. However, given the relationship that existed with AT&T, together with the relationship between Cisco, AT&T, and Caliber, the decision was made in favor of AT&T. Other factors weighing in the decision included the number of points-of-presence (POPs), comprehensiveness of the offering, and demonstrated technical competence and ability to meet commitments.

Technical evaluation   After having tabulated the results from the first steps, it was then important to compare the three network services. This step also allowed CTI personnel to get very important experience with frame relay, a then very new technology with which very few people had any hands-on experience. Each carrier established frame relay permanent virtual connections from Akron, Ohio, to Phoenix, Arizona, and back, a distance of approximately 3,200 circuit miles. CTI then performed a variety of performance tests from simulated small, medium, and large sites as well as simulating worst-case response times and other performance scenarios. The initial testing was performed over a 30-day period, after which time AT&T's InterSpan was selected, and further testing and familiarization was performed only with the InterSpan service.

Migration   The migration plan that CTI developed delivered returns immediately to the company. The general approach was for a staged roll-out, beginning with the locations that used the most bandwidth. The roll-out began after Caliber analyzed each location's size and bandwidth requirement. With that information, access capacities and committed information rates (CIRs) for frame relay connectivity could be determined. To account for any unexpected surprises on CIRs, Caliber Technology took the approach of installing slightly larger than needed capacity and then monitored the network to throttle down the CIR to the optimum level. Generally, central terminal hubs were addressed first, then mid-sized sites, and finally smaller sites.

8.3.2 Technical Aspects

CTI's top technical person had been a systems engineer with IBM for 15 years. She understood the complexity of the task confronting CTI, the possible problems and eccentricities of moving SNA over to a new infrastructure, and the possible complications of integrating all of this with TCP/IP. Even with this monumental task ahead, CTI knew they needed to take a holistic view and to initiate the process not in little pieces, but on a systemwide scale, and move as quickly as possible. For this reason, they took on the task of cataloging all applications, protocols, devices, users, and facilities and planned for a complete turnover. The complete turnover of 1,400-plus sites took over two years to complete. And all of the preparations paid off. The concerns and worries about every little detail translated into a surprisingly smooth transition into the new networking environment.

Planning

The top three concerns of CTI's migration planning were SNA, SNA, and SNA. After the technical feasibility of moving to SNA, they concerned themselves with a standardized addressing scheme for the TCP/IP network, routing protocol issues, and the cost elements of the move. Even though their unified architecture document specified brands and models of routers and other devices, other network-related issues (such as router configuration setup) were left in the hands of AT&T, as agreed during the sales process.

SNA Migration Planning

The four elements that were addressed in greatest detail during the process of planning the migration of SNA to the new network infrastructure were all related to performance and delay: how to encapsulate SNA information in TCP/IP for transport across the network, local acknowledgment, custom queuing, and minimization of router hop counts. Although not frame relay issues per se, these issues are important in migration of traditional SNA away from a leased-line environment to any new network infrastructure, and therefore form part of the underlying considerations of migrating SNA to a frame relay network.

There are two fundamental issues related to SNA networking: a technical issue and a human one. The technical issue is the *time-out*, the length of time that an SNA host is willing to wait before it decides that a remote device has gone out of service for some reason. In this case, a process must be initiated in the host operations center to tell the host to begin talking with the remote device again. Besides having a negative effect on the operator of the device that has "timed out," the process has a detrimental effect on overall performance because the actual method used to determine that the slow-to-respond remote device has gone out of service also degrades overall performance on that communication line.

The human issue is the pacing of the input operators. While many of us, especially those of us who learned to "type" on a computer keyboard, are hunt-and-peck typists, the professional operator at an IBM 3270-type terminal is usually a competent data entry operator who knows exactly how much time is required to submit each screen, the order of input fields, and other issues. This special familiarity not only contributes to their speed and accuracy, but also requires consistency from the underlying information transport mechanism—a consistency that can usually be achieved by a dedicated, fixed-latency leased line, but not always by a frame or packet network susceptible to so many different sources of delay.

The seven following considerations each address an important aspect of guaranteeing low, consistent latency for the IBM terminal operator. Although leased lines are "primitive" in comparison to emerging packet and frame technologies, they do still present some benefits that must be emulated as closely as possible by the newer technologies.

Data Link Switching versus RFC 1490   Among the many nontrivial considerations when migrating from a traditional IBM environment to a frame relay environment is the thought that must be given to encapsulation of the SNA information for transportation across the frame relay network. Two primary approaches exist: RFC 1490 and IBM's Data Link Switching (DLSw). RFC 1490 provides a method of encapsulating SNA directly into frame relay; DLSw encapsulates SNA into IP and then uses frame relay to transport the SNA-encapsulating IP packets.

Both DLSw and RFC 1490 have their pros and cons, and each fits different needs. DLSw is a means of transporting SNA and NetBIOS traffic over an IP network.

Data link switching is an alternative to source-route bridging (SRB) that can be used as a basis to address several problems inherent in the SRB protocol, including

- SRB hop-count limits (SRB limit is seven)
- broadcast traffic (from SRB explorer frames or NetBIOS name queries)
- unnecessary traffic (acknowledgments and keep-alives)
- DLC time-outs
- lack of flow control and prioritization

While these SRB weaknesses may apply to a campus environment, they are more pronounced when SRB is extended across a wide-area network (WAN). Hence, data link switching is typically used to transport SNA and NetBIOS across a WAN (Guruge 1996).

A key strength of DLSw is its ability to dynamically locate SNA/APPN or NETBIOS destinations—such as a 37XX gateway to a mainframe—using the destination's Layer 2 media access control (MAC) address. DLSw conducts this destination location process using a search protocol. This protocol is an optimized version of source-route bridging's (SRB) broadcast search mechanism, executed across the WAN using TCP/IP. This dynamic search mechanism does not, however, make DLSw a plug-and-play technique that can be set up as easily and intuitively as a bridged network. The presence and use of TCP/IP nixes that. The administration and management of 32-bit IP addresses is an integral facet of DLSw. At a minimum, all the IP addresses of the DLSw bridge/routers serving all potential destination LANs have to be defined at each source DLSw bridge/router. In addition to defining DLSw-specific IP addresses, you still have to specify all of the SRB-related parameters, such as LAN segment numbers, bridge numbers and MAC addresses of all the destinations. That's because DLSw and Cisco's DLSw+ are essentially TCP/IP encapsulation techniques for performing SRB across a WAN (Guruge 1996).

It is also noteworthy that while DLSw is widely thought to be a standard, it is, in fact, a creation of IBM that has been granted Informational RFC status by the Internet Engineering Task Force and is not a standard in any sense.

While Data Link Switching addresses the encapsulation of SNA, RFC 1490 provides an encapsulation scheme for all protocols, has a lower protocol overhead than DLSw (as little as 25%), and is more widely implemented by router vendors than DLSw.

RFC 1490 appears to have the greatest support and widest acceptance in the standards-based router network community and is more widely installed than IBM's Data Link Switching. RFC 1490, however, does not obsolete DLSw: they each have a role to play, albeit in different networking scenarios. Packet-switched environments, whether public or private, tend to be RFC 1490's domain. DLSw, meanwhile, tends to be practical in IP-based backbones. While the support for RFC 1490 is more widespread, it is significant in the case of CTI that their chosen router vendor, Cisco, has integrated support for DLSw into their product line and offers enhancements (called DLSw+).

Local acknowledgment   IBM's Systems Network Architecture has, from its inception, been a hierarchical system, with local and remote terminals communicating with cluster controllers, which communicate with communications front-end processors, and eventually with host computers. The way that these communications have been kept orderly and efficient is for the front-end processor to keep a list of all active terminals and to send messages to them (in a round-robin fashion based upon their line, control unit, and terminal IDs) to see if they have anything to send. This is the function called *polling* that we discussed briefly earlier (Figure 8.3).

In a local environment where messages travel over dedicated wires at high speed, and even in a remote environment where the wire from the front-end processor to the cluster controller is a dedicated communications circuit, this process is predictable and consistent; any inconsistencies indicate the presence of a problem. In an environment where some type of packet or frame network has been interjected between the front-end processor and the cluster controller, the transport mechanism is not absolutely predictable, but needs to be (within some fairly rigid tolerance).

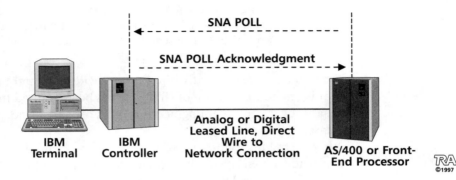

Figure 8.3   IBM SNA Polling

The answer (and one that also saves costly bandwidth) is called *local acknowledgment,* or by its nickname, *poll spoofing* (Figure 8.4).

Local acknowledgment uses two intelligent devices at the edge of the network to provide the appearance of an end-to-end poll that traverses the network, but which actually does not. With end-to-end acknowledgment, the poll goes from the front-end processor to the cluster controller across a dedicated wire or other network and from the cluster controller to the terminal across another dedicated wire—all relatively quickly. With local acknowledgment, the poll goes from the front-end processor to a local SNA adapter, which is a frame relay access device (FRAD) such as a router or dedicated SNA-to-frame-relay adapter, if it is being used in the frame relay instance, and the local SNA adapter responds to the poll. If something has previously been forwarded by the remote SNA adapter to be sent to the host, then it is forwarded. If nothing is to be sent, then a negative acknowledgment is generated. Because the SNA adapter and the front-end processor are connected to each other by a dedicated wire, this process is very fast: each host poll does not need to cross the network. A mirror image of this process is repeated at the distant end of the network, with SNA polls being generated and acknowledged at the remote end of the network as well and information being transported between the two devices supporting the poll spoofing, using a more efficient proprietary or standard protocol.

Some IBM systems programmers are in favor of local acknowledgment, while others feel that it is just a bad "patch" for poorly performing networks. The IBM systems programmers who do not like this approach feel that too big a likelihood exists for the SNA adapter devices to lose synchronization with each other and that these intermediary devices stand in the

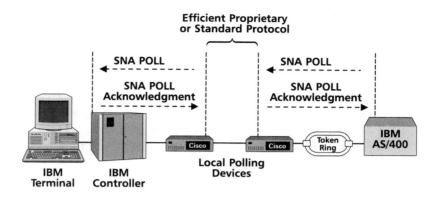

Figure 8.4   Local Acknowledgment (Poll Spoofing)

way of the IBM network management system getting a clear picture of the health and operational characteristics of the network. These opinions notwithstanding, many, many IBM shops use local acknowledgment, as does CTI, to enhance their performance and reduce the costs due to wasted bandwidth used for unproductive polls.

Custom queuing   A key challenge to CTI, or any company, when integrating SNA and LAN internetworks is to preserve the predictable response time of the SNA network while ensuring the throughput requirements of LAN applications. One approach to providing predictable performance is to increase line speeds to assure that adequate bandwidth is available during peak traffic conditions. While this may be a reasonable approach for backbone links because a large amount of backbone bandwidth is shared by many users, it may not be a cost-effective method of attaching remote sites to the backbone. A better approach may be to use lower-speed lines and give mission-critical data priority over less critical transmissions during peak traffic conditions.

Cisco offers two means of ensuring that mission-critical data attains predictable throughput:

- Priority output queuing, designed for enterprises that give mission-critical data the highest priority and are willing to delay less critical traffic during periods of congestion
- Custom queuing, designed for environments that need to guarantee a minimal level of service to all protocols

CTI was one of the early adopters of custom queuing because custom queuing allows CTI to reserve a percentage of bandwidth for specified protocols. CTI can define up to 10 output queues for normal data and an additional queue for system messages such as LAN keep-alive messages (routing packets are not assigned to the system queue). Cisco routers service each queue sequentially, transmitting a configurable percentage of traffic on each queue before moving on to the next one. Custom queuing guarantees that mission-critical data is always assigned a certain percentage of the bandwidth, but also ensures predictable throughput for other traffic.

To provide this feature, Cisco routers determine how many bytes should be transmitted from each queue, based on the interface speed and the configured percentage. When the calculated byte count from a given queue has been transmitted, the router completes transmission of the current packet and moves on to the next queue, servicing each queue in a round-robin fashion.

A key advantage of Cisco's "bandwidth reservation" technique is that unused bandwidth can be dynamically allocated to any protocol that requires it. For example, if SNA is allocated 50% of the bandwidth but uses only 30%, the next protocol in the queue can take up the extra 20% until SNA requires it. Additionally, custom queuing maintains the predictable throughput of dedicated lines by efficiently using packet-switching technologies such as frame relay.

Custom queuing of time-sensitive interactive SNA traffic ahead of less time-sensitive LAN traffic is a very important part of CTI's success with SNA over frame relay, but there is one more level of detail underlying the prioritization process: the recognition of different protocols and communications streams within the overall information transfer. In many cases, this is done in the frame relay network by prioritizing on the DLCIs for different destinations, but in the case of CTI, there is only one DLCI going to one destination, so DLCI-based differentiation is not possible. To make effective use of any prioritization scheme, network administrators must have flexibility in how they allocate traffic to a queue. For example, if an enterprise has both SNA and NetBIOS traffic on a token ring LAN, it may be imperative to prioritize SNA traffic (which is often mission-critical) over the NetBIOS traffic (which is more tolerant of delays). In providing this granularity, Cisco allows prioritization queues to be specified by LAN service access point (SAP), the field in a LAN frame that specifies which protocol is being carried in the frame. In addition, Cisco routers support prioritization of SDLC traffic, any routed protocol suite, and any TCP/IP port. TCP/IP port prioritization enables network administrators to prioritize Telnet traffic ahead of FTP, for example. In environments with traditional SNA, prioritizing at an even more granular level is possible. For example, it may be necessary to prioritize traffic for certain logical units (LUs) to assure that terminal traffic takes precedence over printer traffic. Cisco supports the capability to prioritize by LU address for a given physical unit (PU) when transmitting either SDLC or token ring SNA traffic. Additionally, enterprises may need to prioritize selected SDLC lines over other lines to ensure, for example, that customer service traffic takes precedence over administrative traffic.

Minimization of router hop counts   The final detail-level consideration for optimizing and guaranteeing consistency of performance for SNA traffic is minimization of router hop counts. In a routed environment, it is possible for information packets to travel through several intermediate routers, called *hops,* on the trip from the source router at the remote site to the local router at the central, or host, site. In a non-frame-relay router environment, the issue of the number of hops that an end-to-end connection must make between source and destination is one of geography and cost. One of the cost savings elements when moving from a point-to-point leased-line configuration to a router network is the elimination of costs for direct leased connections from the remote site to the host site.

Instead of the point-to-point lines, traffic is aggregated through intermediate points in a true mesh network type of arrangement that provides both capacity and route diversity. In a public frame relay network scenario, however, routers are directly connected to a high-capacity/low-latency carrier-provided backbone network and therefore minimize hop counts as well as costs.

Standardized addressing scheme   CTI adopted a simplified addressing scheme for TCP/IP. Two registered Class C blocks of IP addresses were used as the basis for Internet access. Initially, all Class C subnetting of unregistered "A" addresses were used. As networks have flattened through the use of switching technology, subnets have been moved to Class B where appropriate (whether or not they need more host addresses).

The ANS fire wall used by CTI accepts unregistered Class A addresses and converts them to registered Class C addresses. Domain name services are used to distribute messages from the fire wall to individual Caliber companies.

Routing protocol issues   One of the technical lessons learned during the implementation process was not directly a function of frame relay, but rather an issue that must be considered when building any kind of router-based network: choice of router protocol. In the original implementation of the network, CTI chose to use Cisco's Inter-Gateway Routing Protocol (IGRP).

IGRP is a protocol that allows gateways to build up their routing table by exchanging information with other gateways. A gateway starts out with entries for all of the networks that are directly connected to it. It gets information about other networks by exchanging routing updates with adjacent gateways. In the simplest case, the gateway will find one path that represents the best way to get to each network. A path is characterized by the next gateway to which packets should be sent, the network interface that should be used, and metric information. Metric information is a set of numbers that characterize how good the path is. This allows the gateway to compare paths that it has heard from various gateways and decide which one to use. There are often cases where it makes sense to split traffic between two or more paths. IGRP will do this whenever two or more paths are equally good. The user can also configure it to split traffic when paths are almost equally good. In this case more traffic will be sent along the path with the better metric. The intent is that traffic can be split between a 9,600 bps line and a 19,200 bps line, and the 19,200 [bps] line will get roughly twice as much traffic as the 9,600 bps line. The metrics used by IGRP include the topological delay time, the bandwidth of the narrowest bandwidth segment of the path, the channel occupancy of the path and the reliability of the path (Hedrick 1991).

IGRP was a fine choice for the network when it was smaller, but as the network grew, so too did the access lists (used for security purposes) and other routing table elements. The size of the routing table updates soon required a great deal of bandwidth and had a negative impact on network efficiency. For that reason, CTI evaluated alternative routing protocols. They took a serious look at the "open shortest path first" (OSPF) algorithm and the Enhanced Inter-Gateway Routing Protocol (EIGRP). Older, inefficient routing protocols such as RIP (Router Information Protocol) were not even considered because their performance characteristics are inferior to IGRP.

One final consideration was that IGRP and EIGRP are both Cisco routing protocols, that CTI's is a Cisco-based network, and that the migration from IGRP to EIGRP could be accomplished most painlessly because EIGRP uses the internal configuration tables of IGRP and the two protocols, because of architectural and implementation consistency, can coexist in the same network during the migration from IGRP to EIGRP. For these reasons, CTI migrated their network to EIGRP.

Technical aspects of cost   While capital costs, budgets, network operating expenses, and similar terms are normally considered the realm of the accounting department and management levels, CTI involved their technical team very heavily in cost assessment, cost impact of alternatives, and cost containment. Doing so ensured that the best technical solutions were delivered at the best possible cost. CTI found that digital 56-Kbit/second leased lines to replace the 9.6-Kbit/second analog lines that dominated the older network topology had roughly the same monthly cost. CTI also found that 64-Kbit/second frame relay access with 32-Kbit/second CIR could be provided at a lower monthly cost than the 9.6-Kbit/second analog or 56-Kbit/second digital solutions. However, the bigger issues that had to be addressed were the migration cost to either the 56-Kbit/second or frame relay solutions. The migration to either new network architecture would be disruptive to the operation of the business, and both would require purchasing or leasing (or an increased service cost to include) new digital CSU/DSUs to replace the 9.6-Kbit/second analog modems. The move to frame relay would also require implementation of expensive routers, an additional cost (both in terms of initial acquisition as well as ongoing maintenance and support) that was not absolutely mandatory with the 56-Kbit/second leased-line approach. The decision point became, "Are multiple protocols, including SNA and TCP/IP, required in the network?" The answer was yes: in many operating companies' networks now and in the unified architecture in the future. The decision by CTI to introduce routers at an early stage turned out to be a prudent one: future disruption was avoided, and the agility and flexibility to handle whatever was asked of the network in a short time frame was ensured.

Migration

One important decision point in the original carrier selection process was the carrier's stated ability to provide comprehensive technical support during the migration. In actual practice, as it turned out, AT&T had overstated their capabilities in this area, and CTI was put into the position of having to coordinate the installation, configuration, and turn-up of its routers with the assistance of AT&T and Cisco. As CTI puts it, "We learned together," but CTI was disappointed that the expertise was not available as promised.

The specific provisioning process used by CTI is the following:

- *Preconfigure the router.* CTI has developed a template for each size location, and this standard configuration, with site-specific details such as addresses, is preloaded into the router prior to the router being shipped to the site.

- *Install the local access portion of the frame relay service.* The local exchange carrier installation of the physical circuit from the remote site to the AT&T point-of-presence is scheduled well in advance of the actual frame relay installation. This is often a big problem area because of the physical remoteness of many Roadway sites from population centers. The local access portion is tested by the local exchange carrier using traditional circuit continuity, loopback, and pattern tests prior to being turned over to AT&T.
- *Install the frame relay UNI.* The frame relay user-to-network interface is installed between the remote site and the AT&T InterSpan network, using the previously installed local access circuit. This includes installing the customer site DSU/CSU if this has not already been done.
- *Install the router.* The preconfigured customer site router is installed and tested.
- *Configure and "turn up" the PVC.* The frame relay PVC is configured between the remote site and the host site. This is the first end-to-end test of connectivity.
- *Configure the new remote site in network management.* The new site is configured in the various network management systems so that the router, DSU/CSU, and line performance can be monitored prior to moving live data to the new connection.
- *"Burn in" new service for one week.* CTI allows the new connection to run without live data for a week or so. During this "burn-in" period, many problems are allowed to surface without having a negative impact on actual operations. Problems that occur most frequently during this time are accumulation of cyclical redundancy check (CRC) errors due to physical problems with the local access circuit or similar indications of local loop problems.
- *Turn up new frame relay service.* After the initial burn-in period, the new service is implemented and monitoring continues just as it does for the rest of the network.
- *Monitor and adjust . . . monitor and adjust . . . monitor and adjust.* Monitoring of performance and adjustment of interface parameters is an ongoing process with all frame relay connections, but more crucial in the initial period after installation. During the first days of the introduction of a new frame relay system (any system, in fact) is when the user's expectation level is set. A user must not have an unrealistically high expectation based on a network or network access connection that is not fully loaded nor should they have an unrealistically low expectation based on interface parameters that are improperly

set. Every effort should be made to establish the network performance levels as they will remain over the long term.

Configuration after Migration

Some CTI sites continue to have SNA only and will for some time, while many CTI sites have both SNA and TCP/IP LANs.

Physical architecture The physical configuration is very straightforward, with SNA controllers and possibly personal computers and RISC 6000 workstations attached to a token ring LAN at the site (Figure 8.5). A router provides the interface to the frame relay network, most of which have an access rate of 64 Kbits/second and a 32-Kbit/second CIR, and the circuits are star configured either to the Akron, Ohio, or Pittsburgh, Pennsylvania, data centers.

Split-T CSU/DSUs are provided on the frame relay access T1 to split a 64-Kbit/second DS0 channel for use by frame relay and other DS0 channels for termination on the PBX or other telephone equipment. Split-T CSU/DSUs are fundamentally normal CSU/DSUs with a small channel bank built in such that as many as three or four data connections and one PBX connection may be split from a standard T1 circuit. This very cost-effective configuration allowed CTI to save money on frame relay access by leveraging T1s that were already in place in many locations and installing new T1s where appropriate for cost-effective shared data/voice use.

Logical architecture The logical diagram after frame relay remains the same as shown in Figure 8.2.

Operations and Network Management

CTI uses a combination of products to provide comprehensive network operations and management capabilities. The network management philosophy of CTI is to use any and all tools at hand to provide a comprehensive view of the operation of the network: physical-level DSU/CSU management is combined with router and SNA management, a change management system, customer network management tools, and HP OpenView to provide many ways of assessing the health of the network. The products used to support the frame relay portions of the network include

- Paradyne's Frame Relay Awareness and COMSPHERE NMS
- HP OpenView NMS
- CiscoWorks Blue
- Net Tech E-View Open
- AT&T InterSpan Customer Network Management System

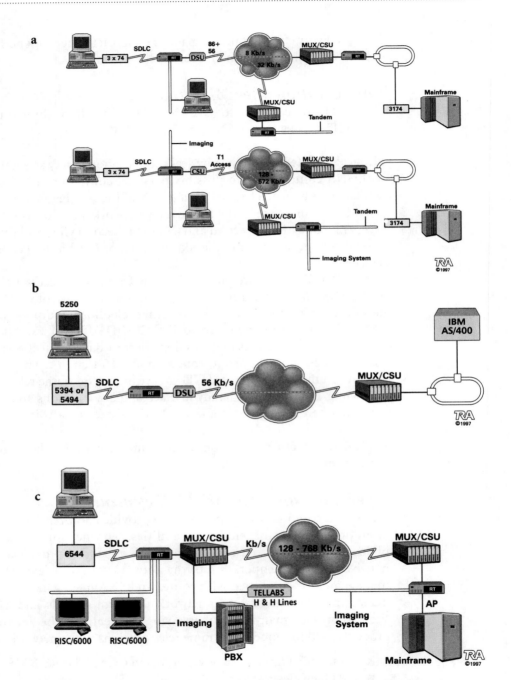

Figure 8.5   Frame Relay Physical Diagram: (a) Frame Relay LAN Interconnection; (b) Frame Relay Terminal Support; (c) Integrated Terminal and LAN Connection

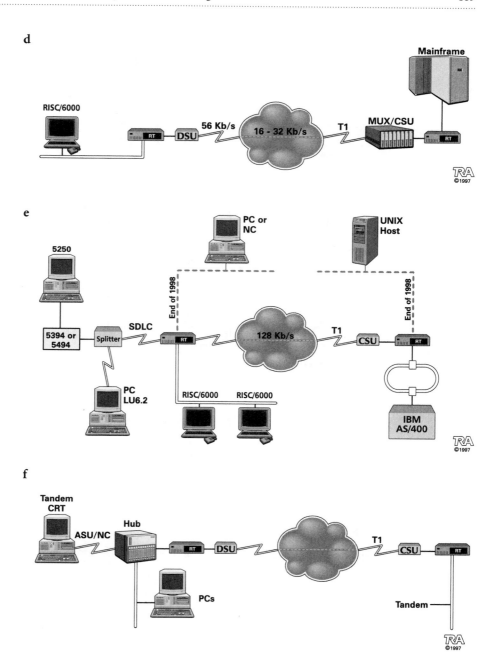

Figure 8.5 *continued:* (d) Frame Relay Workstation Support; (e) Future UNIX Terminal/UNIX PC Support; (f) Frame Relay Tandem Terminal Support

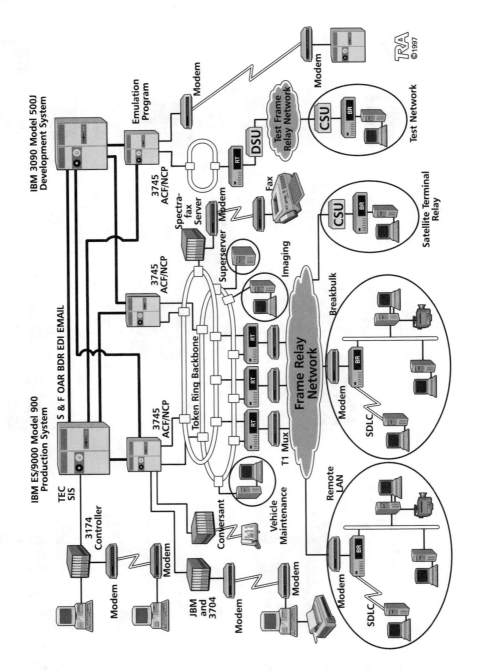

Figure 8.5 *continued:* (g) Post-Frame-Relay Remote LAN Environment

Paradyne's Frame Relay Awareness and COMSPHERE NMS Paradyne offers a comprehensive physical-layer management system called Frame Relay Awareness (FRAW). CTI was one of the beta test sites for FRAW and therefore has a great deal of experience with this newly released product. The Paradyne FRAW is based on the Frame Relay Access Unit (FRAU) 9620 and associated enhancements to their COMSPHERE Network Management System (NMS).

The Paradyne FRAU provides 56/64-Kbit/second frame relay network access, data compression, port aggregation, and advanced network management and statistics. This feature set maximizes frame relay network availability and manageability, enhances cost savings, and reduces the total number of separate devices required to achieve maximum bandwidth utilization.

The FRAU employs a unique PVC-based network management scheme and SNMP connectivity that isn't dependent on external routers, FRADs, cables, or LAN adapters. PVC-based management allows the FRAU to provide a fully integrated view of both the physical and logical frame relay network and to deliver true "end-to-end" management of CTI's frame relay network.

Every FRAU includes a frame relay packet multiplexer, which, in addition to providing frame relay port aggregation, provides the management functions with "logical" visibility and management of all the frame relay frames transmitted or received through the FRAU. This logical PVC-based visibility allows management and testing of individual PVCs without affecting others. Also, the FRAW packet multiplexer acts as a collection point for frame relay packet, PVC, and compression statistics and also provides traditional management, control, and diagnostics of the physical network and DTE port connections.

HP OpenView NMS CTI uses Hewlett Packard's OpenView Network Management System as a collection and coordination point for many of the various SNMP-managed systems within their network, since the frame relay systems and systems using the frame relay network are just a small part of the total. HP OpenView provides a common management structure for all of their systems, allowing CTI to have a single, consolidated network view of most aspects of their network operations.

CiscoWorks Blue CiscoBlue provides a road map for IBM internetworking customers who want to consolidate duplicate networks, effectively manage SNA and non-SNA resources, and integrate IBM networks into higher-speed switched internetworks. CiscoBlue is an extension to the

Cisco Internetwork Operating System (Cisco IOS™) software, the Cisco-Fusion™ architecture, and the CiscoWorks™ Blue network management strategy to provide more efficient use of new carrier services, improved bandwidth management over high-speed multimedia networks, enhanced LAN switching capabilities, and consolidated network management solutions.

CiscoWorks Blue is important to CTI because it provides consolidated SNA and TCP/IP network management. Consolidating information on mainframe and/or SNMP platforms enables a view of the network from both a physical and a logical (SNA) standpoint. New network management tools for response time measurement, configuration, and network design provide service-level measurement, function automation, and network optimization.

NetTech E-View Open   CTI had used Netview for management of SNA. Currently, E-View is being used for SNA management and has been expanded to include AS/400s. CA Unicenter handles IPX with the long-term desired outcome being to accomplish management on one platform.

AT&T InterSpan Customer Network Management system   CTI utilizes AT&T Customer Network Management Service (CNMS) both for long-term network performance monitoring and optimization as well as for near-real-time network status and troubleshooting. CTI's network management center connects to AT&T's CNMS system via a standard SNMP link, thereby allowing access to current network status, performance, and configuration data as well as receiving longer-term reports through the AT&T InterSpan Frame Relay CNMS Advanced Reports feature, which allows CTI to perform an FTP download of PostScript-formatted trended reports on a weekly and monthly basis.

The following statistics are provided via AT&T's CNMS reports with hourly granularity:

- *PVC status.* Provides a status of the active/inactive state of permanent virtual connections. PVC status provides a real-time method of monitoring the health of the network.
- *Port utilization.* Allows CTI to determine the extent to which any access port in the network is being utilized. Contention for access port capacity is an important aspect of overall performance and may represent the effects of widespread network congestion or simply localized problems that can be cured by increasing the access bandwidth or reconfiguring the PVC parameters for the port.

- *CIR utilization by PVC.* The utilization of individual PVCs relative to the committed information rate for that PVC provides an indication of how a connection is performing relative to its historic or expected performance levels as well as relative to the overall port utilization.

- *Frames and bytes transmitted and received by CIR.* These statistics are useful in terms of determining actual throughput of the port and are used to derive the port and CIR utilization percentages. It is useful to have both frame and byte counts because this provides some insight into average bytes/frame, which also affects performance.

- *Frames and bytes discarded.* The "frames and bytes discarded" statistic is a calculated statistic derived by subtracting the number of frames and bytes delivered by the network from the number of frames and bytes presented to the network for transport. This statistic provides a clear indication of the impact of the next four stats.

- *Frames with FECN bit set.* A frame arriving with a forward explicit congestion notification bit set has encountered congestion in at least one intermediate network node on its path from source to destination. This statistic indicates how many of those bits are encountered.

- *Frames with BECN bit set.* The backward explicit congestion notification bit closes the feedback loop by informing the router or other FRAD device whose traffic encountered congestion that there is congestion on the network. Most manufacturers do not set BECN bits on a one-for-one basis with FECN bits because this might cause some thrashing to occur if customer premise equipment responds in some manner to BECN. It is important to understand the exact algorithm used to set BECN to truly understand what is happening in the network.

    The user of these statistics should also keep in mind that the number of FECNs reported on the local end of a given PVC are really unrelated to the number of BECNs reported on the local end of the PVC. It is the FECNs reported on the remote end of the PVC that are meaningful when correlated with BECNs reported on the local end of the PVC, and vice versa, because FECNs and BECNs only report congestion in one direction through the network.

- *Frames sent and received with DE bit set.* Frames presented to the network for delivery in excess of the CIR for the PVC are marked "discard eligible" (DE) and are provisionally accepted by the network for delivery on a "best effort" basis. If congestion is encountered within the network, the DE frames will be discarded before non-DE frames. Coordination of the local-end DE frames sent and the far-end DE frames received statistics for each PVC will give an indication of how well the best effort is performing. If too many DE frames are being discarded, there will be an adverse impact on the user's performance, and an increase in the CIR for the affected PVC should be considered.

■ *Errored frames.* This statistic indicates frames that have been altered in transit and whose frame check sequence is no longer valid. Errored frames are often an indication of a physical-layer problem on the access lines in the absence of any congestion indications, though they could be indicative of some other problems within the switching backbone.

Another important aspect of the AT&T CNMS system is that the same connection, formats, and procedures are used to manage ATM services from AT&T, which fits nicely with CTI's longer-term networking goals.

Operations   CTI is very proactive in their network operations and management. In addition to their own staff, CTI has used on-site technicians from suppliers, such as Paradyne and Cisco, to supplement their own efforts. CTI combines a comprehensive, holistic approach to network health with a specific, detail-level problem determination and troubleshooting approach, utilizing both the tools we have discussed and traditional tools.

8.4 Living with Frame Relay

On the whole, CTI is very pleased with their move to frame relay. CTI continues to have experiences on a daily basis where the flexibility and manageability of their frame relay network remind them how lucky they are to be away from their old static, rigid, and difficult-to-modify leased-line network structure. CTI also finds that original expectations about performance have either been met or exceeded.

8.4.1 Anticipated Benefits

CTI expected to have more flexibility with the frame relay network. They do. The ease with which logical PVC parameters can be modified is unsurpassed, and the flexibility of adding, deleting, or moving sites far exceeds the flexibility and speed with which similar changes could occur in a leased-line network.

CTI expected better performance with the frame relay network. They have it. In some cases, applications' response times have gone from 4 or 5 seconds to below 1 second after implementation of the frame relay network, and the flexibility of parameter changes allows CTI to balance cost and performance issues to optimize network utilization and performance in both a business and technical aspect.

CTI expected cost savings through efficiencies and staff reduction and has achieved 30–50% savings as a result of their move to frame relay.

8.4.2 Unanticipated Benefits

Because CTI plans every aspect of their network operation so thoroughly and does so much research prior to making any move, there are rarely any surprises. For that reason, there is only one unanticipated benefit of using frame relay in the CTI environment. Because CTI uses an integrated access approach to providing their sites with frame relay access and traditional voice DS0s on a single access T1 circuit, as opposed to two separate circuits, they have realized a 10–12% savings in access circuits. For an organization the size of CTI, this represents a substantial savings.

8.4.3 Lessons Learned

CTI has learned two important lessons from their frame relay experiences: work closely with vendors and carriers, and use preconfigured cabinets. CTI has two areas where they would like to see improvements from their carrier: "pay as you go" model for frame relay incorporating switched virtual connections and better coordination of maintenance windows.

CTI's original expectation had been that the end-to-end connections would be handled by AT&T with very little intervention on their part. This was not to be the case, and CTI spent a lot of time, money, and effort to ensure the end-to-end installation of their frame relay service. CTI recommends staying very much involved in the planning and implementation phases as well as tracking deadlines and due dates closely to avoid terrible surprises.

CTI also learned that preconfiguring equipment cabinets at their headquarters site and shipping the systems intact to their remote destination for installation made a great deal of sense, saved on-site time, and contributed to overall higher-quality installations. CTI now routinely preconfigures cabinets and all of the devices in them and is even environmentally conscious by reusing the shipping crates time after time.

8.5 Future Plans

CTI is vigorously attacking perceived shortcomings in their present system as well as continuing to monitor ATM for applicability to future projects. CTI's list of future projects includes

- *ATM.* Monitor ATM standards, products, and service offerings on an ongoing basis to determine cost, business, and technical impacts.
- *Desktop video.* Increasing use of desktop video.
- *Enhanced vendor communications.* CTI will implement an electronic order submission and tracking process with Cisco, AT&T, and other key providers of services and products to the frame relay network as well as other areas of CTI's network operations.
- *Automated problem determination.* Automated tools to coordinate alarms and event messages and improve the first-level problem isolation process.
- *Management awareness.* Continue to interpret the technical aspects of their network operations and improvements to those operations in terms that management understands, and continue to make management aware of the pros and cons of various approaches and the strides CTI is making in many areas.

There is clearly no shortage of work to be done at CTI.

8.6 Conclusion

Our first real-world case study is now concluded. What have you learned? How have you supplemented your theoretical understanding of frame relay with some real-world considerations? Can you generalize the information in this chapter to your own specific situation?

In our next case study, we will see a company, also in the transportation industry, that has moved from an older, outdated X.25 network to a frame relay infrastructure. We will see many similarities and many differences from this case study. We will also deepen and strengthen our appreciation for the simplicity of frame relay and the many ways in which it can be employed in solving real networking problems.

CHAPTER NINE

X.25 to IP over Frame Relay Migration

Greyhound moved from an archaic, unreliable X.25-based solution to a modern, flexible platform. In this case study we will see how Greyhound combines frame relay public network and Internet services to get the proper balance of performance, reliability, control, and cost.

9.1 Case Study Background

Dallas-based Greyhound Lines, Inc., is the U.S.'s largest intercity bus company and the only U.S.-wide provider of intercity bus transportation. The company's primary business is scheduled passenger service, but it also provides charter bus service, package express delivery service, and food service at certain terminals.

The company that would become Greyhound Lines, Inc., was founded in 1914, by Carl Eric Wickman, an immigrant from Vamhus, Sweden. He began transporting miners between the villages of Hibbing and Alice, Minnesota, on his seven-seat Hupmobile. During 1995, the most recent year for which complete statistics are available, Greyhound operated 244 million miles of regularly scheduled service in the 48 contiguous states and three Canadian provinces, serving more than 2,400 destinations. By comparison, fewer than half that many U.S. locations are served by the airlines and Amtrak together. Greyhound employs 12,000 people, including 3,700 drivers and 750 maintenance workers.

The 2,400 Greyhound destinations run a ticket sales application called TRIPS. Prior to the implementation of frame relay in the Greyhound network, the destinations were divided into two groups: automated and manual. The automated sites were connected to a Tandem host in Dallas via a private X.25 network. The manual sites required a human operator to look up fares in a book and manually write a ticket. The decision between automated and manual was made based on sales volume.

The new network that Greyhound has developed is based upon a dual network approach, with sites still categorized based on sales volumes. In the new network, the top 150 ticket sales locations are configured in a star on a public frame relay network infrastructure, with remote sites connected via 56-Kbit/second lines with a single 32-Kbit/second PVC back to the corporate data center in Dallas. The remainder of the sites (including the ticket sales offices that were previously manual) are handled over the Internet.

Even though Greyhound's motto has always been "sell tickets," the new network arrangement has allowed the company to initiate a number of new applications that were not possible on the prior X.25 network. After the main TRIPS application had been successfully migrated to the frame relay/Internet network, Greyhound was able to use the new infrastructure for a number of new applications, including an ordering and package-tracking application for the Greyhound Packet Express (GPX) Service.

The main reason for Greyhound to move to the new network arrangement was that their X.25 vendors were not investing sufficient research and development effort into keeping the products upon which their old network was based up to contemporary support and maintenance standards. Greyhound's old network required a great deal of hands-on network management utilizing archaic management systems, was down frequently, and was increasingly difficult and expensive to upgrade. Additionally, during their research for new network alternatives, Greyhound found that their older X.25 network performed poorly when compared with newer, more streamlined alternatives such as frame relay.

Greyhound has reaped numerous benefits, both tangible and intangible, from the new network, all of which are evaluated later in the chapter. Greyhound understands that the new network is more costly than the old networking arrangement but feels that the additional cost is justified based upon the increased reliability, manageability, and capability of the new combined frame relay/Internet network.

When asked to characterize their overall approach to frame relay, Greyhound said, "Build it and they will come." When they embarked upon their initial mission to move to frame relay, their primary objectives were to replace the increasingly unreliable X.25 network with something more modern, more manageable, and more reliable. Their gut instincts told them that so much more was possible, but it was outside of their initial scope. In fact, had all possibilities been considered before they began, that crucial process would have been delayed.

The new infrastructure could support expanded LANs at the remote sites, companywide email and document distribution, gateways to Internet email, an internal intranet arrangement, and a variety of other capabilities. With a solid Layer 1 foundation based upon Category 5 cabling and sound physical plant management principles, a dual Internet and frame relay public network Layer 2 approach, and an extensible Layer 3 IP environment, Greyhound is poised to make decisions about their networking future that are independent of the network infrastructure they have in place.

9.2 Before Frame Relay

Greyhound operates a call center for customer ticket sales and other customer service needs, but most of the ticket sales are done at the large metropolitan Greyhound terminals, smaller remote terminals, and third-party-operated ticket sales locations within two hours of the trip for which the ticket is being purchased. The X.25 network had an average response range of 6–8 seconds at the automated sites and several minutes for the manual sites. The new frame relay locations are experiencing response times of 3–4 seconds, and the Internet sites, about 200 of which were manual, are experiencing response times of 7–10 seconds, depending upon time of day and other Internet usage patterns.

One critical aspect of this case study is rather subtle but worth pointing out: while the emphasis of this book is frame relay, Greyhound's migration was really from an X.25 to an IP environment. It is important for our case study purposes that one of the two transport methods used for Greyhound's IP traffic is frame relay, and, in fact, many of the benefits that Greyhound will realize, including positioning for future intranet applications, are a function of IP only, or of frame relay and IP together.

9.2.1   Business Aspects

The pre-frame-relay networking environment was not able to be upgraded, or even readily maintained, without a great deal of attention and effort. The pre-frame-relay environment, based upon X.25 packet-switching technology, was no longer providing a reliable ticket sales capability, and management and maintenance were very manually intensive. It was very clear to Greyhound management that another solution needed to be located and implemented.

Requirements

The requirements of Greyhound were largely based on the shortcomings of their prior networking environment. Greyhound's priorities, in order of importance, were scalability, functionality/manageability, reliability, and cost. Note that while cost was certainly an important consideration, it was not first and foremost. Greyhound realized that the scalability and functionality aspects of the right new solution could certainly drive down true costs (such as costs due to network problems or having to purchase a new system due to scalability issues) and that life cycle costs of ownership could more than make up for initial purchase costs.

Scalability   Greyhound defines *scalability* as the ability to add sites to the network without adding additional hardware or making network changes to the headquarters data center. By utilizing a frame relay solution for the larger sites and an Internet-based solution for the smaller sites, Greyhound is making good use of the multiplexed interface aspect of both solutions. Both frame relay and the Internet connection use a single physical interface to carry multiple logical connections. To allow more sites to access the headquarters data center, all that is needed (up to a point) is to add the remote site and make some minor software changes—a fairly fast and easy change when compared to a leased-line environment.

The very first thing that Greyhound did was to have their local exchange carrier (LEC) in Dallas install three T1 lines (each with an information carrying capacity of 1.5 million bits per second, for a total of 4.5 million bits per second) between their Dallas Data Center and AT&T's InterSpan frame relay service (Figure 9.1). This provided a large amount of capacity for carrying information from the network to the Greyhound Data Center.

The next step was to begin adding remote sites to the InterSpan frame relay service (Figure 9.2). The process for each remote site was the same as

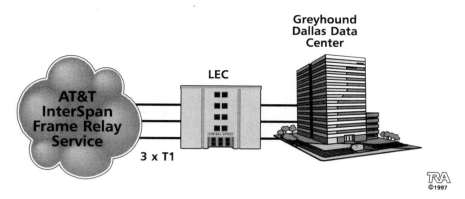

Figure 9.1 Initial Installation Step

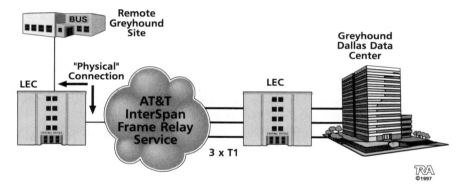

Figure 9.2 Remote Site Installation

for the data center except that the amount of capacity installed between the remote site and the network was substantially less; in fact, the remote site connection is only 1/24th of the capacity of the connection from the frame relay service to the data center, with an expectation that only about half of it would normally be used.

After the physical connection is established between the frame relay service and the remote site, the last step is to define a logical connection between the remote site and the Dallas Data Center (Figure 9.3). The logical connection has several important characteristics. It only uses network carrying capacity when there is information to send, and many logical connections can share each of the three physical connections in Dallas. In fact,

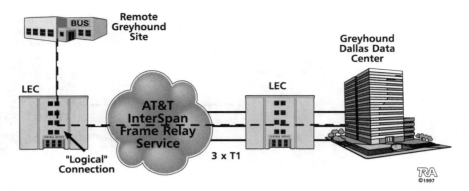

Figure 9.3   Establishing Logical Connection from Remote Site to Data Center

in the Greyhound case, approximately 50 remote sites share each of the Dallas T1s.

As each remote site is added, only a short access line via each remote LEC is needed to connect that site to the network. Only a simple software change needs to be made at the Dallas Data Center to accommodate each new remote site; no hardware changes or additions to the communications configuration need to be made.

One available alternative to frame relay, though certainly less popular with the passing years, is traditional leased lines. If Greyhound had opted to use traditional leased lines instead of frame relay, the scenario would be very different than stated above. If traditional leased lines were used, each site would require a dedicated circuit to be installed from each site all the way back to the Dallas Data Center. Hardware and software changes would be required at the Dallas Data Center because each new leased line would have modem or DSU/CSU hardware and would require a new physical port on some piece of equipment. The lead times would be measured in months rather than in days because a line would have to be engineered and installed to connect both sites to each other; the line would go a much longer distance than a local access line and involve coordination of three different carriers. It would also be more expensive because it would lease circuits from the remote site to the Dallas Data Center for the dedicated use of the traffic between the two rather than using the existing public frame relay network.

Functionality   *Functionality* is defined within Greyhound's context to mean that the system simply does more: the new frame relay/Internet network enabled the use of routers with the Cisco Fusion architecture and Internetworking Operating System (IOS). While it would have been possible to implement routers in the former X.25 environment, the use of more sophisticated architectures, with their additional overhead and demands on the network transport system, would have made performance in that environment even worse. The primary reason is that the two conceptual networking models are basically different. The X.25 model was developed during a time when communications lines were slow, highly prone to errors, and were used by unintelligent terminals. The intelligence, and therefore overhead, was put inside the network so that the costs of the very expensive computer processing power needed to provide reliable and error-free data transmission were shared by all network users. Frame relay is quite the opposite: frame relay is designed for an era where high-speed digital communications make possible fast, lower-error networking between intelligent systems that can determine if there are errors in the transmitted information without the help of the network. And it is so unlikely that an error will occur, compared to the prior X.25 system, that the resources used correcting the problem between the communicating systems are much less than checking and correcting at each intermediate step in the communications process as was done in X.25.

Reliability   Reliability is achieved in the Greyhound environment in two ways: by building the network based upon newer, more modern, and more reliable hardware and software, and by providing more backup systems. By moving from the aging X.25 equipment to more modern router-based networking, Greyhound improved their reliability dramatically. While the X.25 system did utilize a dial backup system, the new frame relay network also has multiple connections between the frame relay service provider and the Dallas Data Center as well as ISDN dial backup at the Dallas site.

Cost   Cost was not the most important aspect, though it was considered very seriously in the requirements for the new network. In the Greyhound context, it would be more realistic to have labeled this requirement as "value" because Greyhound was more interested in increasing scalability, functionality, and reliability than they were in lowering actual monetary outlays for network products and services. As long as the value could be proven, Greyhound was willing to move forward.

9.2.2 Technical Aspects

In this section, we will discuss Greyhound's applications. Although the word "applications" is more commonly used to refer to the applications that are run by the computer, we use the term here to refer to application of the networking technology to providing transport services for a variety of capabilities, of which two are defined below.

Applications

Greyhound has two basic applications: a PC-based terminal emulator that emulates a Tandem 6530 ASCII terminal, and an IBM 3270 SNA terminal and printer application. Both applications share a single network access for cost efficiency. There can be more than one PC at a given site, with as many as 40 personal computers at large sites like New York City's Port Authority Bus Terminal. Both applications exist at all large and medium Greyhound sites; only the PC-based application is used at the smaller Greyhound and independent ticket sales locations.

PC-based tandem terminal emulation   Tandem hosts, like those of other minicomputer manufacturers such as Digital Equipment Corporation and Data General, were developed during an era when there were no standards for how a terminal should communicate with a host. Therefore, each manufacturer was required to develop their own proprietary methods, thereby rendering all such systems incompatible with each other. The specific type of terminal protocol used by the Tandem terminal to communicate with the Tandem host is the 6530 protocol. While no different from the DEC VT-100 terminal protocol or any other similar protocol in terms of its function, the actual codes used to cause each function to occur vary greatly. For this reason, if a company like Greyhound would like to use personal computers as terminals, as opposed to using proprietary dedicated Tandem terminals, it is necessary to use special software to translate the screen and keyboard codes indigenous to the PC to the codes used by the Tandem host, and vice versa. This is exactly what the PC 6530 terminal emulator application does.

SNA terminal and printer   The SNA terminal and printer application is a very straightforward connection of an SNA terminal and printer to the IBM host via a 3745 front-end processor (FEP). Greyhound uses Memorex-

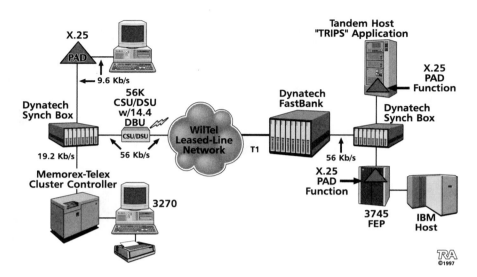

Figure 9.4   Pre-Frame-Relay Physical Architecture

Telex cluster controllers, terminals, and printers as a means of saving money (in lieu of purchasing the more expensive IBM products), but they are functionally equivalent. The SNA terminal and printer application supports the Greyhound bus maintenance application.

Communications Environment

The pre-frame-relay communications environment at Greyhound is typical of X.25 installations everywhere in that there are many separate boxes to perform a variety of functions needed to provide a complete solution (Figure 9.4). This fact in itself diminishes the manageability and reliability of the network. Add to this the fact that the antiquated equipment is based on older hardware and software systems that are now becoming obsolete and the reasons for migrating to a new environment are compelling and obvious.

In the pre-frame-relay environment, the users of the TRIPS ticket sales application used a DOS-based PC running the Tandem 6530 emulation program from PCT Software. The COM1 port of the DOS computer was connected via a serial cable to a Dynatech X.25 Packet Assembler/Disassembler (PAD). The Dynatech X.25 PAD took the raw 9.6-Kbit/second

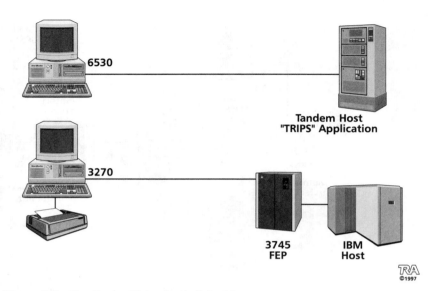

Figure 9.5   Pre-Frame-Relay Logical Architecture

ASCII asynchronous input and wrapped the X.25 protocol around the asynchronous terminal information for transport across the synchronous X.25 network. The output of the PAD was a 56-Kbit/second serial connection, which connected to a 56-Kbit/second DSU/CSU, which allowed connection of the Dynatech FastBanks located on the host premises via leased lines. WilTel only provided leased lines for the private X.25 network; the X.25 protocol handling was performed by customer-provided devices. The outputs of the FastBanks, which take the channelized T1 connections from WilTel and subdivide them into individual 64-Kbit/second DS0s, feed a Dynatech CPX Synch Box, which is a mirror image of the device located at the premises. From the Dynatech Synch Box, a 56-Kbit/second output goes to the Tandem host's X.25 PAD function, and a 56-Kbit/second output goes to the IBM 3745 front-end processor and its X.25 PAD function.

Logical Architecture

The logical architecture is very simple: a Tandem 6530 terminal for the TRIPS ticket sales application and an IBM 3270 terminal for the bus maintenance application (Figure 9.5).

9.3 Frame Relay: Selection and Migration

Once the decision was made to move forward on a new networking initiative, Greyhound spent very little time weighing alternatives and looking at different technology choices, but rather moved ahead quickly with vendor selection and deployment of the frame relay network.

9.3.1 Business Aspects

The business aspects of Greyhound's frame relay selection are really very straightforward. Greyhound was so unhappy with their old system that anything—so it seemed—would be better. The selection process was fairly informal, and Greyhound made their decision quickly and moved to the task of implementation without much fanfare.

Expectations

Greyhound's expectation was that any new system would be more stable and more manageable than what they had. The X.25 system had reached the end of its useful life, both in real terms and in accounting terms, and could be written off with no financial penalty. From both a business and operational perspective, Greyhound was ready to move forward.

Alternatives Considered

Greyhound felt that they had no alternative except for the dual frame relay/Internet initiative on which they embarked. Greyhound felt that leased lines were more expensive and less efficient than the X.25 network that was being replaced and that ATM was very costly and "not ready for prime time." Greyhound made these decisions after some quick, paper-based analyses and moved directly to the process of selecting their frame relay and Internet service providers.

The real decision made by Greyhound was to move to an IP-based networking approach that was delivered to their remote users on two different platforms, each ideally suited to the differing sizes and requirements of the two tiers of user sites. Frame relay was faster, more responsive, and more expensive and was well suited to the requirements of the larger terminals; the Internet was ubiquitous, low speed, low cost, and was very often already installed on the personal computers to be found at the smaller locations.

Carrier Selection Process

Greyhound prepared a formal request for proposal (RFP) that identified the locations of their top 150 sales locations (those that would be the beneficiaries of the frame relay service) and a description of their intended architecture and frame relay network needs: 56-Kbit/second access at the remotes with 32-Kbit/second CIR and multiple T1 access at the Dallas Data Center. Greyhound circulated the RFP to AT&T, Compuserve, MCI, and WilTel. All of the service providers responded, some with proposals that were substantially less expensive than the final winner, AT&T.

One of the things that Greyhound soon realized was that the service providers did not adhere strictly to the RFP guidelines in preparing their bids. As an example, one vendor provided a bid that was substantially below any of their competitors, but further analysis revealed that the respondent had used "zero CIR" pricing. The zero CIR option, while less expensive, would have put the Greyhound data traffic at a disadvantage, and greater risk of discard, when compared to the 32-Kbit/second CIR that was requested. The service provider, who was not awarded the contract, tried unsuccessfully to explain that because their network was so robust, there would never be a situation where data was discarded. This answer was not acceptable to Greyhound.

Another approach that some service providers tried to use to lower costs was defining an asymmetrical CIR, also not what was requested by Greyhound's RFP. The asymmetrical CIR approach provided a lower guaranteed bandwidth from the remote site to the data center for the small information requests from the remote, and a larger guaranteed bandwidth from the data center to the remote site for the large result from the data center. While this is a valid approach, it was not what Greyhound requested.

Greyhound evaluated each bid carefully by reading each document and comparing it to their original RFP. Any remaining questions were answered and gaps in understanding filled in before Greyhound was able to make their final evaluation and award the contract.

When all was said and done the award was given to AT&T. Even though AT&T had not provided the lowest bid, Greyhound had a prior relationship with AT&T and was able to leverage frame relay and voice pricing to yield a very acceptable overall package for Greyhound from a financial and service point of view. Greyhound also wished to reduce the total number of vendors they are dealing with as much as possible to simplify handling of problems. Choosing AT&T, their voice vendor, allowed them to accomplish this goal as well.

Migration

From a business point of view, it was important to minimize or eliminate downtime during migration so as not to have a negative impact on revenues or customer service. Greyhound was able to accomplish this through a combination of using third-party personnel and coordinating their installation activities from Dallas. Another fortuitous situation for Greyhound was an earlier choice of the type of wiring that they used to connect their personal computers to the X.25 system. As will be discussed later in greater technical detail, Greyhound's facilities department chose a more expensive yet more widely usable type of wiring that was not only suitable for connection of the personal computers in the older ASCII terminal mode but in the new LAN mode used in the frame relay/Internet networking arrangement. This decision to use the more expensive higher grade of wiring may have been considered a bit extravagant at the time it was made, but making the proper decision then saved a substantial amount of money and time during the upgrade. As an example, the additional cost of the more expensive wire two years before the migration would have added no more than $200 to the cost of the average site. Taking into account only the 150 sites that were migrated to the frame relay network, this amounted to an additional $30,000. To have replaced wiring at the average site with the new wiring when the migration was made to frame relay would have been far more disruptive to operations and would have cost an estimated $4,000 per average site. The correct wiring decision in the beginning meant that approximately $600,000 did not have to be spent and made the cost justification of the move to the frame relay network far easier. While this last point is a consideration in any type of networking, and not just in frame relay networks, here it made the case to move to frame relay easier because the physical wiring infrastructure at the remote sites was of a sufficiently high quality and generic enough in its design and implementation to allow a number of different scenarios to be supported; in other words, the wiring did not dictate the type of network solution.

9.3.2 Technical Aspects

In order to understand the benefits, from a technical point of view, of Greyhound's move away from X.25 to the more modern, more streamlined frame relay, we will begin by contrasting frame relay and X.25 in some fair degree of technical detail. We will then discuss the traditional planning and migration stages that moved Greyhound into their present networking environment.

X.25 versus Frame Relay

Much of the efficiency of frame relay comes not from the things it does, but from the things it does not do. The X.25 packet-switching protocol was designed as a method of protecting data in transit over low-speed, high-bit-error-rate analog transmission facilities. There is still a heavy investment in X.25 in the United States and even more so in Europe, South America, and the Pacific Rim countries. To increase speed and efficiency, the designers of frame relay streamlined it, compared to X.25, and have left many of the functions of X.25 to protocols that are higher on the OSI stack than frame relay's Layer 2. In fact, as shown in Figure 9.6, frame relay's definition is entirely within OSI Layer 2, the data link layer, and uses existing Layer 1 standards to provide the physical bit pipe for moving the frame relay formatted bits; X.25 defines capabilities at both Layer 2 and Layer 3, the network layer.

The basic differences between frame relay and X.25 are the following:

- They are based on different cost models.
- They were designed for different types of networks.
- They were designed for functionally different roles in the network.

X.25 and frame relay are similar in that both are standardized methods of statistically multiplexing information formatted as variable-length units and both form the foundation for publicly available network services. If you were more interested in similarities than in differences, it would be more realistic to compare frame relay with X.25 Layer 2 definitions only, which are where the original frame relay definitions that were developed to work with ISDN came from, the latest incarnation of which was called LAP-F prior to being decoupled from ISDN standards to provide a stand-alone frame relay. But it is the differences, not the similarities, that are responsible for the speed and performance of frame relay, so we will take a closer look at the differences.

Different cost models   The X.25 protocols grew out of the work done by Paul Baran and others at the Rand Corporation on survivable networks and the Arpanet in the 1960s. The X.25 protocol is more than a quarter of a century old, having been developed in the early 1970s and first published by the CCITT (the precursor of the modern ITU-T) in 1974. At that time, the specialized computers that were used as network switches were far less

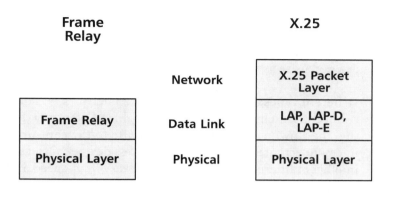

Figure 9.6   X.25 Layers Compared to Frame Relay Layers

capable, in terms of processing power and memory, than many handheld scientific calculators are today, and their cost was measured in fractions of millions of dollars: half a million, three quarters of a million, a million, and so on. In the time period during which X.25 was developed, even the biggest and most powerful switches were capable of processing only several hundred packets per second, as opposed to today's low-end routers, which can process in the range of thousands of packets per second, and the big expensive specialized computers had to be shared by many users in order to be cost-effective. At the time, interactive terminals were not intelligent, and the idea of computing power dedicated to a single user was absolutely unheard of.

Today the cost model is moving toward lower-cost networks and more capable end systems. With personal computers and workstations today being so powerful, it is easy and cost-effective to take protocol processing power out of the network and place it on the desktop. This results in lower-cost, higher-performance networks but places a greater burden on the individual processors in the intermediate or end systems.

The second cost aspect is the cost of fixing errors. In pre-frame-relay networks, it was sensible to check for errors between each pair of communicating systems because errors were very likely to occur and the cost of bandwidth was very high. Protocols such as X.25, therefore, needed to check data integrity at each intermediate hop. Frame relay, on the other hand, discards errors if they are detected, and a higher-layer protocol will retransmit the information if it is necessary to do so. The net effect is better performance overall. Even though the overhead cost to detect and correct an error when it does occur is higher, the total number of errors encountered is substantially lower than in prior networks, and the bandwidth is less expensive as well.

Different types of networks   The X.25 network was designed to interconnect unintelligent terminals incapable of detecting, let alone correcting, their own errors. Frame relay, quite to the contrary, is designed to interconnect intelligent frame relay access devices, such as routers or other intelligent intermediate systems, over very high-speed and reliable communications facilities.

Functionally different roles   While it was necessary for X.25 to provide definitions for both Layer 2 and Layer 3, frame relay typically forms the inner core, or second to the inner core, of a multilevel switching and transport system often split up over many devices acting in different roles. As an example, a typical public frame relay network will have an innermost switching core composed of Layer 1 ATM switches, a secondary core composed of Layer 2 frame relay switches, and an outer, or access, core comprised of Layer 3 switches, or routers belonging to customers and normally residing on the customer premises.

The basic functional blocks of frame relay and X.25, as defined according to the OSI layers, show that X.25 was designed to be more of an all-encompassing single solution, while frame relay was designed to act as a data link layer transport capability to be used with a wide variety of Layer 3 protocols such as IP.

Planning
The planning process was fairly straightforward. The first step involved performing benchmark tests to determine which sites should be on the frame relay network and which sites should be on the Internet. Greyhound determined that sites with greater than five personal computers would be on the frame relay network. The 153 sites that qualified were then scheduled with AT&T in such a manner that on average three sites each day would require Greyhound centralized support for installation.

Migration
The central site was installed first, the central site routers and other devices were installed and tested, and Ethernet access to the Tandem host and token

ring access to the IBM host via the 3745 front-end processor was installed and tested. Because the move was a migration of the remote sites to a new networking paradigm, but utilized the same host applications, there were no applications changes of any kind required on the hosts. Greyhound was ready to begin welcoming remote sites to the network.

Greyhound's remote site installation was smooth and virtually painless not only because of good planning but also because installers orchestrated by the frame relay carrier coordinated some of the more frustrating parts of the installation. The three steps of the installation process outlined by Greyhound were LEC facility installation and turn-up, AT&T GIS FR install, and PC migration and testing.

LEC facility installation and turn-up   In order to make the migration to the new network as fast as possible, Greyhound made a contract with AT&T InterSpan and AT&T GIS to install both the frame relay service and the routers. While Greyhound guesses that there were probably the normal problems with coordination of the LEC circuits and that, as other frame relay customers have reported, some LECs were easier or more difficult to deal with than others, it is not possible to prove these points. Nor is it important to do so, as these were issues with which Greyhound did not need to concern itself because they were hidden from view by AT&T as a part of the contract. AT&T coordinated the LEC facility installation and turn-up and then turned over the new access circuit from the Greyhound premises to the AT&T InterSpan service directly to AT&T GIS for the frame relay service installation. Greyhound was notified of this turnover but was not required to do anything other than note AT&T's progress.

AT&T GIS FR install   The second step of the installation process, and also included in the contract with AT&T, was to have AT&T GIS personnel go on site and install the new router and DSU/CSU that would be used with the new frame relay service. Because the new frame relay service was being installed on new access circuits and did not have any impact at all on the WilTel access lines that were being used to access the old X.25 network, all work could be accomplished nondisruptively during daylight hours while work progressed with no downtime and with no adverse effects on revenues.

When the new DSU/CSU and router were installed, AT&T GIS would coordinate the provisioning and testing of the single 32-Kbit/second PVC from the remote site to the Dallas Data Center and would then call Dallas for verification of the install. Dallas tested the new router using Telnet, a capability that allows the data center to remotely access the router and perform configuration and other management tasks. After the router was successfully tested by the Dallas Data Center, Greyhound dismissed the GIS technician, and the installation, from an AT&T point of view, was completed.

PC migration and testing   The next step was to contact the company responsible for Greyhound's PC maintenance and support and have them go on site to migrate the personal computers from the old X.25 network to the new frame relay network. This process involved a technician going on site and performing some simple installation and verification steps. Because frame relay was being installed in sites that typically had five or more personal computers in operation simultaneously, there was minimal operational impact. The installer would migrate one PC to the new system, test it, move one of the human operators to the new PC on the new network, and proceed in this fashion until the installation was completed. The installation process involved

- installing an Ethernet network interface card in the PC
- loading Ethernet LAN and TCP/IP driver software
- installing Windows
- installing a new Windows-based Tandem 6530 emulator
- wiring the new PC to the integrated Ethernet hub on the Cisco router
- testing the connection
- performing the above series of steps until all personal computers were migrated
- familiarizing users with the operation of Windows
- moving the Memorex-Telex SNA controller to the serial 1 port of the Cisco router
- verifying the operation of the SNA 3270 workstation and printer

When the process had been completed, the technician was dismissed, and WilTel was contacted for the removal of the old X.25 access circuit.

The impact of a good physical infrastructure   Although often ignored (and not in the most technical sense related directly to frame relay), a good physical infrastructure (that is, wiring) within the premises can be a substantial aid in installing the proper solution. In Greyhound's case specifically, years before the move to frame relay Greyhound facilities planners had the foresight to install a more expensive Category 5 wire that was not only suitable for their low-speed asynchronous ASCII terminal application, but could also be used, years later, for a migration to 10-Mbit/second Ethernet and can also support future higher speeds if needed by Greyhound. The financial ramifications of this decision have already been discussed in a prior section; however, the operational ramifications are just as astounding.

Had Greyhound needed to rewire all of the operator positions to accommodate their new networking initiative, they would most likely have run all new wiring to these positions (instead of replacing existing wiring) to minimize impact. This additional step, however, would have required coordinating another company or organization because companies who do PC maintenance either do not do inside wiring, or at the very least have a completely different department for this function. It would also have required working during off-hours to minimize problems from dust and other airborne debris from the removal of ceiling tiles, dust and noise from drilling walls, and other kinds of disruptions. Although Greyhound was required to go through all of these disruptions when their wiring was installed in the first place many years ago, a good decision then kept them from going through this a second time and may keep them from yet a third possible iteration in the future.

Coordination of remote site installs   Greyhound's approach generally seems to be characterized by good planning, reasonable expectations, and the flexibility to deal with problems when they occur. This approach is very useful in keeping down stress on the part of those coordinating a large multisite frame relay installation and ensuring its ultimate success. Greyhound planners knew from past experience that a rigid schedule requiring multiple parties to appear on site at fixed times was unrealistic. Instead, Greyhound managed the frame relay installation as a series of sequential events that were loosely coupled in time and coordinated all activities via pagers worn by Greyhound employees in Dallas.

The process was performed basically this way: AT&T would coordinate the LEC access line installation at the remote site and fight any battles and solve any problems needed to get the LEC access line working. This was done behind the scenes, and the details were not visible to Greyhound and, therefore, not a problem with which they needed to worry themselves. AT&T GIS was dispatched by AT&T InterSpan to install the router. AT&T GIS would arrive on site within the next day or two, not on any rigid schedule, would install the router and PVC, and perform their own preliminary testing. Any needs they had while on site would be handled by calling a beeper of a coordinator in Dallas. The PC technician would coordinate in a similarly informal manner. Pagers were used extensively, and with great success, avoiding the need for rigid coordination, as well as avoiding tying up resources and playing "telephone tag."

One other aspect of the Greyhound install was the rate at which they were able to do installations. After the initial couple of installations, the pace of installs was rather hectic but manageable. Greyhound installed, on average, three sites each day, in multiple time zones. By spreading the installations by time zone, coordinating via pagers, and using outside contractors, Greyhound was able to bring their sites over to frame relay as quickly as possible.

There was a general consensus of all of the companies who were interviewed for this book, both the ones that appear on these pages and the ones that didn't make it, that the process of letting the carrier perform a complete turnkey installation was full of problems and that, in the end, the customer needed to stay involved with the process to make it work. Greyhound, in stark contrast with the norm, was very successful with contracting the carrier to perform the installation. The reasons for this seem to include the fact that Greyhound set reasonable expectations, kept flexibility in the schedule, and in general had a "don't worry" attitude. This approach resulted in much less stress on Greyhound's part; a superior installation; and installation times, overall end-to-end project times, and resource costs that are very much in line with companies who took a direct, active role in all aspects and rated their carrier's performance inadequate in the area of turnkey installation.

Configuration after Migration

The physical architecture after frame relay was very different (Figure 9.7). The Greyhound network had gone from being a "dumb terminal" based X.25 network to a Windows PC-based TCP/IP router network with the promise to be a platform for so much more because it embraced an architecture common to large multivendor inter- and intranetworks using common protocols and transports.

Physical architecture   After the migration, the remote side of the connection looks very different from a physical standpoint. The PC is running Windows and a Windows-based 6530 emulator with a TCP/IP stack and Ethernet network connection. The Ethernet connection goes directly, via star-wired Category 5 twisted-pair wiring, to an integrated Ethernet 10-Base-T hub in the Cisco 2505 or 2507 router. There are several additional devices connected to the router besides the personal computers: the SNA

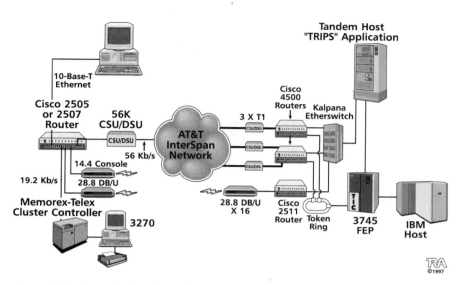

Figure 9.7 Frame Relay Physical Architecture

cluster controller is attached to the serial 1 port of the router, the 14.4-Kbit/second dial-in remote router configuration and management modem is attached to the console port of the router, a 28.8-Kbit/second dial back-up modem is attached to the AUX port of the router, and the 56-Kbit/second Cray 3080 DSU/CSU providing connectivity to the AT&T Inter-Span network is connected to the serial 0 port. Each remote site has a single 32-Kbit/second PVC with a 56-Kbit/second access line.

At the host site, the changes have been sweeping as well. The Dallas Data Center is connected to the AT&T frame relay service by three T1 facilities. Each T1 facility carries approximately 50 of the 32-Kbit/second PVCs from the remote sites. The aggregate bandwidth of the PVCs is only modestly more than the actual bandwidth of the T1. This configuration allows PVCs to burst more readily than if heavier oversubscription were used and allows Greyhound more growth room before additional T1s must be added.

Two T1s terminate in a Cisco 4500 router; the third T1 terminates in a second Cisco 4500 router. A Cisco 2511 router provides 16 dial-in ports to support the dial backup capability for up to 16 remote sites simultaneously. Internal Ethernet hubs and a Kalpana Etherswitch on the site allow routing of incoming information between Cisco routers and the Tandem host while an internal token ring media access unit (MAU) in one of the Cisco 4500s provides direct token ring connectivity for the IBM 3745 FEP.

The multiple router/Ethernet/token ring architecture works very well because all traffic everywhere within the Layer 3 routing network is IP-based: the remote PC to Tandem 6530 traffic uses direct IP, while the SNA traffic is IP-encapsulated, thereby allowing all traffic to move anywhere within the routing network. Tandem terminal emulation traffic is placed into IP inside the PC, sent to the remote Cisco 2505 or 2507 routers, and routed across the Layer 2 frame relay network to emerge at the host site 4500 router. At the 4500, it is routed onto the Ethernet connection to the Kalpana Etherswitch, where it is switched to the Tandem host. The SNA traffic, on the other hand, starts as SNA from the remote cluster controller and is IP-encapsulated at the remote Cisco router, and the IP packet is routed onto the frame relay network. At the host site, one of two things can happen to the IP-encapsulated SNA. If it happens to enter the host site on a frame relay access connection that is connected to the router housing the integrated token ring MAU, then the IP is stripped off, and the SNA traffic is placed onto the token ring connection, which allows it to be processed by the 3745 FEP. If it does not enter on a router housing the MAU, then it is switched via the Kalpana Etherswitch to the router housing the MAU and then is routed to the IBM FEP.

Greyhound is quick to point out that it is the Cisco Fusion/IOS combination that delivers the full set of features important in running their network, not simply the use of routers in general. Simply stated, Cisco Fusion is an architecture—that is, a set of principles governing the way that a network should operate and a definition of the products that are used to implement those principles and how they are interconnected and the functions performed by each. The IOS is one of two sets of software, implemented on a variety of hardware platforms, including the routers used by Greyhound, that brings the concepts of the Cisco Fusion architecture to life. The second software piece that allows the promise of the architecture to be realized, and one not currently used by Greyhound, is CiscoWorks, the comprehensive network management capability.

The capabilities provided by the routers that are most important to Greyhound are routing, building access lists, and filtering. The routing and access list aspects are more important in the Internet portion of the network than they are with frame relay because of the open nature of the Internet and the higher likelihood of security problems from that network than from the frame relay network. The filtering capability, however, is very important because it allows Greyhound to maximize the utilization of the relatively costly wide area network frame relay connections by ensuring that they are used in the most efficient possible way. Filtering basically keeps any information pertinent to the local site at the local site and ensures that WAN resources are only used for information that must be transmitted to Dallas.

Logical architecture   The changes to the Greyhound network were only related to how remote terminals access the host-based applications, and therefore the logical architecture remains unchanged from Figure 9.5.

Operations and Network Management

Greyhound has found the frame relay network to be highly reliable, which is not surprising considering the level of unreliability that had become "normal" with the prior aging X.25 network. Day-to-day monitoring of the network is done with surprisingly simple tools, and more sophisticated tools have been budgeted to make the process even easier and more automated.

Day-to-day management is done with SunNet Manager, which monitors the status of the central site and remote routers as well as a number of homegrown applications developed by Greyhound on their Sun UNIX platform.

Greyhound downloads AT&T's Customer Management System (CMS) reports monthly to view trends in utilization and performance. The CMS reports are downloaded from AT&T in a PostScript format so that they may be printed directly on a PostScript-capable laser printer. Greyhound does not utilize AT&T's direct Simple Network Management Protocol (SNMP) network management system.

9.4 Living with Frame Relay

Now that frame relay is working, Greyhound is turning their networking thoughts to two other areas: how to make better use of frame relay and how to keep frame relay's popularity from killing it. When frame relay was originally installed, it was installed in a dual mode with the Internet. The performance of the two systems varies widely, though both are dramatically better than their predecessors: frame relay is better than X.25 and the Internet is better than manual. Greyhound would like to expand the use of IP over frame relay to allow more and more sites to realize the performance of frame-relay-based IP and is evaluating ways that might be accomplished cost-effectively. The second aspect of frame relay is that it performs so much better than X.25 that it has made a rich field for application development, and Greyhound's network operations group is constantly policing new applications to be sure that they can be implemented without negatively affecting either networking budgets or the main reason for any type of network to exist in the first place—the job of selling tickets.

9.4.1   Anticipated Benefits

The initial benefits of scalability, functionality, and reliability/manageability at a reasonable cost have all been realized by Greyhound. In fact, Greyhound is quick to point out that frame relay has, in their network, performed "better than advertised." Greyhound's dual frame relay/Internet approach has solved myriad problems and, in effect, provided them with a router-enabled, IP-based Layer 3 routing network that effectively includes all automated sites. The question that remains is, "How will Greyhound get the most benefit from this infrastructure in the future?"

9.4.2   Unanticipated Benefits

While there were no surprises at Greyhound regarding frame relay, there is one unanticipated benefit of the Internet side of Greyhound's dual network approach worthy of mention. An unanticipated benefit that has been realized as a result of putting the previously manual sites on the Internet is the cost savings in keypunch operator time at the headquarters office because of the information now being keyed in over the Internet at the time of the ticket sale. Costs of this aspect of ticket accounting have been reduced, accuracy has been increased, and more timely sales figures can now be generated for Greyhound management. This benefit, though not attributable directly to frame relay, is an important aspect of this case study because it represents a technology that has been paired with frame relay to provide a comprehensive solution for Greyhound. Frame relay is not always the answer, nor is it always the entire answer.

9.4.3   Lessons Learned

Of all of the lessons learned by Greyhound in their move to frame relay, the biggest one is the importance of controlling the forward motion of those who would move to exploit the new capabilities made available by frame relay. Unlike the older X.25 network, the new frame relay network provides an ideal foundation (in terms of performance, connectivity, and protocols utilized) for client-server applications, and Greyhound has become somewhat aggressive in rolling these new applications onto the network. Even though the old and new networks both feature a PC running a Tandem ASCII terminal emulator at their core, the new implementation puts TCP/IP into the picture and allows multiple activities to be performed simultaneously by using the Windows multitasking environment rather than a dedicated single-task DOS environment inherent in the older networking approach.

In the same way that park rangers must ensure that park resources are not overburdened and that there are ample resources for all, the networking department at Greyhound has had to police the way in which resources are used on the frame relay network. Just as park rangers are wary of negative impact on native species, so too is Greyhound's networking department careful of anything that may have a negative impact on their native species—the TRIPS ticketing application. The biggest potential hazard Greyhound sees is a sloppy client-server application. Greyhound's networking department has been made very aware, through experience, that client-server has a long way to go before it can coexist gracefully with other network-based applications because it tends to be developed by programmers with a "bandwidth is free" LAN-oriented mind-set.

The heart of the debate centers around the choice of client-server models used by the applications developers. Client-server, in its most basic form, simply means that a client (often referred to as a *requestor*) asks for something and the server gives it to them. In the case of a file server arrangement, the client workstation would ask for a file and the file server would send the entire file. In the case of a print server, the client would request printing and send the file to be printed, and the print server would print the file. In the case of a transaction server, the client would ask for the server to perform some process and to return the result (such as a database lookup of a single record or field in the record).

The older client-server model that accompanied early LANs required the passing of an entire application or database file, or a very large part of it, to the PC for processing. An example would be a PC wishing to process a dBase II database file: the entire file was copied from server to client across whatever network linked client and server, and the client processed the complete file for some period of time and then returned the entire file to the server for storage. This approach is very bandwidth-intensive and in many cases not necessary because the complete file may contain much more information than is needed by the client.

In the newer client-server model (and the one that the Greyhound networking department would like to see used more liberally within their environment), much of the processing of the complete file is performed by the server, and the information returned to the client is very small and only represents the record (or records, or fields in the record) needed by the client; that is, the network is only used to transmit actual information needed by the remotely located client. Although the newer client-server model is more complex and difficult to implement from an applications standpoint, it is more efficient, uses fewer network resources, and many more applications may be implemented before requiring a change to the network infrastructure.

Unlike many organizations in which highly pitched internal battles rage between the applications development staff and the corporate networking staff, the major battles in Greyhound are kept to small skirmishes by everyone's focus on two major facts: the network exists for the purposes of the TRIPS application (selling tickets), and a longer effort at the beginning of an application's life in developing a WAN-ready application is better than spending more money every single month of the application's life in recurring charges needed to put sloppy client-server applications on the network.

9.5   Future Plans

Greyhound's future plans fall into two basic areas, network management and enhanced frame relay functionality, and there are two planned initiatives under each category. In the network management area, Greyhound will begin to use CiscoWorks and is evaluating NetHealth. In the enhanced services area, Greyhound is pondering implementation of switched frame relay access and voice over frame relay.

9.5.1   CiscoWorks and NetHealth

Greyhound has budgeted for CiscoWorks, Cisco's network management system specifically designed to help get the most out of the Cisco router products, and is reviewing the implementation of NetHealth, an additional network management tool that will assist in correlating present network problems with historic problems so that Greyhound can anticipate trends and configure systems accordingly.

CiscoWorks will ease some of the network management processes now done manually via interactive Telnet sessions across the network or via the out-of-band dial-up connection to the console ports on the remote routers.

9.5.2 Switched Frame Relay

Presently, response times are approximately 3–4 seconds on the frame relay network and 7–10 seconds on the Internet. Greyhound is beginning to evaluate ways to get additional sites on the frame relay network to help boost performance. Greyhound's current performance versus cost criteria states that five or six personal computers are needed before a move to frame relay can be realistically considered. One of the underlying assumptions is that a dedicated LEC access is used to connect the remote site to the AT&T InterSpan frame relay network. Greyhound is just now addressing the following questions:

- If dedicated access frame relay is cost effective for sites of five or six personal computers or more, what will be the size of the sites for which dial-up frame relay makes sense?
- How much of a performance increase will be realized with dial-up frame relay as opposed to the Internet-connected sites?
- What portion of the lower Internet performance is attributable to the dial-up function, and what portion is attributable to slower Internet performance?
- What is the actual cost of dial-up frame relay compared to dial-up Internet?

The answers to these questions and any others that might come up will guide Greyhound in their ultimate networking decisions.

9.5.3 Voice over Frame Relay

Greyhound has prioritized their networking agenda; voice over frame relay is third, behind enhanced network management and monitoring, and switched frame relay access. The active investigation of voice over frame relay has not yet begun at Greyhound, but they have formulated some initial ideas of where it may or may not fit into their long-term strategies. Greyhound sees some promise in the cost reduction possibilities inherent in voice over frame relay but is concerned that the quality of the service will not make it a viable solution for their voice requirements.

9.6 Conclusion

One thing that both of the first two case studies have in common is size: CTI was extremely large and Greyhound was large. The impact of frame relay is directly proportional to the number of sites involved. If a cost savings exists for frame relay over a single leased line, then a greater cost savings exists for 100 frame relay connections over 100 leased lines. But frame relay is not just the domain of large and extra-large organizations; many small companies are realizing the benefits of frame relay as well, like the small telecommunications consultancy in the next case study. Their applications, though only involving a very few offices, are still as mission-critical as the extra-large firm's applications, and the smaller cost savings is just as important to a small company as the huge savings to a huge company. Let's continue to investigate frame relay applications in one of its many forms in the next chapter.

Small LAN Internetworking Environment

TeleChoice is representative of thousands of small, distributed firms who are beginning to adopt frame relay because of its good performance-to-cost ratio and availability anywhere in the domestic United States and many other countries globally. And, unlike many similarly sized companies, TeleChoice has the technical acumen to explain what happened.

10.1 Case Study Background

TeleChoice, Inc., is a telecommunications consulting firm with offices in Verona, New Jersey; Richmond, Virginia; and Tulsa, Oklahoma. TeleChoice was founded in 1985 with the objective of providing long-distance carrier selection, network design and configuration, telecommunications management, and expense reduction programs to end user clients. The company today numbers about three dozen employees and is growing at the rate of one about every other month.

TeleChoice is an Apple Macintosh shop. Their normal suite of applications includes Word, Excel, PowerPoint, Persuasion, Up-to-Date (a networked calendaring program), a shared Touchbase contact database, and QuickMail. TeleChoice is using the AT&T InterSpan public frame relay solution to provide a level of reliability and performance that TeleChoice feels would have been unaffordable with a small, leased-line private networking solution. TeleChoice links their three domestic U.S. offices into a single, cohesive AppleTalk/IP environment via 56-Kbit/second and T1 access circuits with 32-Kbit/second PVCs.

The industry averages of 9.8 ports/customer and 4.8 PVCs/port (Taylor 1995) are skewed somewhat by the very large customers who have completed their test phases and are now moving rapidly into frame relay deployment. For this reason, the network topology of TeleChoice is much more representative of the size of the majority of customers who are beginning to adopt frame relay. TeleChoice is also representative in three more important ways:

- This case study represents the results of the initial several months of frame relay network use.
- TeleChoice is moving from a dial-up modem environment to a frame relay environment.
- TeleChoice is representative of distributed service firms, a very important market segment for frame relay. The distributed services market segment includes law firms, advertising agencies, consulting firms, and similar small, distributed operations.

TeleChoice is, however, as atypical of small companies beginning to use frame relay as it is typical. TeleChoice is a telecommunications consultancy that is knowledgeable in frame relay and has high visibility with their carrier. Unlike many small companies, when TeleChoice encounters problems in their selection, planning, or implementation processes, they are able to apply resources to the problem and rapidly find a fix that is appropriate to the situation. Many companies of similar size must turn to their carriers, consultants, other companies, or books like this one for answers. It is exactly because TeleChoice understands frame relay and can articulate the issues that they were chosen as the subject of this case study.

10.2 Before Frame Relay

TeleChoice's early network had evolved into a hodgepodge of unreliable and slow dial-up modem connections that gave the growing firm only the most basic connectivity, limited real-time coordination or interaction, and wasted a lot of their employees' time simply dealing with the issues of communication setup and troubleshooting.

10.2.1 Business Aspects

TeleChoice's business requirements are the same regardless of their communications infrastructure. A choice of dial-up, frame relay, leased line, X.25, or Internet IP would not change the basic business requirements, but variations do come into play with the exact capabilities of the chosen infrastructure, how it is implemented and used, its costs, and how it is managed. In this section we will look at the business requirements of TeleChoice and the environment in which they operated prior to moving to a frame relay network. We will also discuss the known inadequacies of their prior dial-up environment and will do so with the knowledge that TeleChoice has already migrated from this environment to a frame relay environment.

Requirements

With a distributed environment and limited resources in a small company like TeleChoice, the flow of communications—not just binary information, but communications between people—is extremely important. For these reasons, a reliable and flexible communications network is extremely significant to TeleChoice. TeleChoice needs an infrastructure that facilitates communication between people in real time; a highly distributed environment that does not penalize people at remote sites; central administration of all sites; the easy exchange of documents and collaborative work on the same documents; and the centralized storage, retrieval, and management of documents. Let's review these requirements in a bit more detail.

Real-time people-to-people communications   TeleChoice has real-time people-to-people communications requirements that go beyond normal telephony requirements and, in fact, dovetail with them. Because of TeleChoice's distributed environment, almost all internal company communication is via the QuickMail and QuickConference applications. QuickConference allows TeleChoice employees to "talk" with each other in real time via the computer keyboard, even though they might, for example, simultaneously be on a conference call. For example, two TeleChoice consultants in different offices might be on a conference call with a client. The two consultants can "chat" back and forth on the keyboard during the voice conference call to be sure that they are providing as much information to the client as possible with the maximum coordination. In the pre-frame-relay environment, this communication was hindered by the slow nature of the dial-up communications as well as the fact that the dial-up connection might be dropped at a critical moment and need to be reconnected.

Highly distributed environment without penalizing remote users   In order to attract the most experienced consultants (and to allow those consultants to work as close to the customer as possible), it is important for TeleChoice to provide a management information system with an underlying communications infrastructure that does not penalize users, in terms of connectivity or capabilities, because of their distance from the central New Jersey office. From time to time, TeleChoice consultants may work away from their regular offices, of course, but in general the office locations are known and fixed and are in the same location for a long time. Prior to the implementation of frame relay, TeleChoice operated two remote U.S. offices via dial-up modems and will add two more offices this year. The dial-up modem environment represented a penalty to the remote users in terms of both speed and reliability.

Central administration of all sites   In the pre-frame-relay environment, TeleChoice was forced either to burden their consultants with network and systems administration duties, to perform these duties over the less-than-desirable dial-up lines, or to hire additional, and costly, information management personnel for the remote offices. The desired option, central administration of all sites, was therefore an unobtainable goal prior to the implementation of frame relay. In the pre-frame-relay environment, TeleChoice had the unfortunate combination of performing some administrative responsibilities over undesirable dial-up lines and of burdening their remote staff with the balance of the duties.

Collaborative work and easy document exchange   TeleChoice's business revolves around the development of documents. The creation, editing, updating, and tracking of a variety of documents (word processing documents, spreadsheets, graphics files, desktop publishing documents, and emails, for example) in a timely and consistent manner is critical to TeleChoice's ongoing operation.

Version control is as important in this regard as is any other aspect of document control and will be increasingly important as TeleChoice grows. A lot of the business TeleChoice does pertains to creating documents, and very often those documents are worked on by a number of different people within the company and must be readily available to all of those different people. It is also important that when one person is working on a document, another person isn't working on the same document, resulting in different edit versions.

Centralized document management   Document management and storage, in addition to just connectivity, is of particular importance to Tele-Choice because all clients' files are retained indefinitely. Often someone needs to access a study that had been done several years ago—possibly by someone else in the company—and either redo that study or work from it to create a new document. So the organization, availability, and flow of information within the company is critical to the success of the overall business.

10.2.2   Technical Aspects

We will now take a look at the applications used by TeleChoice and how they were supported in the pre-frame-relay dial-up environment. We will look at the problems encountered in the dial-up environment and get some sense of TeleChoice's expectations in moving to frame relay.

Applications

While TeleChoice makes use of the full suite of ordinary business applications in their day-to-day work, there are two specific applications whose operation is greatly influenced by the communications environment in which they operate: the QuickMail email program, with its associated real-time chat capability, and a centralized Touchbase contact database.

Email and real-time conferencing   The QuickMail email program is Tele-Choice's most used application after Microsoft Word. In the dial-up environment, the QuickMail program was relied upon heavily for file transfers. In lieu of a true file transfer (which required the individual wishing to transfer the file to initiate a modem connection and then copy the file to the appropriate remote destination, thereby tying up the user's Macintosh computer and time for the duration of the call setup, transfer, and call tear-down), it was more common to send a file as an attachment to a Quick-Mail document. This process took only seconds for the user to execute, and the transfer from the sender to receiver was done automatically by

QuickMail. The drawbacks to this approach are that several versions of the same file might be in transit at any one time and that there was a time lag due to the length of time required for the update interval for the Quick-Mail dial-up to occur. In the dial-up environment, neither file transfers nor email were accomplished in anything approaching real time.

Additionally, one of the features of QuickMail that was most attractive to TeleChoice, the QuickConference capability for interactive real-time "chat," was virtually unusable beyond the main New Jersey office because of the bandwidth restrictions of the 14.4-Kbit/second analog dial-up environment.

Contact database   Like QuickConference, the centralized contact database, Touchbase, is also significant to TeleChoice for internal coordination. And, like QuickConference, the use of a centralized Touchbase database in the prior dial-up environment was problematic because of the dial-up nature of the access and because the contact database is centralized. TeleChoice's objectives are that contact information in the centralized Touchbase database can be updated from any office and that notes and contact information are available to any individual within the company. Prior to calling a client, the TeleChoice employee knows who called the client last, the nature of the call, when the needed follow-up is due, and other pertinent details—an especially critical capability in a distributed company, where it is impossible to walk down the hall and talk with the rest of the account team.

Communications Environment

Prior to the move to the frame relay network, Figure 10.1, TeleChoice had separate Apple EtherTalk/LocalTalk-hybrid or EtherTalk-only networks in their remote offices with Apple Macintosh clients. Each Apple Macintosh client was equipped with an internal dial-up modem. In the case of the EtherTalk/LocalTalk hybrids, the Macintosh computers were connected either directly to an Ethernet segment via an EtherTalk card/connector or to an Apple LocalNet/PhoneNet network, a network that operates on four-wire telephone cable over a built-in port at 230 Kbits/second using a modified HDLC-like protocol. The hybrid sites used Dayna bridges to tie together the EtherTalk and LocalTalk segments.

In addition to the Macintosh personal computers for individual use, each site had a dedicated mail server—another Macintosh computer with an external U.S. Robotics 14.4-Kbit/second dial-up modem. Periodically, or when the mail queue was full, the mail server would dial up the main office in New Jersey and exchange mail. The individual workstations in the remote offices, or from travel locations, could dial in individually to New

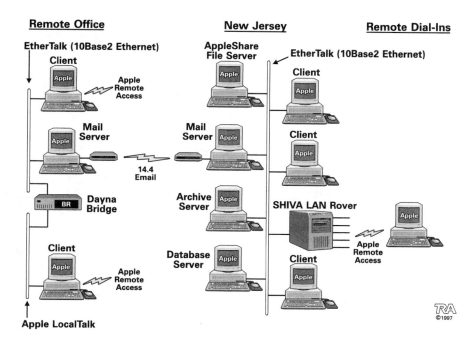

Figure 10.1 Pre-Frame-Relay Physical Architecture

Jersey via Apple Remote Access if they needed access to network resources such as files.

In New Jersey, there was a similar network, larger, of course, and with a dedicated mail server, a dedicated primary AppleShare file servers and two other minor servers: an archive server, which holds historical (library) files that are not frequently accessed, and a database server.

In New Jersey, a Shiva LAN rover with eight ports accommodated the dial-up users and allowed them to access the New Jersey LAN remotely, as well as supporting dial-out functions from New Jersey to other systems.

Logical Architecture

Sitting at the keyboard in their office, the TeleChoice users of the old network had several choices, as shown in Figure 10.2. They could compute locally; send email, often with attachments as opposed to doing real-time file transfers; or go through a problematic dial-up process and use the New Jersey LAN at 14.4 Kbits/second. In dial-up mode, they had access to all servers and system resources in New Jersey, but over a communications facility that was sluggish and prone to going down.

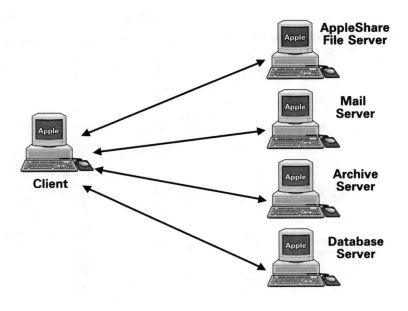

Figure 10.2   Pre-Frame-Relay Logical Architecture

10.3   Frame Relay: Selection and Migration

In this section, we will discuss TeleChoice's expectations of their move to frame relay as well as how they accomplished their migration. We will also look more closely at the four biggest challenges that TeleChoice encountered in their move to a frame relay environment: improving their systems personnel's understanding of the WAN environment and how their system operated in that environment, the move from a remote LAN to a distributed client-server environment, configuration of the remote equipment, and conversion from AppleTalk to Ethernet to support an all-IP environment.

10.3.1   Business Aspects

TeleChoice was at a crossroads. TeleChoice had the option of hiring more consultants to handle their growing business (not easy since TeleChoice operates in a highly specialized field where consultants are neither inexpensive nor easy to come by) or making the consultants they did have more efficient. It was clear that growth would mandate the hiring of more consultants in the future; however, their first step was to improve the efficiencies of their operating environment.

Expectations

Before frame relay, TeleChoice had a remote analog dial-up LAN connectivity environment with all of the associated connectivity, file transfer, and coordination problems previously mentioned. TeleChoice's expectation was that if they moved to a new full-period nondial network, specifically a frame relay network, they could realize their plans for how they wanted to be organized as a company, the way they exchanged information, and subsequently the way they did business. TeleChoice's expectations were that the frame relay network would allow them to accomplish the following specific goals:

- Improve the way they communicate with remote offices and eliminate the penalty for remote workers
- Expand the applications that the remote offices had available to them
- Provide a more controlled information environment
- Centralize the processes of controlling, administering, and backing up information
- Centralize MIS resources and expertise
- Off-load the burden of systems administration from consultants
- Improve consultant efficiencies, thereby making money and enhancing their contributions to the bottom line
- Lower the costs to run the business

Carrier Selection Process

TeleChoice did not go through a lengthy carrier selection process: they simply chose AT&T and moved directly to implementation planning. By not going through a lengthy and exhaustive formal evaluation and selection process, TeleChoice was better able to focus their resources on the implementation of their frame relay network and cut weeks, or possibly even months, off of the implementation timetable. Although significant technical distinctions between carriers do exist, these distinctions have much less impact on very small, low-bandwidth, single-carrier domestic networks than they do on other networks. While it is not advisable for customers with large, complex networks to just jump into frame relay in the manner TeleChoice has done, it is true that any of the public frame relay network offerings that provide the needed geographic coverage will work quite well for the small user with a limited number of sites and low bandwidth requirements.

For the small network user, the two most important criteria will be the extent to which the carrier is willing (and capable) of assisting in getting the network set up and the price of the service. Important capabilities to consider in carrier selection might extend to the point of the carrier not only helping to configure, but also providing and managing, the customer premises equipment (which would then be referred to as "customer-located equipment" to imply carrier ownership and management), such as bridges or routers. Pricing may also take into account voice, voice mail, Internet access, and other services offered by the carrier, which might be bundled to achieve convenience of one-stop shopping and possible consolidated billing and discounting.

Migration

TeleChoice wished to migrate from their analog dial-up environment to their new frame relay environment in a manner that minimized the negative impact on their consultants and the amount of time that their operation was in a transitional phase. In order to accomplish this, TeleChoice chose to leverage their own internal expertise, as well as that of AT&T. In addition to existing expertise, TeleChoice added an MIS director to their staff at about this time with prior expertise in migration to a frame relay environment.

10.3.2 Technical Aspects

Prior to a final decision, TeleChoice informally considered both private lines and frame relay. (They never seriously considered X.25 although there's no reason why they couldn't have: TeleChoice doesn't have very high-speed applications, and they do have operations outside the United States. TeleChoice also did not seriously consider ISDN or IP connection via the Internet.) TeleChoice found that the private line solution was actually a little bit more expensive than frame relay and provided no additional benefits. Because TeleChoice knew that they would eventually want to interconnect their international site, and that they were going to add remote U.S. offices over the course of the next couple years, they didn't feel a private line solution was going to be as flexible or scalable a solution as frame relay.

Another important selection point for TeleChoice was that they are a company that deals with telecommunications technology. Because they have a lot of experience with frame relay from the technology and the services standpoint, they decided it would be better to actually have experience in using frame relay as well. Additionally, TeleChoice wanted to be able to support a new business unit involved with testing different technologies and equipment over a network environment and needed a network that would be very flexible and could easily be reconfigured to support any given test—and that definitely wasn't private lines, and definitely was frame relay.

Planning

TeleChoice began with a typical design process for small frame relay networks, one discussed in a fair amount of detail here because it differs significantly from the process for larger networks.

"For small remote sites, the design process may be as simple as estimating the CIR based on the level of connectivity in place today" (Heckart 1994, p. 122). While this general rule of thumb is a good starting point, and in many cases can yield the final answer, TeleChoice was not only migrating to a frame relay network, but was changing their architecture as well. While the dial-up connections were 14.4 Kbits/second, they were also very problematic, and their true value could be rated well below a full-period 14.4-Kbit/second dedicated leased line. TeleChoice opted to implement their network initially with 32-Kbit/second CIRs. A single 32-Kbit/second PVC would be configured in a star arrangement back to the main office from each remote office. Other PVCs could be added at a later time between offices if office-to-office traffic warranted it, but anything other than a star configuration is unlikely to be needed because all communications in the network are with servers that will be centralized in the frame relay configuration. Centrally administered, star-configured networks are very common in frame relay networks, representing over 65% of all frame relay customer network topologies (Taylor 1995).

The next planning step was to choose the access rate, often called *port speed*, required. Lieberman and Szoke (1996) state:

An application's effective bandwidth will vary based on port speed, CIR, and traffic load at any instant on the carrier's network. The carrier makes a commitment to provide at least the bandwidth of the CIR. And the carrier delivers in excess of 99.9% of the data that is within that CIR. You can choose a port speed greater than the CIR. If so, the application can burst to the port speed. However, if the network is congested, the carrier makes no guarantee that the traffic beyond the CIR will be delivered. You have to weigh the benefits of adjusting the CIR one way and the port speed the other with price and performance.

Heckart (1994, pp. 123–124) gives an alternative rule of thumb:

Take the total CIR and choose a port connection speed that will provide a subscription level between 100 and 200 percent. For small remote sites, depending upon the applications and the protocols being used, it is not uncommon to see subscription rates of 300 to 500 percent.

Taking all of these considerations into account, TeleChoice opted for 64-Kbit/second access at the remote sites and a full T1 with 128 Kbits/second of channelized bandwidth dedicated to (nontest) frame relay at the headquarters site. This arrangement would guarantee greater than 32-Kbit/second throughput at the remote sites—a 32-Kbit/second CIR plus whatever else the network was able to deliver on a "best effort" basis above and beyond the CIR. This arrangement also made it possible to double the remote CIRs in the future, if desirable, and still be within the 64-Kbit/second port speed.

Consideration was also given to many other aspects of the migration/implementation as well:

- Router selection and configuration
- Migration to Ethernet with IP
- Human logistics
- Software licensing
- Email services
- Service cut-over
- Testing/certification

We will now take a brief look at each area.

Router selection and configuration   What type of a device (router, bridge, other specialized FRAD device) would be required to provide connectivity from the premises to the frame relay network? What type of DSU/CSU would be required? Would a stand-alone CSU/DSU be required, or is it possible to get an integral DSU/CSU that could be deployed inside the router, bridge, or specialized FRAD?

To support the connection to the frame relay network, TeleChoice chose the Ascend Communications Etherframe 50, a combination router and CSU/DSU, for the remote offices and the Ascend MAX 4000, a combination router and T1 CSU/DSU, for the main office in New Jersey. TeleChoice also made arrangements for a remote dial-up connection to be available at each remote site so that the Ascend devices could be accessed remotely by New Jersey–based personnel without the need to place TeleChoice IS personnel at each site for the duration of the implementation process.

Migration to Ethernet with IP   What changes would be needed in each of the offices to support Ethernet only and to move away from the existing AppleTalk/LocalTalk environment? How could the changes be made with a minimum impact on each user? Which Macintosh stations would need to be replaced, if any, to take advantage of the new operating environment?

TeleChoice replaced Dayna bridges and other adapters, as needed, with EtherTalk cards and made appropriate software changes to the Macintosh stations.

Human logistics   What will the effects of interim and final changes be on the consultants? What carrier personnel will be needed, where, and when? What TeleChoice personnel will be needed, where, and when? Which steps, exactly, will be the responsibility of AT&T, and which will be the responsibility of TeleChoice? What personnel training was needed prior to beginning their first implementation?

TeleChoice chose to take each installation on a case-by-case basis, intending to learn from their first installation and apply what they learned to subsequent installations. They chose to schedule personnel accordingly.

Software licensing   What impact will the consolidation and reconfiguration of servers have on software licenses? Software that is licensed on a per-server basis will obviously be affected, and, in fact, server centralization and consolidation could represent a cost reduction. Software licensed on a per-user or maximum-user basis will obviously not be affected, but there could be some benefits to converting individual, per-user licenses to site licenses or server licenses.

Email services   How will the new server configuration affect the mail server, and how should accounts be transferred from one server to another? How will duplicate mail be avoided during the migration? How will near-normal communication be achieved? How will lost mail be minimized during the transition?

Care had to be taken to assure that no accounts or mail messages were lost in the transition process and that there were no conflicts between the dial-in systems and the new frame relay network. Although the specific steps needed in the TeleChoice migration were mandated by the Quick-

Mail system, the steps will be similar for any mail system. These steps include ensuring that all mail queues are cleared before bringing down or relocating any mail server, that no user maintains multiple accounts or log-ins, that no mail servers are connected to more than one service (dial-in or frame relay) simultaneously, and that the configuration is proper for the service to which they are attached.

Service cut-over   How would the service be cut over? In what order, and by whom would different steps be performed? On what schedule? What fallback position was available to allow normal operation if the installation of the new service failed?

TeleChoice was replacing a number of dial-up systems with a full-time, 24-hour, seven-day-per-week system. While the dial-in system still existed as a backup from individual Macintosh computers, the use of dial-up servers was discontinued immediately after the turn-up of the new frame relay network. This service cut-over needed to be coordinated with each office to minimize the likelihood of negative impact during the cut-over period. The change affected their operations tremendously during the migration process. A lot of planning was done and great care was taken to be sure that the servers on either end wouldn't become confused and mail wouldn't get routed improperly. This required careful scheduling of the implementation phase to make sure that servers and users were turned off in the remote offices, and new servers and services at the central site were turned on in a specific order.

Testing/certification   How would the operation of the new installation be verified? How would an installation be judged a success or failure? How would it be determined if further fine-tuning were needed?

A process was put into place to verify the integrity of the new frame relay service and to certify that it was operational. The first level of testing was to show that the physical access to the frame relay network was operational, followed by tests of the end-to-end permanent virtual circuits. The final step was to test actual applications prior to going live with the new network.

Migration

TeleChoice had a basic idea of their requirements and knew that they wanted, and needed, to move very quickly. TeleChoice called AT&T and explained what they wanted to do and the kind of additional support that would be needed because of the test lab facility. (The test lab facility necessitates AT&T making some changes more frequently and on shorter notice than most customer configuration changes.) AT&T was willing and able to meet all requirements TeleChoice put before them: support for all sites, fast installation, and quick turnaround on changes for the test lab.

TeleChoice moved quickly from the remote LAN connectivity environment to the remote client-server environment in one continuous motion. TeleChoice centralized a lot of equipment and functionality that previously had been distributed, centralized the management of those systems, and off-loaded some of the burden of installing and managing the network from the remote offices back to the central site.

The first two implementations of remote connectivity took over a week each. Additional implementations were a lot faster than the first two because TeleChoice learned a great deal about how to configure the remote equipment, how the whole network works from the logical level down through the physical level, how the LAN protocols were integrated over the WAN, and how they interact. All of this education was applied to future implementations, which took only a day or two each.

Prior to the move to the frame relay network, TeleChoice used a lot of Apple Remote Access connections to allow remote users to dial in from wherever they were and access their email as well as the network servers. After the frame relay network, the dial-in network was left in place for use by mobile consultants but was no longer needed by users in the individual offices.

Configuration after Migration

After migration, TeleChoice uses 56-Kbit/second access, with 32-Kbit/second PVCs at remote offices and an integrated access T1 at their headquarters office. The integrated access T1 allows the 24 individual 56/64-Kbit/second DS0 channels within the T1 to be allocated for different aspects of carrier access. Because the local access T1 provided to TeleChoice at their headquarters by their local exchange carrier follows the protocols and format of the North American Digital Hierarchy, the individual channels can be split at the LEC and can be redirected to specific locations. Several will stay at the LEC and will provide interconnection to local telephone service, some will be connected to the long-distance telephony network, and some will be redirected to the AT&T InterSpan frame relay service to provide network connectivity. The integrated access T1 represents an opportunity to save money on present voice and data service while providing some room for future growth with a minimum lead time and very little negative impact on present services.

As a part of the move to a frame relay network, TeleChoice centralized their file and mail servers in New Jersey. Frame relay's substantially higher bandwidths (56-Kbit/second frame relay access with 32-Kbit/second PVCs versus the 14.4-Kbit/second dial-up) and dedicated, full-time, nondial access combined to provide far greater throughput with much higher reliability. The centralization of the servers also meant that the servers could be professionally administered by personnel dedicated to that task, as opposed to being administered by the remote site consultants. This new arrangement guaranteed that backups would be performed regularly and consistently, that backup media would be properly archived and protected, that new system and applications software would be administered consistently, and that the information that is the lifeblood of the organization would be more secure and protected in a central location.

TeleChoice is now running a heterogeneous AppleTalk-over-IP network, and the remote offices and the main office are seamlessly interconnected. With the exception of speed, there is no difference in functionality between offices. People can instantly share files without a concern for dial-up access, mail goes through a lot faster, and some new applications can also be supported for group coordination and real-time communications that would have been impossible previously.

Physical architecture   To support the connection to the frame relay network, TeleChoice chose the Ascend Communications Etherframe 50, a combination router and CSU/DSU, for the remote offices. At the remote offices, the Etherframe 50 connects to the EtherTalk segment using a standard Ethernet interface and to the frame relay network using a four-wire RJ45 data connector to the dedicated 56-Kbit/second frame relay access line (Figure 10.3).

At their headquarters office, TeleChoice has implemented the Ascend MAX 4000. The MAX 4000 has a T1 interface on the frame relay network side and an Ethernet interface on the LAN side. The T1 bandwidth is used in a channelized format (Figure 10.4). One of the twenty-four 64-Kbit/second DS0s of the T1 is dedicated to supporting the remote office LAN interconnection, four of the DS0s are used to provide Internet access at 256 Kbits/second, and two more of the DS0s are used to support a frame relay test environment at TeleChoice Labs, colocated with the headquarters office.

Logical architecture   In the new architecture, each user sees all system resources as directly attached to a single, cohesive LAN infrastructure, as the user is, rather than imagining resources to be across some great void of

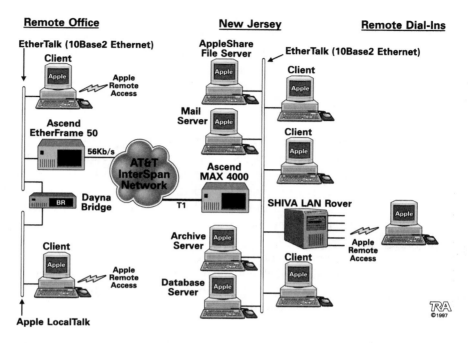

Figure 10.3 TeleChoice Frame Relay Physical Architecture

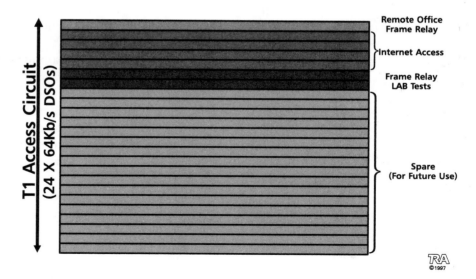

Figure 10.4 Channelization of TeleChoice Access Bandwidth

time and space. In the new architecture, all resources are immediately available, which has a very positive effect on the usability of the LAN and allows the implementation of some additional applications that were not so usable in the prior networking environment. The logical configuration diagram of the new network is identical to the logical view of the old network approach.

Operations and Network Management

TeleChoice manages every device individually and does not feel that the size of their network has grown to the point where a centralized network management system is needed. TeleChoice has about 40 devices in the network today, most of which have a human personally assigned to them who will call if they encounter a problem.

Network management architecture   Although they do not have a centralized network management system, there are still several tools that TeleChoice utilizes to provide remote support to the users of their network. Among these tools are the frame relay network itself, which provides the speed and transport capacity to be able to use Timbuktu remote control software, allowing centralized staff to support people at all locations.

Network performance is good, and after the initial installation the reliability and stability of the network remain good. TeleChoice utilizes the statistics built in to the Ascend boxes as well as some simple traffic-monitoring tools to monitor what is going on in the network.

Operations   The centralized network support team utilizes Timbuktu remote control software to access remote computers and to centrally take control of the remote computer. Now, if one of the network users has a question about how to use or get into an application, or if they're having a problem with the general operation of their computer, instead of trying to explain it over the phone, the MIS person can go over the network, take control of the computer in real time, see exactly what's going on, and then fix the problem quickly and efficiently.

In the past, prior to the implementation of frame relay, it was possible to use Timbuktu as well, but this required the remote user to dial into the central site, which changed the exact operating environment, often interfered with the operation the remote user had questions about (such as how to dial up a certain site), and added to the time needed to answer the question or solve the problem. Not only is the frame relay approach faster than doing it via modem, many remote users were more willing to live with problems or work around them than they were to deal with a new problem—the dial-up modem connection—in order to solve their original problem.

10.4 Living with Frame Relay

Overall, frame relay has met or exceeded TeleChoice's expectations, with some additional benefits that were unanticipated as well. By providing additional, full-period bandwidth, frame relay has improved the way TeleChoice communicates with remote offices and eliminates the distance penalty for remote workers. The additional bandwidth made available by frame relay expands the applications that the remote offices have available to them; creates a more controlled information environment; allows the centralization of the processes of controlling, administering, and backing up information; and concentrates MIS resources and expertise in one location. All of these steps off-load the burden of systems administration from consultants, thereby improving consultant efficiencies.

10.4.1 Anticipated Benefits

The core of the problems with the prior dial-up network was the use of older, analog dial-up technology for more modern applications for which this type of access is ill-suited. Bad telephone connections, large files or email messages with large attachments, and the time delays and potential problems that could be encountered made older, analog dial-up ill-suited to the applications of TeleChoice and combined to compound the problems. Just establishing a connection and transferring a file might take anywhere from 30 seconds to 4 or 5 minutes, and email messages, files, and email messages with files attached required much more time than that to be downloaded.

TeleChoice estimated that in an eight-hour day, a consultant might spend as much as an hour or more establishing the analog dial-up connection and exchanging messages in the pre-frame-relay environment. Although it is easy to talk about setting up a connection and doing other work in parallel while communications occurs, the harsh realities are that the consultant needed to wait for the file exchange to occur before they could begin their next jobs.

By saving only one hour of a consultant's time during each workday, TeleChoice was able to avoid hiring an additional three consultants by moving to the frame relay network (considering that they had about 24–26 remote consultants at the time the new network was implemented). This additional efficiency also provided the needed funds to hire the additional consultants that would be required to support even more growth.

The results can be measured in a number of financial ways. One of the most accurate is to measure the impact of the move to frame relay as a lower overall cost to run the business as a percentage of revenues. Calculating the costs of frame relay plus other network costs as a percentage of revenues takes into account both the decrease in cost and increase in profits in a single calculation. Neither calculation alone would be an accurate representation of the true impact. The impact attributable to frame relay could be compared to the estimated bottom-line impact of competing technologies to develop a comparative estimate, but this calculation was not done by TeleChoice in the actual case study.

10.4.2   Unanticipated Benefits

Another benefit, and one that cannot be quantified in terms of time saved or other direct bottom-line impact, is TeleChoice's increased firsthand, frontline knowledge of frame relay. As a telecommunications consulting firm, TeleChoice now has direct insight and experience with the problems and the issues that end users face in implementing frame relay because they are one. TeleChoice feels this makes them a bit more insightful in dealing with end users as well as giving feedback to equipment vendors and to carriers about how they can improve their service and their support processes. For TeleChoice it's been very important and resulted in a demonstrable competitive advantage.

10.4.3   Lessons Learned

Because of their involvement in the industry, TeleChoice felt like they entered into the process of implementing frame relay with open eyes and a fairly good understanding of what it would take to do the implementation. Even so, TeleChoice did have more problems with the actual implementation than they had anticipated, and they learned lessons that could be very beneficial to other frame relay customers, or prospective frame relay customers, of any size. The lessons learned by TeleChoice can be summarized into the following areas:

- TeleChoice uses a less common hardware platform, operating system, and protocol than most frame relay users.
- Good carrier technical support is critical.
- Better implementation planning should have been done and would have eased installation problems substantially.
- A common vocabulary between all parties ensures good communication during the implementation and later troubleshooting processes.
- A single individual responsible for coordinating installation activities would have eased coordination problems between TeleChoice, the carrier, and the equipment manufacturer.
- Minor postinstallation problems must all be cleaned up before the installation can be considered a success.

We will look at each of these items in some degree of depth with the idea that TeleChoice's lessons can be applied to other frame relay networks and, in some ways, to network implementation in general.

Less Common Platform

Retrospectively, TeleChoice feels that a lot of the unforeseen additional problems encountered during the installation phase were due to the fact that they are an Apple Macintosh shop and use equipment that is not the most common platform in frame relay networks. There was a lot less experience by both the carrier and the equipment vendor in hooking up to and working on Apple-based frame relay networks than there would have been had TeleChoice implemented a frame relay network based on the more common DOS platform. It must be pointed out, however, that Apple Macintosh computers are very prevalent in this market segment—a market segment that includes small, less technical companies who gravitate to the more user-friendly, yet still very powerful, Mac platforms.

Good Carrier Technical Support

TeleChoice emphasized that they were very impressed and very happy with the support provided by AT&T. TeleChoice is a small company and AT&T is a very big company, and when TeleChoice had problems, even if AT&T didn't have an immediate solution, AT&T did play the role of coordinator, and they brought the necessary parties together and stayed involved until the problem was resolved. TeleChoice feels that this says a lot for AT&T's willingness to support their customers, even when that customer isn't necessarily a big player. An argument could be made that, because of TeleChoice's preeminent position as consultants in the industry, they received attention and levels of service that would be uncharacteristic of what most small customers would receive, but an informal survey of several similar-sized customers seems to indicate that AT&T does, in fact, provide a similar level of support for customers of similar size. The carrier's technical support capabilities, staffing, hours of availability, levels of support available, costs, and actual procedures form the foundation of one of the most important remaining areas of service differentiation between carriers.

Better Implementation Planning

Although TeleChoice feels that AT&T did a good job of being the coordinator of the implementation process (and when problems were encountered, that AT&T stepped in and brought all the parties together to get the problems resolved), many of the implementation problems could have been foreseen and avoided entirely. TeleChoice feels that the preinstallation planning and consulting phases could be improved dramatically. As the service matures and as companies like TeleChoice adopt frame relay, the more proactive all of the players (equipment vendors, the local access providers, and the interexchange service provider) should be in avoiding problems in the first place. TeleChoice feels this is mandatory for the widespread adoption of the technology to continue. TeleChoice has communicated these thoughts to AT&T, and as a result, AT&T has taken steps to modify its implementation process with the hope of making it easier and faster for small, nontechnical companies to install and benefit from frame relay service.

Some of the items that appear simple but that confounded the implementation of TeleChoice's frame relay service and could have been eliminated by better planning included

- getting the equipment configured, out to the site, and plugged into the network
- site survey and site preparation
- providing remote dial-in lines for equipment configuration

These problems represent especially big hurdles in a nontechnical office environment, which is increasingly where frame relay is being installed and implemented. In fact, frame relay is moving down-market and is being adopted by companies that don't have huge MIS departments or MIS people out at every remote site. Configuring the equipment is something that should be staged at the main site, and the equipment could then be installed more easily at the remote site by less technical personnel with minimum training. It is also possible that smaller firms could save time and money overall by engaging a network integrator, or possibly the same firm contracted to provide service on their personal computers or other office equipment, to be responsible to move equipment to the site and assist in the installation. These types of companies often have remote personnel that are available for less than the cost of an airline ticket.

Finding the proper location for equipment, and siting the equipment upon arrival, is not a trivial task and requires a knowledge of power requirements, heating and cooling, security and system reliability concerns, and any local fire or building codes regarding the type of equipment being installed. These site planning requirements are often neglected until the last minute, or ignored entirely, and lead to a less-than-desirable installation. The war stories and anecdotes within the industry about automatic teller machines plugged into outlets on the same electrical circuits as lights and turned on and off by wall switches, or about cleaning people who routinely unplug file servers to plug in their vacuum cleaners, are too numerous to recount here, but the main point is that these types of planning items should be in the critical path, and not afterthoughts.

Another aspect of implementation planning that did not receive sufficient advanced consideration (but that retrospectively TeleChoice feels would have been advantageous) is planning for remote dial-in lines for configuration and testing of the remote Ascend routers. Although it was possible for nontechnical on-site personnel to get the units connected to phone lines and assist in getting dial-up access during the installation process, advance consideration of this key point could have streamlined the implementation process and minimized the impact on the time and other resources of the remote offices.

Common Vocabulary

While it is true that there are far fewer parameters to consider in frame relay implementation than, say, X.25 or SNA, there are still many areas for possible misunderstanding. During the implementation of their frame relay network, TeleChoice and AT&T suffered from many minor problems that they soon discovered were problems of human, not electronic, communications. TeleChoice learned that Ascend and AT&T have different terms and parameters for the same thing and could often be agreeing but appear to be disagreeing. For example, the names used by each for the exact flavor of local management interface to be used was different. One group called the original StrataCom/Cisco prestandard Frame Relay Forum version of LMI simply "LMI," while the other called the Annex D variant "LMI." Problems were easier to solve once a translation was established and meanings were clarified.

Installation Coordination

TeleChoice encountered a number of problems that were, in reality, fairly minor but were compounded by the lack of overall coordination between TeleChoice, AT&T, and Ascend. Multiple simultaneous changes can, very often, not only create different problems, but can, in many cases, mask the fix to the problem and make it impossible to duplicate. TeleChoice, for instance, had problems with the Ascend MAX 4000 at the main site and the Etherframe 50s at the remote sites. TeleChoice solicited Ascend's assistance and found that there was a system software version problem that required the upgrade of the system software. During this time, AT&T made some changes in attempting to resolve the problem that interfered with the work Ascend was doing. After that problem was fixed, it was determined that some other changes had been made regarding the proper encapsulation of the AppleTalk over IP—changes that should not have been made and for which no one seemed to be willing to take ownership.

Minor Stability Problems

The only other problems were related to AT&T and were some spurious stability problems with one of the offices. For some reason that could not be determined, the frame relay network kept randomly failing. AT&T rehomed the connection to a different StrataCom IPX node within their network, and the problems went away permanently.

10.5 Future Plans

TeleChoice has some very specific future plans for frame relay regarding expansion in three ways: increasing the size of the CIRs, increasing the number of locations in their network, and increasing the types of traffic going across their frame relay network.

10.5.1 Increasing the Size of CIRs

By comparison, the environment that TeleChoice has is substantially faster than the prior dial access environment, and, for the most part, it supports their business requirements. There is a trade-off between greater speed (and, therefore, saving some time) and the additional money that the frame relay network costs. TeleChoice feels that right now, from a business perspective, they've probably got a pretty good balance. The price that they can afford to pay and the level of network performance that they're getting are fairly equivalent. Of course, they would like to have greater network speeds and envision the broader range of applications they could do if they had more speed (including some desktop video teleconferencing), but at the same time, for their core business applications, what they have now works a lot better than anything they've ever had before.

However well the frame relay network is handling present needs, TeleChoice foresees a time when growth will require more bandwidth. For this reason, TeleChoice is going to increase the committed information rate of its PVCs this year, probably to 64 Kbits/second everywhere, at which time they will also evaluate ways to increase the bandwidth even more in the future. Right now, access is limited at the remote sites because their dedicated access line is limited to 56 Kbits/second, which would preclude increasing the CIRs to 64 Kbits/second. TeleChoice will evaluate ways to economically increase access, maybe up to 128 Kbits/second. Two possibilities are T1 access lines and ISDN dedicated access. T1 access lines are the more traditional method and would allow future expansion up to 1.5 Mbits/second but are more costly than ISDN dedicated access in most markets. The ISDN alternative would be to use a 2B+D ISDN line: two 64-Kbit/second B (or bearer) channels, which can be combined for a total throughput of 128 Kbits/second, plus a 16-Kbit/second D (or signaling) channel, which is used for call setup and other signaling.

10.5.2 Increasing Number of Locations

This company is growing at a very rapid rate, in excess of 100% a year, so TeleChoice plans to continue to open remote offices, both domestically and internationally. Those new offices will, at the very least, need to be connected back to New Jersey, and possibly to other remote sites, depending on the future architecture of the network.

It is also anticipated that their new business unit that deals with testing of applications and equipment, TeleChoice Labs, will continue to grow, and so will its reliance on the frame relay network; the frame relay network will continue to play a very visible and important part in supporting that business unit.

10.5.3   Increasing Applications

There are two additional applications that may be applicable to TeleChoice. One is videoconferencing, but it appears as though videoconferencing will remain on the wish list for a while and will not see serious consideration during the next year. The other is voice over frame relay, which TeleChoice has discussed internally but hasn't yet tested or decided on implementation of, although that's something in which they are interested. TeleChoice estimates voice over frame relay would eliminate almost 100% of intracompany calls. The cost of the intracompany calls via regular dial-up services each month minus the cost of the additional frame relay network bandwidth and equipment needed to support voice over frame relay, TeleChoice estimates, could save $12,000 to $15,000 per year in their specific case and would require a hardware investment of approximately $15,000, which would yield approximately a one-year payback period.

TeleChoice's opinion is that frame relay's future is very bright and that the options available to end users are only going to improve. When they become available, TeleChoice intends to take advantage of some of the newer options such as dial-up and ISDN access to the public frame relay network.

10.6   Conclusion

The TeleChoice case study has many things in common with previous case studies, and we are beginning to see some important patterns emerge. The most important pattern, in a broad respect, is the use of frame relay as a transport for an IP network. Frame relay is as useful in this regard for small organizations like TeleChoice as it is for large companies like Greyhound. The second pattern we can see is a strong interest in voice over frame relay, but a reluctance to implement voice over frame relay before products are widely available, standards fully settled, and the impact on present operations fully understood. There is a great deal of interest in packet voice, both frame relay and Internet voice, but many customers have yet to take decisive steps. A third pattern is an emphasis on good migration planning and execution: planning, testing, staging, and installation coordination are, and will continue to be, the keys to success in the implementation of any technology. And probably the most important pattern of all: the main reason companies are adopting frame relay as rapidly as they are is cost. The reasons may vary in their exact description, but there is always an obvious or underlying correlation to cost savings or cost containment.

The previous case studies have dealt with customers of varying sizes who utilize public frame relay network infrastructures. The next case study will discuss a customer so large that it has become its own carrier and begun to sell network design and transport services to other companies, as well, on a global basis. At some point, a critical mass is reached at which a carrier or service provider frame relay network solution no longer makes sense. The subject of our next case study has clearly reached that point.

CHAPTER ELEVEN

Global Multiservice Backbone Network

The focus of this case study is on frame relay's role as one of many services provided by a global frame-based multiservice network. The "public networking" model of frame relay is executed here with debis Systemhaus being the carrier for internal customers, like Daimler-Benz, as well as for external customers.

11.1 Case Study Background

Every minute of every business day the huge machine that is Daimler-Benz InterServices (debis) cranks and churns and generates over DM 112,000 (about $62,000). With 1995 revenues of almost DM 11.7 billion ($6.5 billion) and a worldwide presence of over 200 branch offices in 23 countries, the network of debis is indeed global in scope and broad in the range of services and capabilities that must be supported. What began as a world-spanning network infrastructure for the Daimler-Benz Companies, including auto manufacturer Mercedes-Benz, has grown to be a true carrier service, managed by the Systemhaus division of debis. Its network traffic is split approximately 50/50 between Daimler corporate traffic and outside customer traffic.

Debis AG is comprised of seven business divisions—Systemhaus, Financial Services, Insurance Brokerage, Trading, Marketing Services, Telecommunications and Media Services, and Real Estate Management. Established on July 1, 1990, debis has achieved substantial growth during the first five years of its existence, increasing its annual revenues threefold since the company was established. The number of employees has risen over the same period from 3,600 to 10,196, of which almost 2,000 work in debis's foreign branches.

Based in Berlin, debis AG is pursuing a strategy of establishing a global presence in network services and comprehensive outsourcing through strategic alliances with other companies such as Cap Gemini Sogeti, the largest manufacturer/independent supplier of IT services in Europe and which also operates in the United States. Debis's goal is to open new markets, win international customers, and guarantee the highest possible level of service to its customers all over the world.

The information technology branch of debis, debis Systemhaus, was established in 1990 to offer services that are not tied to the products of any individual manufacturer. In order to strengthen the company's market position in Germany and to obtain access to international markets, debis Systemhaus entered into a strategic alliance with Cap Gemini Sogeti in 1992.

The range of products offered by Germany's largest independent IT service company addresses the specific needs of each sector of the economy and covers a broad spectrum of information processing, network service provision, and full-scale outsourcing. By leveraging its core competencies in consultancy, development, and marketing, debis Systemhaus offers its customers a single source for information technology solutions. For example, debis Systemhaus will take over responsibility for the maintenance and servicing of applications systems. Debis Systemhaus will not only design, implement, and service the customer's IT-related corporate functions (for example, the computer center and network services), but it will also take over day-to-day operational responsibility.

The needs of debis Systemhaus's internal and external customers are as diverse as any subset of customers, not only because of applications but also because of the wide variety of international transmission facilities and interfaces required. It was the goal of debis Systemhaus to design and build the most flexible consolidated backbone transport network possible and then to provide service interfaces, as appropriate, to carry all varieties of traffic. Debis Systemhaus carried out an exhaustive study and lab tests, and the result was the deployment of two entirely different networks interconnected via frame relay user-network interfaces (UNIs). The domestic German network consists of Cisco/StrataCom IPX switches; the international network consists of Netrix switches. Both networks provide a full spectrum of data and voice services, but debis Systemhaus did not find the Cisco/StrataCom IPXs to be cost-effective enough for many of the smaller international locations, nor were the Netrix switches big and robust enough for the high-demand domestic German sites.

This case study varies to some extent from the others because it is the story of an end user providing their own internal carrier services as well as services to outside companies. This case study is also unique because the debis Systemhaus network is not strictly a frame relay network in the truest sense: it is a multiservice network implemented to cost-effectively consolidate a variety of other networks, with frame relay being only one of the service interfaces offered. An area of great focus in this chapter will be the backbone selection criteria for the high-demand domestic German network—a process that is critical to the success of any carrier or service provider offering and a process that small- to medium-sized frame relay users rarely, if ever, see.

11.2 Before Frame Relay

Prior to the implementation of their consolidated backbone network, debis operated four completely separate WANs: SNA, router LAN internetwork, X.25, and voice.

- *SNA:* The SNA data network operated over dedicated leased lines and supported over 100,000 SNA terminals worldwide attached to local and remote cluster control units, and eventually to IBM 3745 front-end processors and then to a variety of IBM host computers.
- *LAN internetwork:* The preconsolidated-network LAN internetwork also operated over leased lines as well as Internet connections and consisted of approximately 1,000 routers (about 90% Cisco) providing a corporate intranet and outside Internet connections. Internet connections are provided via security fire walls.

- *X.25:* The private X.25 network is still widely used in Germany and the United Kingdom and had to be consolidated into the new network as well. The user departments were unwilling to replace production systems that were in place and operational simply to accommodate some new networking technology.
- *Corporate voice:* The fourth of the originally disparate, unconnected networks that debis Systemhaus wished to consolidate was the corporate voice network. In addition to millions of call-minutes per year of human voice calls, the corporate voice network is utilized extensively for voice band data: high-speed fax and analog modem connections. It was imperative that any new network support the full range of call types needed by debis Systemhaus and their clients.

11.2.1 Business Aspects

The end goal of debis Systemhaus was to save money without sacrificing—and hopefully enhancing—flexibility, connectivity, and reliability. Debis Systemhaus hoped to achieve this goal through the consolidation of the separate networks; the elimination of redundancy of equipment, transmission facilities, and staff; and a more effective management of the combined bandwidth.

Requirements

Because debis Systemhaus is to operate as a carrier/service provider for internal and external customers, they must be able to provide an infrastructure that will allow for the migration of current legacy technologies as well as support for future technologies. To provide a comprehensive service offering, debis Systemhaus needed to be able to provide an infrastructure that could support "anything" and be highly manageable.

The debis Systemhaus requirements appear to generally follow the requirements of other frame relay users, but there is one important difference. In most cases, the frame relay users are choosing a service or hybrid public/private network for their own use, and they can modify their own application requirements somewhat to achieve a perfect balance between the application and the transmission system. In the case of debis Systemhaus, it is one of several subsidiaries and will not be operating a network for its own requirements, but rather will have to provide a network that will meet the needs of its internal and external customers with no ability to change their requirements if they do not meet the needs of the transport network, unless the demands are completely outrageous.

One challenge that debis Systemhaus faced was that providing services to very particular internal customers is more challenging than providing a network for external customers. Internal customers are often politically connected or have preset expectations that external customers do not have. An internal customer must be much happier than an external customer to provide the same rating on an evaluation form: an internal customer's "7" rating of satisfaction might be equivalent to a "9" rating for an external customer. And there is also the issue of having to provide a level and style of service to internal customers that does not suggest that they are being taken for granted because they must use the internal systems and have no choice in selecting outside providers or doing the network themselves.

Cost savings   Cost savings is the number one objective and was first and foremost in the evaluation, both from the business and the technical standpoints. Tariffs for telecommunications services are very high, especially for service between countries, and represent an important source of cost savings to justify the move to a new technology.

Flexibility and reliability   The ability to support any kind of interconnection between any set of sites in the network as well as the flexibility to extend the geographic scope of the network were also important. One aspect of flexibility, and cost and reliability as well, that was important in the evaluation process was the extent to which the network could be configured and managed remotely because of the cost, both in terms of time and money, of moving equipment and personnel between countries. In many cases, the time and money costs of moving personnel and equipment are prohibitive. Customs delays, high airline ticket prices, visas, and other issues can compound the already difficult problems of implementing and managing a network.

A mature hardware platform with remotely configurable modules, reliability options such as power supply, common logic and port/trunk card redundancy, and downloadable software upgrades is highly desirable as a method of getting around the problem of having to physically move people and equipment from place to place. All of these things were, of course, a part of debis Systemhaus's evaluation process.

Predictable quality of service   Because debis Systemhaus is to act as a service provider, they are on the other side of the service-level agreement. The other frame relay customers profiled in this book have been in the position to specify service levels, either in their contracts for service or in separate service-level agreements, and it has been the responsibility of the carrier to ensure that service levels are met. In this case study, it is our case study focus company, debis Systemhaus, who will have to manage the network in such a way that they provide a predictable quality of service, within agreed guidelines. This includes all of the aspects of monitoring normally associated with network management as well as internal rerouting in case of failures, redundant components, and very careful bandwidth management. Debis Systemhaus took bandwidth management as a special area of focus, not just for their own network, but also in a global consulting practice that applies the expertise and knowledge gained from their own network to the networks of other organizations.

Geographic independence   While debis Systemhaus wanted a consolidated, integrated backbone network that delivers traditional data, bursty data, voice, and video information using a single, unified communications infrastructure, they also wanted a high-speed/high-capacity network that reduced or eliminated the detrimental impact of geographic distances.

Companies grow, merge, divest, and expand operations. As they go through these phases, the communications systems delivering the information that is the very lifeblood of a healthy company must grow and expand along with them. This has created not only building and campus networks, but regional, national, and global networks as well.

Many of debis Systemhaus's own employees, as well as those of their internal and external customers, are located remotely, and the ideal was not to penalize offices for being located remotely from the headquarters location, but rather to create a consolidated backbone network that delivers the same information and services at the same speeds regardless of the point from which a user accesses the network—in other words, to create the appearance of a single large network that is independent of location or physical differences. Users at PCs in Berlin and Bogota get the same menus, access the same applications, and use the same data—and ideally at or near the same response times.

Manageability and reporting   The remote configuration, monitoring, and reporting aspects of a network of this size and geographic scope cannot be understated. Debis Systemhaus focused a lot of attention on this area. It was the intention of debis Systemhaus not only to provide a highly manageable network with excellent availability, internal rerouting in case of failures, and bandwidth management, but also to provide the reporting and billing information needed to allow network users to be billed for their use of the network on a usage basis, if desirable, in order to distinguish between the new network and the old leased-line networks.

"Future-proof"   The final requirement of the management of debis Systemhaus for their new network was that, to the extent practical, the network be "future-proof"—that is, that it is an architecture with the longest possible useful life and that it be upgradable and adaptable to future requirements with the minimum impact on existing customers and services.

11.2.2   Technical Aspects

Because the debis Systemhaus network is a carrier network that must be able to support any type of information transport, it was necessary to evaluate a new network architecture from a much higher level than most frame relay customers. The approach was to first look at the types of information that would be transported and then to choose a suitable backbone transport architecture to handle the various information types.

Traditional Data

The first major category of information requirements could be labeled "traditional data." Traditional data would encompass IBM's Systems Network Architecture (SNA) data, such as Synchronous Data Link Control (SDLC) framed data, needed by 100,000 terminals in the debis Systemhaus network; X.25-formatted packet data; and information transfers between asynchronous ASCII hosts and "dumb" asynchronous terminals, such as those between DEC VAXs and DEC VT-100 terminals, also used extensively by debis Systemhaus and its customers. Traditional data would also encompass an entire alphabet soup of other protocols, such as Houston Automatic Spooling Program (HASP)/Remote Job Entry (RJE), 2780/3780, Binary Synchronous Communications (BSC), Burroughs Poll/Select, HP Asynchronous Block Mode terminal protocols, Universal Data Link Control (UDLC), and many other specialized protocols.

Traditional data requirements vary widely based on the type of terminal and host computers being used but can be characterized in some general ways. In general, bandwidth requirements do not exceed 19,200 bits/second, bandwidth consumption is fairly flat (that is, traditional terminal traffic exhibits very low burstiness), and traditional terminal communications only connect one discrete point to one other discrete point at any one time. And while many of the customary stand-alone terminals are being replaced by personal computers, the terminal-type connection, even though accomplished through a PC with terminal emulation hardware and/or software, is still the predominant type of connection in data processing and data communications today.

A trend in terminal-type communications is toward a single terminal (usually a PC) being able to access two or more, often dissimilar, host computers at one time. Traditional data is, therefore, the first type of information that must be accommodated on the debis Systemhaus integrated backbone.

Bursty Data

A second type of data is bursty data. Bursty data, characterized by large instantaneous demand for bandwidth and very large peak-to-average ratios, is common in local area networking, host-to-host communications, and certain other specialized applications. Bursty data can be generated by a variety of protocols, from the LAN-oriented protocols, such as TCP/IP, Novell's IPX/SPX, Sun Network File Service (NFS), Apple's Apple File Protocol (AFP), DEC's Local Area Transport (LAT), and many others, to more traditional protocols such as SDLC and BSC.

Bursty data connections can tolerate variable delay, require bandwidth-on-demand, and are often supported today on very costly dedicated circuit connections that do not allow leftover bandwidth to be shared by other connections when it is not being used. An additional characteristic of LANs and host-to-host communications is that they often require that a single site be partially or fully mesh interconnected to several other sites. Bursty data, then, is the second type of data that this carrier network must accommodate.

Circuit Data

The third distinct type of data is circuit data. A circuit provides a fixed amount of bandwidth that is constant over time and with very little latency. Circuits are important for supporting applications, such as traditional voice and video, that will not tolerate any latency.

Circuits do not require bandwidth-on-demand because their bandwidth requirements are constant. Circuits, for their duration, require a fixed amount of bandwidth, which is not sharable with other applications, and connect one point to another. Special circuits such as multipoint circuits are a concatenation of simple point-to-point circuits.

Another type of circuit-based communications, voice communications, is a predominant application for the debis Systemhaus network. Voice information on an integrated network is transported as digital data. The analog voice data is sampled at the source, and digital bytes are generated for transport across the backbone.

The two most popular methods of converting analog voice into digital bytes are pulse code modulation (PCM) and adaptive differential pulse code modulation (ADPCM). Standard PCM samples require 64 Kbits/second of bandwidth per voice call; ADPCM typically requires 32 or 24 Kbits/second of bandwidth per call. PCM and/or ADPCM samples are then transported across our integrated backbone with the rest of our information.

Bursty Voice

Voice communications might be able to use bandwidth-on-demand, or they might utilize a fixed-bandwidth connection. The distinction is based upon how silence is handled in the network. In a network where the nodal hardware that readies the PCM and ADPCM samples for transmission across the network transfers samples representing silence, then a fixed-bandwidth connection is required.

On the other hand, nodal hardware that has a mechanism for suppressing silence, and therefore not requiring bandwidth to send the samples representing silence across the network, can take advantage of bandwidth-on-demand. In other words, the connection will use bandwidth only when one or both people on a voice call actually talk. Studies by Bell Laboratories have shown North American speakers on telephone calls generally speak only 38% of the total time during a call. The other time is spent listening, or where both parties are silent. Using the Bell Labs numbers, if ADPCM encoding is used (32-Kbit/second voice) and a silence suppression mechanism is also used, only approximately 38% of 32 Kbits/second, or approximately 12 Kbits/second, of bandwidth is utilized per call. Subsequent studies done by companies developing Internet and voice-over-frame-relay products that have an even tighter tolerance for distinguishing silence than was possible when the Bell Labs studies were conducted have shown that as little as 22% of bandwidth is actually utilized; the balance is silence that can be suppressed and not take up costly bandwidth.

Another very important characteristic of voice communications is its requirement of fixed delay. A voice communication is intolerant of delay because the human mind has no way of interpreting small voice samples with different arrival times into meaningful words and sentences. Examples of the effects of variable network delay, or latency, on voice are choppy speech, apparent "cutting in and cutting out" of the voice call, and unintelligible dialog.

In addition to normal digitized speech, there are special categories of communications that occur over voice connections that must be taken into account as well. High-speed voice band data communications (generally, speeds greater than 4,800 bits/second, but in some networks 2,400 bits/second) generated by modems and fax transmissions assume 100% of the bandwidth will be available to them. Special consideration has to be given to accommodating these types of transmissions in the voice network.

Voice requires connection of only one location to one other location at one time. Even multilocation teleconferences are comprised of several point-to-point calls from teleconference locations to a single site where they are bridged together.

Requirements Summary

Let's review the four major categories of information that must be supported by the debis Systemhaus service, or any general carrier network, and the associated characteristics (see Table 11.1). Traditional data, such as SNA, X.25, and various other protocols, has low (generally less than 19.2 Kbits/second) bandwidth requirements and low burstiness and can tolerate variable delay. Traditional data historically has only connected two discrete points, but is increasingly connecting one terminal with many different hosts.

Bursty data, such as host-to-host transfers and LAN-to-LAN communications, has high bandwidth requirements (generally 64 Kbits/second to 2 Mbits/second), high burstiness, and can tolerate variable delay. Bursty data connections often require partial or full mesh interconnection of many sites in order to provide any-to-any connectivity as needed.

Circuit connections for applications such as video have high bandwidth requirements (generally 64 Kbits/second to 2 Mbits/second) and no burstiness and cannot tolerate delay. Circuit connections only connect two discrete points.

Table 11.1 **Generic Information Transport Requirements**

Category	Examples	Bandwidth Required	Burstiness	Latency	Number of Points Connected
Traditional Data	SNA, X.25, ASCII	Generally Low <19.2 Kb/s	Low	Variable	One to One One to Many
Bursty Data	LAN-to-LAN, Host-to-Host, Frame Relay	High: 64 Kb/s to 2 Mb/s and Up	High	Variable	Many to Many
Circuits	Voice (PCM, ADPCM), Video, Voice and Data	Fixed Low to High	None	Fixed	One to One
Bursty Voice	Silence Suppressed Voice	Low	High	Fixed	One to One
Bursty Video	Compressed Video	Low to Medium	Medium to High	Fixed	One to One

Voice communications have moderate (64 Kbits/second) to low (10–12 Kbits/second) bandwidth requirements, may exhibit burstiness if silence is suppressed, and cannot tolerate delay. Voice communications only connect two discrete points.

Frame relay is an interface protocol that provides efficient transport of variable units of data (frames) from several logical sources to several logical destinations over one physical connection. Frame relay will provide up to 55 Mbits/second of bandwidth-on-demand, with 2.048 Mbits/second and below being typical in the debis Systemhaus network, and frame relay is a variable latency service. So, based upon the foregoing discussion of requirements, frame relay is a good choice for our traditional data and bursty data requirements, but not for all of the requirements of debis Systemhaus. Although great strides are being made in areas such as voice over frame relay, many of the voice requirements are still traditional PCM/ADPCM voice, and many of the circuit requirements are still for traditional fixed latency circuits that cannot typically be guaranteed by frame relay, except when the circuit speed is very low and the backbone transport speed is very high.

Backbone Architecture

What debis Systemhaus opted for was a multiservice backbone architecture, as shown in Figure 11.1, that provides support for any type of service, with frame relay being only one of the interface options. This architecture provides the most flexibility as it allows any type of service to be provisioned either by direct access to the backbone network (either at the "edge" of the network via service multiplexers located within the network, or, more conveniently, on the customer premises, as shown in the lower-right corner of Figure 11.1) or to the high-speed switching core of the network, as needed based upon customer demand.

The next step was to evaluate options for the backbone network: the choices are circuit switching, high-speed packet switching, frame switching, and cell switching, such as ATM. Although the choice of ATM as a backbone switching technology might seem obvious, it most certainly was not: debis Systemhaus researched each of the options very carefully. During the time frame of the evaluation, standards for SONET/SDH had breathed new life into traditional TDM circuit switching by making it a simple, viable alternative at very high speeds; high-speed variants of packet and frame switching were emerging, and true standards for all needed aspects of ATM (including the very key specifications for voice adaptation and many aspects of operations, administration, provisioning and maintenance, intercarrier signaling, and service interworking) were not yet available.

11.3 Consolidated Network Selection and Migration

The debis Systemhaus selection and migration process was for a carrier-class backbone network that would accommodate frame relay as well as any other information that was presented to the network to transport. The considerations and process, therefore, were very different from previous case studies; in fact, they more closely resembled the types of deliberations that the carriers providing the frame relay services to our previous case study subjects may have experienced.

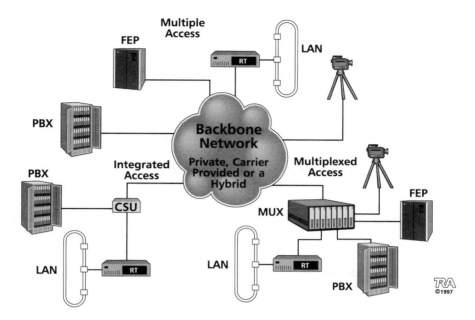

Figure 11.1 The Backbone Network

11.3.1 Business Aspects

The communications networks of debis Systemhaus and its internal and external customers have evolved over time. The evolution has been driven by business needs and changing technologies. Enterprise networks of the past, and many that still exist today, are clearly divided based upon the type of information they carry.

For instance, debis Systemhaus was operating a voice network, with its own technicians, engineers, management, and budget; as well as an SNA data network, with its own technicians, engineers, management, and budget; a LAN router network, with its own technicians, engineers, management, and budget; and a leased-line data network, with its own technicians, engineers, management, and budget.

Many forces, both technical and financial, are causing the lines between these networks to blur to a point where the separate networks within a given company are inextricably interwoven. From the technical side, users of traditionally all-voice networks increasingly need to transport new formats of information such as high-speed voice band data and fax information. These new requirements have caused a reevaluation of what the voice network does and whether it really should be treated totally independently of other networks. The data side of the network is also carrying voice information in the form of digital voice, voice data files, such as voice mail, and integrated voice/data applications. Enabling technologies such as T1 TDM, high-speed synchronous transfer mode (STM), and ATM/cell relay are also allowing voice and data to be combined with no loss of information integrity or substantial added delay.

From the financial side, as competition increases and profits fall, companies are tending to downsize support staffs and look for other ways to decrease costs. Often, this means combining historically separate voice and data staffs, and the networks they support. In many cases, in addition to reducing costs and overhead, a more easily managed and capable network emerges from the joining of multiple networks to provide integrated voice, data, video, and image services to the enterprise.

The consolidated network goal of debis Systemhaus is a network in which voice, data, video, and image information is combined on common communications facilities using common switching equipment. Although video is not a current requirement, it is a foreseeable future requirement.

A discussion of network integration requires us to look at the extent to which these different types of communications traffic are commingled on the common facilities. The traditional, hands-down choice for integrated networks is circuit switching. Traditional circuit switches use networks of channelized T1 and E1 facilities to interconnect concentration points at relatively high speeds.

11.3.2 Technical Aspects

The technical evaluation was performed in such a manner as to be consistent with the business requirements stated above. The backbone architectural direction had been set, and it was the function of the technical selection process to select first the technology and then the hardware platform for the realization of the architecture.

Backbone Selection Process

The first step was to review the options available and the pros and cons of each as an integrated multimedia backbone transport. The candidate technologies are

- circuit switching/time division multiplexing
- packet switching
- frame switching
- cell relay

A discussion of each individually will be followed by a discussion of their suitability as a backbone technology for the integrated multiservice debis Systemhaus network.

Circuit switching/time division multiplexing The simplest way of sending information from one place to another, especially across a WAN, is via a fixed communication path or circuit (Figure 11.2). The term "circuit" implies a bidirectional communication path where both endpoints of the circuit may act as either sender or receiver. A circuit can be described as either a logical circuit (a connection from point A to point B, disregarding the equipment actually used to make the connection) or as a physical circuit (taking into account all of the electronic componentry and wires used to make the connection). But whether a circuit is logical or physical, it is a fixed path between two points with a fixed and very small delay; most of the delay is attributable to the distance being traveled, and almost none is attributable to modifications made to the signal or information being transported. Examples of communications circuits in our everyday lives include data leased lines connecting two computers or connecting terminal equipment and a computer, a copper cable connecting an ASCII terminal and an asynchronous host, an IBM 3270 terminal connected via a multipoint circuit to an IBM host computer, a 64-Kbit/second LAN-to-LAN connection via a channel within an E1 digital transmission frame, or possibly a voice connection from Atlanta to London.

Circuits have characteristics that make them very desirable for certain types of communication. Circuits are *protocol transparent,* which means they transfer bits from sender to receiver without modification or interpretation. Circuits can provide very high throughput with very low associated delay (latency). The delay associated with a given circuit is affected by

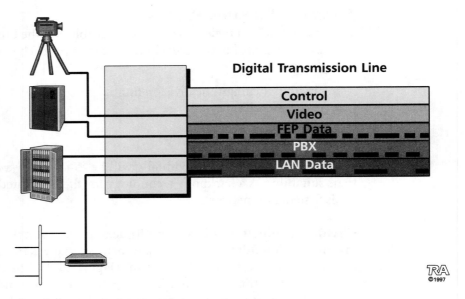

Figure 11.2   Backbone Transport Options: TDM

very few physical factors. Therefore, latency of a circuit is virtually constant. This is very important from a network design standpoint. Circuits are also very simple: you can, figuratively speaking, start at the sender and follow the "wire," or at a minimum a constant bit rate connection, through its entire path, even though it may go several thousand miles, and eventually arrive at the receiver.

Even with all of the good news about circuits, there are also some possible drawbacks. Circuits are capable of providing substantial amounts of bandwidth, such as a dedicated fiber circuit providing gigabits per second of data transfer capability, but the cost of providing the bandwidth increases with the amount of bandwidth required. This leads to a second limitation: the inability to share a circuit's bandwidth among users. Sharing the bandwidth would allow sharing the cost, which reduces the cost per user. Another possible drawback of basic circuits is that they only connect two endpoints at any one time, which precludes circuits from providing capabilities such as mesh networks, rerouting, or conference calling without the use of additional equipment.

There are two distinct types of circuits: fixed circuits and switched circuits. The only fundamental difference is the duration of the circuit, or the length of time it connects the two endpoints. Fixed circuits, such as the data leased line mentioned above, are generally established through some type of installation or provisioning process and are in place for days, months, or years. A switched circuit, on the other hand, is established by some sort of dialing or operator command and is generally in place only for seconds, minutes, or hours. Other than duration, however, fixed and switched circuits have identical properties: they provide fixed bandwidth, are protocol transparent, and provide low latency for the amount of bandwidth. They are also simple end-to-end arrangements that can be traced from point A to point B and cannot be shared among users without additional equipment.

Packet switching   The second choice for the debis Systemhaus backbone network is a packet-switching network (see Figure 11.3), similar to their existing private X.25 network, but with higher-speed backbone trunks. Packet switching utilizes physical circuits as its basic building blocks but uses individual physical circuits to carry information for several logical circuits. Packet-switching hardware is an example of the "additional equipment" that we referred to in the discussion of circuits that would be needed to allow circuit users to share data.

Unlike simple circuits, packet switching allows bandwidth to be shared among multiple users, can be measured and billed based upon actual usage per connection, and provides more or less bandwidth per user, as needed. And, also unlike circuits, protocol-intelligent packet-switching equipment interconnects the user's device to a packet-switching network. These special devices are often called packet assembler/disassemblers (PADs). PADs interpret the incoming information and perform certain operations that allow a single packet-switching connection to be shared by multiple users.

The process of bandwidth sharing, which is implemented by the interpretation and direction (or switching) of packets, frames, and/or cells, introduces additional variation in packet network latency. The additional latency is affected by such factors as the size of the incoming packet, the number of users desiring to transmit simultaneously on a channel, and the bandwidth being consumed by internal network communications. Even though the factors affecting latency can be modeled and estimated, the design, implementation, and management of a packet network is more complex than for a circuit network. This complexity, however, has its benefits: lower per-user costs and the assurance that the user's data is transmitted reliably through the network. Reliable transmission is ensured by

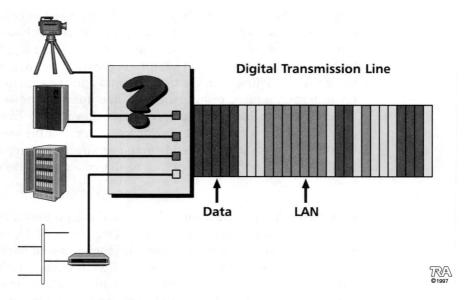

Figure 11.3   Backbone Transport Options: Packet Switching

retransmitting data between points in the network where it may have been corrupted.

Examples of packet-switching networks are those based upon X.25 and corollary CCITT and proprietary protocols and IBM's Systems Network Architecture with SDLC and related protocols.

Unlike circuits, in which the capability of the circuit to transport data is measured in bits, kilobits, megabits, or gigabits per second, packet network throughput is measured in packets per second (PPS). PPS can be translated to bits per second by multiplying the length of the packet in bytes or octets (units of eight bits) by eight bits per byte (octet) and then multiplying the result of that calculation by the number of packets per second. Bytes cancel each other and packets cancel each other, leaving bits per second, which can then be used to size the underlying physical circuit required to carry the multiplexed packet-switching information.

A user requiring little or no bandwidth transmits very few or no packets, decreasing the user's share of the circuit usage at one moment in time. A user requiring a higher throughput, however, transmits more packets, or longer packets, increasing that user's share of the circuit usage for a moment in time. Packet switching is best suited to data communications that can tolerate the variable latency associated with packet switching. Packet switching is not a good choice for traditional voice, video, or image communications.

Frame switching   Frame switching, not to be confused with the frame relay interface, uses the same variable-length units of information as packet switching; however, frame switching, like frame relay, relies on higher-layer protocols for retransmission of errored frames. If a variable-length *packet* is corrupted as it passes through the network, it will be retransmitted between intermediate packet switches inside the network; a frame switch will discard a corrupted *frame,* relying on a higher-layer protocol on a device outside the network to retransmit the frame, if needed. Some higher-layer protocols contain mechanisms that can correct certain single- and multibit errors in received frames, thereby alleviating the need for retransmission for most errors encountered while using error-correcting protocols. Error correction schemes, however, do require more overhead bits in the transmitted data.

A frame switch will discard a frame with a corrupted data payload or a corrupted address. Although this approach may not make intuitive sense to anyone who has been in data communications for a long time, it does make logical sense. Early packet protocols were designed for use on low-quality analog transmission facilities. With low-grade early analog facilities, it was likely an error would occur at some point in a transmission path. Therefore, the additional overhead of rechecking a packet's data integrity and retransmitting it, if needed, was almost a necessity. With the increasing deployment of digital facilities and fiber optic capabilities around the globe, the likelihood of an error during transmission has dropped dramatically.

At the same time, the processing power in the end system (for example, a 486-based PC communicating with an Intel Pentium-based server) has increased to the point where the end system may now process a sophisticated protocol stack such as TCP/IP. Such intelligence in the end system allows the responsibility of retransmission to be removed from the network and placed with the end system, the increased reliability and accuracy of the transport network reduces the likelihood that a retransmission will be needed, and the higher-speed transport will allow an end-to-end retransmission to be done much more quickly, if it is needed.

Using a sophisticated protocol such as TCP/IP with a traditional packet-switching protocol such as X.25 is much like using both nails and screws—the additional cost and overhead are not warranted. Both protocols offer error checking and retransmission, and the packet-switching network introduces additional overhead at each intermediate switching point in the network. It is also important to realize that the X.25 protocol has internal flow control mechanisms that will control the bandwidth given to a particular connection, while the aim of TCP/IP is to perform end-to-end flow control and provide as much bandwidth as possible, pushing the limits of the network. This is why frame switching has become prevalent, because frame switching does not have the retransmission overhead of packet switching.

One possible problem in both packet switching and frame switching occurs when an extremely long packet or frame is entering the packet or frame switch. The processor in the switch is tied up, and therefore unable to perform other tasks, until it reads the end of the incoming packet or frame. Other tasks that might be frozen out would include servicing other incoming data, switching data to other outbound circuits, and synchronization and management functions. This situation, called *unpredictable freeze-out,* can be alleviated somewhat by the use of a multiple-processor architecture (for example, a discrete I/O processor on each port and trunk card), but it still creates problems in actual operation. The problem of unpredictable freeze-out is less likely when processing interactive terminal traffic because of the short size of packets or frames (generally only several hundred bytes at the very most). Unpredictable freeze-out becomes more pronounced when processing maximum-length packets or frames being transmitted between Ethernet (maximum frame size 1,518 bytes), FDDI (maximum 4,500 bytes), token ring (maximum 8,196 bytes), or token bus (maximum 8,192 bytes) LANs.

Many manufacturers have avoided the effect of extremely long transmission units by parsing frames longer than a certain size into two or more frames for transmission and reassembling them at the destination so that the parsing is transparent to the destination device. The good news is that this process reduces the negative effects of very long packets, but the bad news is that it is presently done on a proprietary basis so its effectiveness is limited in mixed-manufacturer environments.

Frame switching is suitable for data communications and is seeing increased promise for transmission of voice, video, and image communications as well.

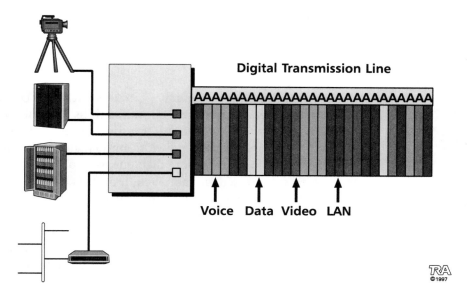

Figure 11.4 Backbone Transport Options: ATM/Cell Relay

Cell switching The fourth and final building block for communications systems considered by debis Systemhaus is the cell. A cell is a unit of information transfer in which the cell length and format of addressing and overhead information is identical, regardless of the content of the cell.

Cell switching performs no content check on the cell's data payload. A CRC on the header portion of the cell will indicate the integrity of the address and overhead portion of the cell. The only instance in which a cell's information will not be delivered is if the address is corrupted.

Cell switching, also referred to as fast-packet switching, cell relay, asynchronous transfer mode (ATM), or asynchronous time division multiplexing (ATDM), uses an adaption layer to perform standardized parsing of incoming data streams into fixed-length cells for transmission across a cell-switched network, which is often called a *cell-switched backbone.*

Cell switching or cell relay (see Figure 11.4) is well suited for all types of information transmission. Because information is transported in a cell relay network in fixed-length cells, a cell-relay-based network can provide fixed-latency services, such as voice or video or other circuit-type information, and variable-latency services, such as packet and frame switching or other packet-type information. A cell relay network may also switch cells from a user across the network backbone. Cell switching is a very important building block in integrated networks because of its ability to transport voice, traditional data, bursty LAN data, image, and video information equally well.

Backbone technology summary   Circuit switching/TDM is suitable for voice, data, video, and image communications. Circuit switching/TDM offers fixed, low-delay end-to-end transport but is wasteful of bandwidth and has no multiplexing or bandwidth-on-demand properties.

Packet switching allows more than one user to access the bandwidth by transporting addressed, variable-length packets from each user, provides for packet retransmission at intermediate points if data is corrupted, provides bandwidth-on-demand, and can be measured on a usage-per-connection basis. Packet switching is best suited to data communications.

Frame switching retains the fundamental characteristics of packet switching, but does not retransmit corrupted data within the frame-switching fabric. Frame switching relies on the higher-layer protocols for retransmission. Frame switching is well suited for data communications and is showing promise for use in voice, image, and video communications as well.

Cell relay switching is a high-speed switching mechanism that switches small, efficient, fixed-length cells with identical formats regardless of content: voice, data, video, or image. Cell relay, often referred to as fast-packet switching, ATM, or ATDM, is a foundation for all emerging modern communications.

Because frame and packet switching are not suitable for traditional telephony or circuit data requirements, they are eliminated from final consideration, and the decision is made between TDM circuit switching and ATM cell relay.

Results   The final result for the high-capacity/high-utilization density was to choose the T1/E1 narrowband ATM product offered by StrataCom, now part of Cisco. The product provided the variety of interfaces needed as well as the bandwidth efficiencies and an evolutionary path to full ATM, when needed. Overall bandwidth management efficiencies for the mix of traffic types that debis Systemhaus has put on the network are 180%, which means that each deutsche mark that they spend on transmission capacity on the network delivers 1.8 times the capacity that their old system was able to achieve.

11.4 Living with Frame Relay on a Consolidated Network Backbone

Debis Systemhaus completed the migration to the new network with a minimum of difficulty by leveraging the expertise and wisdom gained on their initial network installations at the sites migrating to the new consolidated network backbone. The debis Systemhaus network continues to expand to meet the needs of internal and external customers, and the revenues continue to grow as well.

One area where debis Systemhaus is still experiencing difficulties, and an area they think needs some improvement, is in the standardization of billing for usage-sensitive traffic. The tools available to perform the measurements of utilization, as well as the integration of the measurement tools to a financial billing system, leave a lot to be desired.

11.4.1 Anticipated Benefits

As mentioned earlier, debis Systemhaus improved their overall network efficiencies on all connections by 180% and realized an attendant savings in costs. Some of the cost savings were put into rerouting bandwidth to increase the efficiencies of the backbone network and its survivability during outages, some of the savings were passed along to the internal and external customers as an incentive to put their traffic on this network, and some of the savings were returned to the company as profit.

11.4.2 Unanticipated Benefits

Unanticipated benefits in the debis Systemhaus network fall into two areas: reliability/availability and bandwidth efficiencies for noncircuit data types.

Reliability/Availability

A combination of the highly redundant and resilient architecture of the chosen hardware platform, high-speed rerouting around failures, and use of switched ISDN to back up network access lines has resulted in much higher than anticipated network reliability and availability figures. For any given month, the average availability exceeds 99.99%. This has not only given existing internal and external customers the confidence to put even their most mission-critical application on the consolidated backbone network, but it has also made attracting availability-minded new customers, such as financial institutions and government agencies, to the network even easier.

Noncircuit Bandwidth Efficiencies

The second set of unanticipated benefits comes in the area of bandwidth efficiencies for noncircuit traffic, such as frame relay. While the overall bandwidth management efficiencies are a respectable 1.8 times, the bandwidth efficiencies achieved for typical frame relay applications such as LAN-to-LAN router connections and SNA over frame relay are many times in the 10 times to 15 times range, and in rare cases even higher. These results make it clear that a shift from traditional circuit data to shared-bandwidth frame relay is a key to further savings. A less significant, though substantial, level of savings could also be achieved by moving from traditional voice telephony, which is presently supported via 32-Kbit/second ADPCM connections with silence suppression, for a statistical average of about 12 Kbits/second per connection, to voice over frame relay, which is being used by other companies with great success at 6.5 to 8 Kbits/second per connection averages.

11.5 Future Plans

True 53-byte standards-based ATM is in the future for debis Systemhaus and is being introduced on a very limited basis where needed. Debis Systemhaus feels that the main driver for full-fledged ATM will be video applications, which are just now materializing in their environment.

11.6 Conclusion

The issues and areas of focus in this case study were very different from those of other case studies: this network was a large, multiservice backbone supporting frame relay as only one of its many interfaces. Issues of multiservice support that were important in this case study do, however, affect frame relay in carrier environments where other information types are also being carried on the same network infrastructure. Questions about traffic prioritization, backbone network engineering, latency and fairness issues, and other shared network issues arise more often in this environment than in even the frame-relay-only network environment.

The debis Systemhaus network is based upon ATM transport, and the engineers at debis Systemhaus have plans for further expansion of the ATM aspects of their backbone network. The next case study takes an in-depth look at another service provider/carrier class backbone networking environment, but the engineers discussed in the next case study are not so enamored with ATM; in fact, they have very strong feelings in favor of frame switching as a backbone transport and reluctantly implement ATM today largely because frame switching and/or IP are not yet available at the high speeds needed for the traffic demands placed on their network by their customers.

CHAPTER TWELVE

IP LAN Internetwork

From a philosophical point of view, the Internet is the closest humankind has yet come to one single global/universal mind. This chapter explores how some of the nerve centers of this universal mind are interconnected with synapses of frame relay and ATM.

12.1 Case Study Background

Pondering the configuration diagram of UUNET Technologies' network (Figure 12.1) is very impressive indeed. The observer will see all of the usual items associated with large-scale networks: 622-Mbit/second OC-12 fiber rings; numerous large Cascade 9000 frame relay switches; Fore ASX ATM switches; dual Fiber Distributed Data Interface (FDDI) rings; thousands of customer analog and ISDN switched connections; customer 56-Kbit/second, T1, and T3 connections; high-speed links to other carriers such as Metropolitan Fiber Systems' HLI network and WorldCom's WilPak, and LEC and CAP frame relay nets; and enough Cisco 75xx and 47xx routers to make any network technician's heart skip a beat. It is not until you realize that the diagram represents a single metropolitan hub in the UUNET network that the scale of this network really begins to become apparent. And when you realize that there are several of these hubs, each one individually costing as much as the entire UUNET network itself was worth only 18 months or so ago, you begin to get an appreciation not only for the scale of the network but also for its rapid growth.

Though today it is a massive multi-layered IP network with regional frame relay switching running across an ATM core switching fabric with aggregate capacity measured in multiple gigabits per second, UUNET had much humbler beginnings. Founded in 1987 and headquartered in Fairfax, Virginia, UUNET Technologies, Inc., is a supplier of a comprehensive range of Internet access options, applications, and consulting services to businesses, professionals, and online service providers. UUNET's customers choose from a variety of applications and services including

- turnkey World Wide Web server hosting
- WWW content development services
- front-end client and LAN software options
- network integration and consulting services
- a wide range of network access options

UUNET's long-term technology strategy is to provide a single source of easily accessible, useful, secure, and reliable Internet communications for the full range of applications, from commercial/consumer transactions and information dissemination to business collaboration and database research access. To that end, UUNET is expanding its high-performance network infrastructure, in part through an agreement with Microsoft; integrating and expanding its suite of value-added products and services; investing in its network operations and technical support infrastructure; and building and leveraging relationships with strategic partners. UUNET is owned by WorldCom, which also owns Metropolitan Fiber Systems.

UUNET's network infrastructure allows local Internet access to users in 845 cities, 516 of them outside the United States. The company's Internet access options include its dedicated leased line and AlterDial® analog and ISDN services. In addition, UUNET offers a comprehensive Internet security product family including the Gauntlet™ Firewall System (a hardware and software fire wall solution that protects a company's internal resources and information from unauthorized access) and a complete security consulting service.

The company's technical staff monitors network status via its Network Operations Center, which operates 24 hours per day, seven days per week,

UUNET GLOBAL NETWORK

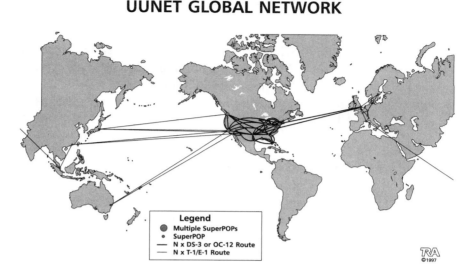

Figure 12.1   UUNET Global Network

and is backed up by uninterruptible power systems and diesel-powered generators.

This case study represents a single network larger than all of the other networks discussed in this book combined, and then some. This case study, although probably not as directly applicable to your situation as the other case studies, is important for a number of reasons. First, although the network is measured in terms of very large numbers, the architecture can be scaled to fit a wide variety of cases. Second, the architects of this network are so far out on the technology curve that they are developing solutions to problems that will not become issues in smaller networks for years to come. Third, this case study is not about an end user network, but rather a carrier network, and it will give the end user a feeling for what issues exist inside the mysterious "cloud" that appears on virtually all network drawings.

12.2 Before Frame Relay

UUNET is positioned as a backbone network for customers who aggregate Internet traffic. These customers may be corporate customers whose employees dial in to UUNET, corporate customers with their own networks who have already gathered together the traffic of their own internal customers to place on one or more UUNET connections, smaller Internet Service Providers (ISPs), or even large network service providers in their own right. Before the big boom in Internet services and connectivity, the typical customer, be they ISP or corporate accounts, was 56 Kbits/second. Typical customers now connect at T1 rates of 1.5 Mbits/second or T3 rates of 45 Mbits/second.

12.2.1 Business Aspects

Unlike a general-purpose carrier positioned to transport any type of information, UUNET specializes in one type of information only: packets conforming to the agreed-upon conventions of the Internet Protocol. While there may be other information contained inside the IP packets, the format of the information received and transported by UUNET is pure IP. This focus on IP-only traffic makes the UUNET network fairly simple by comparison to networks that transport all types of information. This model of transporting only a single protocol allows UUNET to provide one fairly narrowly focused service and all of the supporting services required to do one thing very well.

Requirements
UUNET states that their top network requirement is scalability. When viewed in a greater level of detail, the three issues that emerge, in order of importance, are scalability, capacity, and compatibility, but none at the sacrifice of reliability or network availability.

Scalability   UUNET views their role as one of building an industry, incorporating many companies in a single enterprise, and not as one company buying products from other companies and providing networking services. UUNET works hand in hand with suppliers of networking products as well as other service providers to look ahead at tomorrow's issues and to be sure that they are positioned for those coming challenges. The most important aspect of any decision UUNET makes from a network engineering and provisioning standpoint is to be sure that today's solutions will be supplemented, not replaced, by tomorrow's technologies—in other words, that today's systems are scalable.

Enhancement, not replacement, is the key to UUNET being able to grow without leaving a trail of used equipment in its wake. UUNET uses an outward push approach that involves constantly updating the core of the network so that existing networking systems are being pushed closer and closer to the customers. This approach works very well as customers' needs mature and customers begin to demand more and more sophistication.

A look at UUNET's network evolution will help make their approach more clear. UUNET has been through three major steps of network evolution since their founding in 1987, which can be characterized in terms of the technologies that formed the core of the UUNET network: the Router Era, the Frame Relay Era, and the ATM Era.

The Router Era was characterized by lower-speed customer connections, typically 56 Kbits/second, connected to UUNET routers, which were interconnected by 10-Mbit/second Ethernet LANs and 100-Mbit/second FDDI rings within the UUNET facility, and then interconnected to other UUNET sites via T1 or fractional T1 long-haul leased telco circuits. During the Router Era, all aspects of networking were incorporated in the routers, and routers formed the core of the network switching fabric at the time.

Customer requirements were slightly different, depending on the customer, but tended to be 56-Kbit/second leased-line interconnection for corporate customers and 56-Kbit/second leased lines or fractional T1 lines from smaller ISPs. During this era, it must be remembered, the Internet had not yet been commercialized, electronic mail between academic researchers represented the bulk of network traffic, and bandwidth-intensive applications like World Wide Web browsers were only in the concept stages.

The next step, the Frame Relay Era, is characterized by the insertion of frame relay switching into the core of the network. By utilizing a core switching capability that was decoupled from the routers themselves, UUNET was able to gain much more control of the operation of the switching aspects of the network and to leverage the capability and power of the routers. By utilizing frame relay's ability to control the flow of information within the network (to a far greater extent than possible with routers), UUNET was able to make the operation of the network more deterministic, to better utilize resources and to provide a more reliable, consistent, and higher-speed service to their customers.

The move into the Frame Relay Era was driven in large part by the commercialization of the Internet and the surge in customer growth. The typical customer had gone from a 56-Kbit/second or fractional T1 demand to a T1, and in many cases T3, demand, and the total number of customers had also grown very rapidly. Bandwidth-intensive applications like the World Wide Web browser from Netscape and Microsoft had become the norm, and the actual information content of the connections from customers had become much more dense. In the Router Era, customer connections would typically transmit an email message every now and then, and the biggest issue was connectivity more than it was capacity: a 56-Kbit/second line would not be transmitting information bits constantly but rather "fill in" bits that could be ignored by the router. The commercialization of the Internet brought big demands from customers sitting at personal computers waiting for responses, and with it much more tightly packed data circuits. If data circuits were utilized 10% to 20% during the Router Era, it would be a lot, but circuits connecting to UUNET during the Frame Relay Era could be very nearly 100% utilized.

While the Router Era was characterized by T1 or fractional T1 interconnection between UUNET sites, the Frame Relay Era was characterized by 45-Mbit/second T3 connections between UUNET sites and a big jump in the number of UUNET sites.

The third evolutionary step was the ATM Era. Just as frame relay supplemented the router capability and created a new network core based upon frame switching in the move from the Router Era to the Frame Relay Era, so too does ATM supplement the capability of frame relay and create a new core for the network. As much as UUNET would like to have scaled their frame relay network to higher speeds, their research and work with the leading manufacturers in the industry indicated that ATM was the only technology currently available that could provide the next leap in network capacity. UUNET was faced with a move to ATM in 1997 or with the prior frame-relay-based switching core bulging to an unmanageable 700-plus 45-Mbit/second T3 lines. UUNET views the move to ATM in the core of the network as a mandatory tactical move to allow the network to grow and support more traffic to and from more locations.

The ATM Era is also being driven by an increasingly sophisticated customer base—a customer base that relies more and more every day on the Internet and Internetlike services to move the information that is the foundation of their businesses. And UUNET is seeing greater and greater demand for customer T3 terminations as well as interconnect arrangements with other carriers. The ATM Era is characterized by 622-Mbit/second OC-12 fiber optic connections between UUNET sites.

Capacity   Although capacity would seem to be the primary issue, it really is not. The ability to scale the capacity upward is far more important. A high-capacity system that is static would be surpassed very quickly by a dynamic yet scalable system, and UUNET is very aware of this fact.

Compatibility   UUNET does not promote one technology over any other, but rather leverages the right combination of available technologies to do their overall job. For this reason, it is important that all products and systems be compatible on some level, and preferably at the highest possible level, IP. As an example, in many metropolitan areas, customers purchase an interconnection to UUNET from a local exchange carrier (LEC) or competitive access provider (CAP). The customer purchases a T1 access circuit from the LEC or CAP. The T1 circuit leaves the customer premises on copper wire and goes to a central office or point-of-presence where it is multiplexed with data streams from a number of other customers and placed onto a metropolitan fiber ring. At the point nearest the UUNET facility, the signal is taken off the fiber, demultiplexed into its original form, and sent to UUNET as one of 28 T1 channels within a channelized T3 circuit or as an individual T1, depending on the size of the UUNET facility and capacity from the carrier.

The breaking down of the metropolitan fiber ring into individual channels and transport to UUNET in a T3 or T1 format is the highest level of compatibility today between the LEC/CAP and UUNET. There is additional equipment cost and delay as well as potentially lower network reliability because of the total number of devices and systems involved compared to systems that would be compatible at higher levels. If, for instance, UUNET were able to become an "IP central office" and to take IP traffic directly off of the metropolitan fiber ring, the end-to-end connection would be greatly simplified, more reliable, less expensive, and with less delay.

IP central offices, among other futuristic initiatives, such as IP over SONET, may be more than just talk in the packet-oriented future where higher- and higher-speed packet and frame technologies reduce traditional arguments about delay to the stuff of the historic low-speed past, and packets and frames riding over extremely high-speed transport systems carry all types of information: data, video, and telephony.

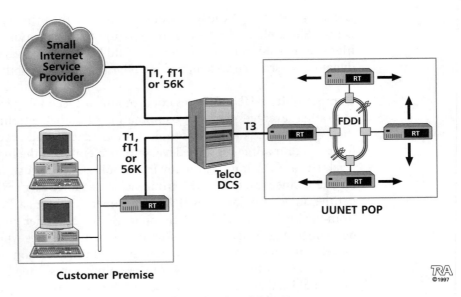

Figure 12.2   Pre-Frame-Relay Physical Architecture

12.2.2 Technical Aspects

Despite the apparent complexity of their network, UUNET has one and only one application: moving IP packets.

Communications Environment

Prior to widespread implementation of frame relay in the UUNET network, UUNET was primarily a traditional Internet service provider offering an IP service based upon router technology. In that era, customer connections were predominantly 56 Kbits/second, with a few T1 and fractional T1 accounts for, more often than not, other smaller ISPs (Figure 12.2).

The customer and smaller ISP connections would come into a telephone company central office (CO) and would be groomed (combined) on a Telco Digital Cross-connect System (DCS) into channelized T1s for delivery to the UUNET site. At the UUNET site, several routers would be linked together by a high-speed medium such as 10-Mbit/second Ethernet or 100-Mbit/second FDDI rings. Local traffic would be routed to other routers in

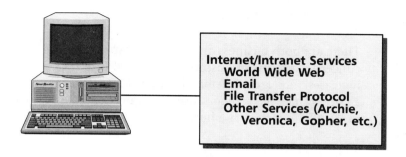

Figure 12.3 Pre-Frame-Relay Logical Architecture

the same room and switched back out to other local sites, and traffic going out on the long-distance network would be routed to other UUNET sites with a similar internal architecture.

Logical Architecture
The pre- and post-frame-relay logical architecture is exactly the same: access to Internet/intranet services, such as World Wide Web browsing, electronic mail, file transfer services, remote access services such as Telnet, and other file management and information retrieval services such as Archie, Veronica, and Gopher (Figure 12.3).

12.3 Frame Relay: Selection and Migration

UUNET's use of frame relay is as part of an IP carrier network and is strategic in nature. The engineers and managers at UUNET prefer frame-based protocols in general, and frame relay specifically, for their efficiency compared to alternative transports. For instance, even though ATM is being deployed heavily in the core of the network, for tactical reasons UUNET is greatly concerned with the convergence of network cost constraints, increases in demand, customer pricing pressures, and ATM inefficiencies when compared to a pure frame relay network infrastructure.

12.3.1   Business Aspects

There are both business and technical aspects to all of UUNET's areas of concern. In terms of business impact, all three concerns—network cost increases, increases in demand, and ATM inefficiencies when compared to a pure frame relay network infrastructure—can be equated to money and to UUNET's success as a business.

Network Cost Increases

As UUNET is in the traditional "middle person" role in networking, they are experiencing the traditional problems associated with that role. The companies from whom UUNET purchases bandwidth are moving out of the cheap data transport 1980s when the largest carriers were selling bandwidth at what amounted to bargain rates because of grossly overconfigured domestic fiber networks with capacity to spare, and are moving into the high-demand 1990s, a time period where demand is increasing exponentially and new investments are being made in the fiber plants to increase their capacities, and these same carriers are trying to recover costs and to make profits. This creates a need for a greater focus on bandwidth costs as the cost of bandwidth rises.

In the simple language of business, the problem can be stated this way: During the 1980s, bandwidth supply was high and demand, while growing, was still low compared to the amount of bandwidth available. This kept bandwidth prices depressed. In the 1990s and beyond, demand will be high compared to available bandwidth. This will allow the carriers to demand higher prices from their customers.

Increases in Demand

The two main reasons for increases in demand are more network-intensive applications and aggregation of lower-speed traffic. Both of these converge to define the issue of increases in demand.

Early Internet applications were based on simple text communications, represented as short email messages or relatively simple interactive sessions between unintelligent terminals and remote computers. These fairly simple applications that placed comparatively little demand on the transport network have been replaced with information-rich communications such as sizable multimedia emails with attachments (images, spreadsheets, desktop publishing documents, and even application programs) or World Wide Web pages formatted using HTML that include images, sound, and

Java-based animations and often exceed 100 KB each. Additionally, the easy-to-use point-and-click nature of the Web browser allows even the most inexperienced second grader to request dozens of large HTML pages per hour.

The second leading reason for growth in bandwidth demand is aggregation. Even if each user were only able to create a modest demand for bandwidth, the sheer number of users now online has grown tremendously. The number and variety of people in our society who rely regularly on the Internet is staggering—and so is the aggregate demand of their individual uses of the Internet.

ATM Inefficiencies

In years gone by network connections, especially higher-bandwidth connections, were purchased because they were more cost-efficient, and not always because they were needed for their larger capacities. This is no longer true. Even though UUNET uses ATM in their backbone for tactical reasons (because ATM is the only technology available today at the higher speeds needed in the UUNET backbone), UUNET is far from pleased with the additional overhead that ATM brings along as a result of its original multimedia mission to this IP-packet-only environment.

Any inefficiencies in network bandwidth utilization can be directly tied to costs—and, more specifically, not to start-up costs, but to recurring costs, so that any inherent network efficiencies take their financial toll every month. In the case of ATM specifically, these inefficiencies can be brutal. For example, the most common IP packet sizes on the UUNET network are 64 bytes (for acknowledgments used in interactive and file transfer protocols), 384 bytes (seemingly a common maximum transmission unit size for devices that divide large packets or frames into smaller ones for network efficiencies), and 1,500 bytes (the maximum frame size that will be generated by Ethernet networks).

If the 64-byte packet were transmitted by frame relay, it would only require an additional 5 bytes of overhead (the 2 bytes of flags would be replaced with frame relay flags, the 3-byte frame relay header and 2-byte frame check sequence would be added). This would represent only 7.8% additional overhead (Figure 12.4) (calculated as the ratio of the additional 5 bytes to the original 64-byte IP packet). If this frame is transmitted over ATM, however, the overhead is much worse. If an ATM switching fabric, such as that introduced into the UUNET backbone to allow the use of OC-12 circuits, were used to transmit the 64-byte IP packet, the

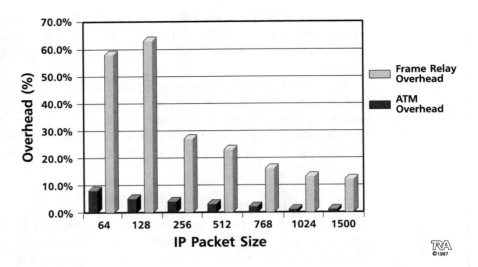

Figure 12.4   Frame Relay versus ATM Overhead for Selected IP Packet Sizes

inefficiencies of ATM for the single protocol environment begin to become apparent. In this specific case, the overhead attributable to ATM would be 10 bytes of protocol overhead (because the 64-byte IP packet would require two ATM cells to transport, each having 5 bytes of overhead) plus 32 bytes of "padding" overhead (because the 48-byte payloads of the two fixed-length ATM cells would not be completely filled by a 64-byte frame). In this case, the ATM overhead would represent 57.8%.

In the instance of the 384-byte IP packet, frame relay overhead would be 1.3%, while ATM overhead would be 10.41%. In the instance of the 1500-byte IP packet, the frame relay overhead would be .33%, while the ATM overhead would be 13.06%. The only thing that needs to be done now to transform this from being a technical discussion into being a business case is to multiply the respective percentages by the monthly cost for a transmission facility to determine the amount of money being spent every month simply for the protocol overhead: for instance, if monthly network transmission costs were $1 million, a frame-relay-only solution would cost $13,000 per month for protocol overhead, while an ATM solution would cost $104,100 per month for protocol overhead, assuming that only 384-byte packets were transmitted.

Product Selection Process

When UUNET had settled on their frame-relay-centric architecture, they brought candidate switches from "all the usual suspects" into their lab in Fairfax, Virginia, and subjected them to rigorous testing. These devices were tested not only to see if they complied with published specifications regarding their basic functionality but were also stress-tested for processing load, network management capabilities, reliability, power usage, temperature generation, and myriad other tests great and small. When all was said and done, UUNET chose the B-STDX 9000 switch from Cascade Communications, Inc. When asked why the Cascade 9000 was chosen, the lead test engineer expressed the engineering team's feelings that the switch performed extremely well. The consensus was that the Cascade B-STDX 9000 was sufficiently scalable and had exceptional performance because it was designed and built from the ground up as a true frame relay switch, the only one among the units tested.

A similar evaluation process was executed when the Fore Systems ASX switches were selected to provide the ATM switching core, and with similar results.

Migration

The migration from an all-router network to a network with a frame relay core was accomplished by outfitting key existing routers with frame relay capability and connecting them to the new Cascade switches. The ATM switching core was implemented in a similar fashion, with T3 links being provided from the new ATM "hubs," the term used by UUNET for their equivalent of points-of-presence or central offices, to the non-ATM hubs to ensure the greatest reuse of equipment in the new network and the minimum negative impact on the existing customer base.

12.3.2 Technical Aspects

From an OSI model perspective, UUNET is adding increasingly better levels of performance and control over the course of time and leveraging them to keep costs as low as possible while providing a technically superior backbone network. This approach is due in part to their single-protocol focus, but it is also being driven by their remarkable growth and need to deploy an architecture that is scalable and manageable.

Technical Aspects of the Migration from the Router Era to the Frame Relay Era

The initial network, circa 1987, was based solely on router technology. The router platform provided all physical layer (Layer 1), data link layer (Layer 2), and network layer (Layer 3) capabilities. For router manufacturers, the focus area of the majority of research and development dollars flowing into router technologies was Layer 3, and not a great deal of work was being done on expanding the Layer 2 or Layer 1 capabilities of the basic router. With a single-protocol approach (that is, solely IP routing), much more of the processing power of the routers in the network could be focused on the routing function, and much less of the processing power would be utilized on protocol discrimination and multiprotocol routing because this job would already have been accomplished by routers or other access devices outside the network prior to the delivery of an IP packet to UUNET.

Comer (1988, p. 67) states that the Layer 3 protocol used in UUNET, the Internet Protocol,

> provides an unreliable, best-effort, connectionless, packet delivery system, analogous to the service provided by network hardware. The service is called *unreliable* because delivery is not guaranteed. The packet may be lost, duplicated or delivered out of order, but the Internet will not detect such errors, nor will it inform sender or receiver. The service is called *connectionless* because each packet is treated independently from all others. A sequence of packets sent from one machine to another may travel over different paths, or some may be lost while others are delivered. Finally, the service is called *best-effort* because the Internet makes an earnest attempt to deliver packets. That is, the Internet does not discard packets capriciously; unreliability arises only when resources are exhausted or underlying networks fail.

Although IP networks were designed explicitly to make good on the "best-effort" promise, there were certain issues related to the scaling of IP-based networks that caused problems. Four of these were solved by UUNET with frame relay: the networkwide ripple effects of topology changes, the smoothing and efficient handling of traffic flows, network efficiency related to router hop latency, and wide performance ranges due to the nondeterministic nature of IP traffic.

IP performance relating to topology changes   One aspect of IP routing that greatly affects performance of router networks as they grow is that IP routers each keep a topology table, a "map" of the network. When any event occurs that changes the network topology, every router needs to be made aware of the change. Although the specific name and format of the message may differ depending upon which routing protocol is being used, the net effect is the same: whenever a network-topology-affecting event occurs, bandwidth- and performance-stealing inter-router messages are generated to all routers so that all routers are aware of the change and may route accordingly.

This problem was solved by frame relay because the entire frame relay network is viewed by the router as a giant physical leased line (access) with a number of smaller logical leased lines (PVCs) inside. When a problem occurs inside the IP network, the Layer 2 rerouting is performed transparently to the Layer 3 frame relay network, and therefore no router notification is performed and no router event notification messages are generated. This limits the router topology event messages only to provisioning events, when bandwidth is added, deleted, or rearranged, and truly catastrophic network failures, which rarely occur.

Path-oriented routing of traffic flows and traffic shaping The connectionless nature of IP allows the network to be highly dynamic and flexible in case of network changes, but it creates a very challenging environment to monitor and manage. Because IP packets can go in any direction and may be duplicated or discarded, traffic studies are all but impossible, and building a rational model of a network, especially one that is growing, in order to judge the impact of network changes or additions is almost impossible as well. This problem is only a small one when the network is small; managers of such small networks often resort to educated guessing and adjust their approach based upon the results they observe. This approach, however, does not work in a network of any reasonable size.

Additionally, when the route metrics of a given route change, the route becomes more attractive and is therefore used more heavily, up to the point of saturation. This thwarts all attempts to level loads across the network and use all routes and bandwidth equally. An example would be a router network based on 56-Kbit/second terrestrial circuits. When the first T1 link is added to the network, it becomes a better route because its available bandwidth metric is approximately 24 times better than the 56-Kbit/second routes, and the routers use that route if at all possible, abandoning the 56-Kbit/second routes and possibly saturating the T1 circuit.

These problems are solved by frame relay because frame relay provides deterministic paths through the network, based upon PVCs that UUNET has implemented using Cascade-supported capabilities based on standard frame relay parameters.

Traffic shaping is a set of rules that describe traffic flow and provides UUNET a mechanism to ensure the traffic transmission behavior of guaranteed and best-effort packets. Guaranteed packets must be delivered according to some time constraint and with high reliability. Best-effort packets are delivered to the best of the network's ability after the guaranteed packets have been delivered. In Cascade nomenclature, there are three types of frames, coded by color: green, amber, and red, like a traffic light.

Green frames are never discarded in the network except under the most extreme, catastrophic circumstances. Green frames identify packets where the number of bits received during the current time interval, including the current frame, is less than the committed burst size.

Amber frames identify packets where the number of bits received during the current time interval, including the current frame, is greater than the committed burst rate but less than the excess burst size. Amber frames are forwarded with the discard eligible (DE) bit set and are eligible for discard if they pass through a congested node.

Red frames identify packets where bits received during the current time period, including the current frame, exceed the excess burst size. Red frames are forwarded with the DE bit set. When Cascade's Graceful Discard feature is enabled, red frames are forwarded by noncongested nodes but are discarded first by congested nodes. If the Graceful Discard feature is not enabled, then red frames are always discarded.

The meaning of the DE bit is maintained to ensure compatibility with other networks to which UUNET, or other Cascade networks, might be interconnected, but the Graceful Discard feature potentially provides better throughput, enhanced performance, and better utilization of network bandwidth.

Router hop latency   In the former router-only network, as the router network grew, so too did the number of intermediate routers, or hops, that an IP packet had to traverse on its way through the network. The growth of a mesh-interconnected router network causes three basic problems:

1. The routers had to be larger, more expensive, and more complex to handle the total number of ports required to fully or partially mesh-interconnect the routers.
2. The amount of tandem/transit traffic (that is, trunk-to-trunk or non-terminating traffic) traversing a router taxed the router's resources and diminished its overall capacity.

3. The two items above result in a higher accumulated delay because a packet must be read entirely into a router before it is processed and forwarded, resulting in increased delays as the number of hops increased, and can, in fact, also be a problem in some frame relay switch implementations.

UUNET solved this problem by using frame relay and implementing PVCs connecting city pairs such that the various routers at the edges of the network appear, from a Layer 3/IP routing standpoint, to all be adjacent, which in fact they are because they are all directly connected via Layer 2 frame relay PVCs acting in the role of the former point-to-point leased lines, but far more cost-effectively and efficiently. And this can be done very cost-efficiently because several logical PVCs can be statistically multiplexed onto a single high-speed frame relay access connection.

Improving service levels and availability Service levels and availability are improved dramatically in the UUNET network as a result of the combination of the three characteristics above plus the implementation of fault-tolerant system configurations inside the network, use of route diversity and rerouting in the backbone network, and the use of uninterruptible power supplies and, in the case of large hubs, diesel backup power generation systems.

Migration

Migration was as described above. The existing routers were rehomed to Cascade B-STDX 9000 switches inside the network, forming a Layer 2 switching fabric. ATM switches were introduced as a third evolutionary step as a means of taking advantage of 622-Mbit/second OC-12 backbone capacity both within the long-distance national domestic U.S. network and within specific metropolitan areas as well. Because of the heavy demands being placed on the networks and dramatic growth, UUNET jumped right over the intermediate 155-Mbit/second OC-3 technology and went straight from a nationwide 45-Mbit/second T3 frame relay network to a 622-Mbit/second OC-12 network using ATM. ATM switches play three basic roles in the UUNET network:

1. Fore Systems ASX 1000s are used for core transit switching, where the wide area OC-12 bandwidth is terminated directly on the Fore switch.

2. Fore switches will also be used for connectivity inside hubs, where Fore switches connect various pieces of equipment inside the hub to provide intermachine connections.
3. ATM switches create regional and metropolitan networks within UUNET's architecture.

Configuration Issues

Cascade utilizes an enhanced "open shortest path first" (OSPF) algorithm inside their network. As frame relay frames are received into a Cascade switch, the frame's original frame relay header is stripped and a Cascade-specific frame header replaces it. The new Cascade-specific frame header provides support for Cascade's green/amber/red packet designation (as described earlier) and for OSPF routing information as well as maintaining the state of the original frame header bits so that an accurate frame relay standard header can be created when the frame once again leaves the Cascade portion of the network.

The OSPF routing protocol allows Cascade nodes to optimize traffic flows inside the frame relay network. OSPF route bandwidth is determined using a calculation, called *virtual bandwidth* by Cascade, which takes into account oversubscription and network control overhead. The calculation prescribed by Cascade is

$$\frac{0.95\% \times \text{Configured Bandwidth}}{K\%} = \text{Virtual Bandwidth}$$

where Configured Bandwidth is effectively the CIR, K equals the amount of oversubscription possible due to statistical multiplexing and tends to vary inversely with the size of the connection, and the result, Virtual Bandwidth, is the amount of bandwidth reserved by the OSPF algorithm each time a connection is added. It is important to allocate sufficient bandwidth for network control traffic and LMI, especially for highly saturated links.

Configuration after Migration

UUNET has developed an architectural concept that they call a "routing engine." The routing engine comprises several devices within the hub interconnected internally and externally to form the routing engine. The routing engine at each hub is interconnected by frame relay or ATM. One of the more subtle aspects of this architecture is that devices are arranged in groups as "peers" that leverage the dual redundancy features of the routing engine architecture so that network maintenance and upgrades can be

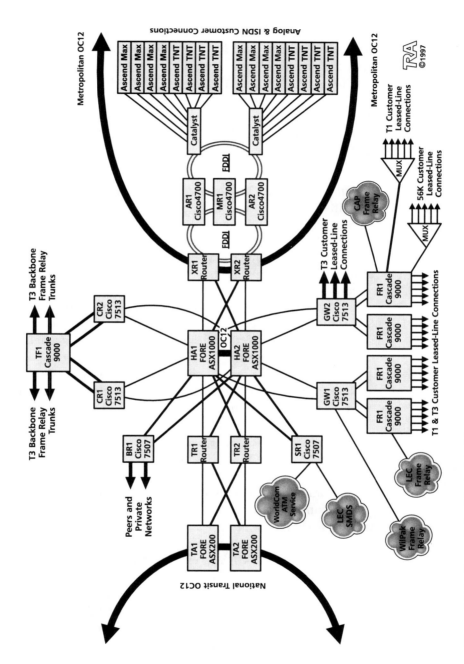

Figure 12.5   Frame Relay Physical Architecture

performed in such a way that only peer devices are affected, and if the peer devices involved are used for customer terminations, then only those directly connected customers need to be notified, and not the entire user population.

Physical architecture   Going in a counterclockwise direction, beginning with the national transit OC-12 network connections on the extreme left side of Figure 12.5, we will describe the function of each of the components found in a typical UUNET transit/metro hub:

- *National Transit OC-12 Interconnection:* Fore Systems ASX 200 ATM switches provide a point of termination for the national transit OC-12 fibers, and the pair of dual redundant switches are mesh-interconnected via OC-12 fiber cables within the hub to a pair of Cisco 7500 transit routers.
- *Metropolitan OC-12 Interconnection:* Dual redundant, fiber-interconnected Fore ASX 1000 switches provide connection between the hub and the metropolitan OC-12 ring. This partitioning is needed because of the increase in localized traffic in the Internet environment. While traffic in the precommercialized academic research Internet was global, a lot of the traffic on today's Internet is very localized—people reading their local hometown daily newspaper on the Internet, for instance, or checking local traffic reports, weather, or other information of local interest. The other area where we see this type of traffic "localization" is in the traffic that flows between the very large Internet IP carriers. The traffic flows between Sprint, Internet MCI, and UUNET are so great, in fact, that they took their traffic off the national Internet backbone ("for the good of the Internet") and made bilateral agreements to route traffic between themselves on direct routes.
- *Special Services Router:* Special services routers, such as the one shown in Figure 12.5 interconnecting the UUNET hub with the MFS HLI service and LEC SMDS services, allow for interconnection of different customer aggregation solutions. These routers allow for service measurement and service insulation/isolation for a variety of different services that can deliver IP traffic to UUNET.
- *Gateway Routers:* Dual redundant gateway routers are dual OC-3 connections attached to Cascade 9000 frame relay switches used to aggregate customer frame relay traffic in T1 and T3 formats either from the customers directly, through LECs and CAPs, or through the mul-

tiplexing of lower-speed 56-Kbit/second connections. The dual OC-3 connections provide an aggregate of 310 Mbit/second between the access Cascade switches and the Cisco 7500 gateway routers.

Large corporate customers, other ISPs, and other frame relay networks can also connect directly to the gateway routers. One of the big benefits of frame relay is the efficiency of bandwidth utilization as a function of oversubscription. Large customers, other networks, and ISPs have already squeezed the oversubscription benefits from their traffic and are providing sustained 45-Mbit/second T3 traffic flows. In these cases it does not make sense to connect them to the Cascade frame relay switches, but rather directly to the gateway routers.

- *Analog and ISDN Customer Connections:* Moving around the diagram to the right are the analog and ISDN customer connections, where the dial fabric meets the backbone network. The analog and ISDN customer connections come into the hub (or may be remotely located in a separate facility if this is desirable for collection of traffic in a different local calling area) on ISDN primary rate interfaces (PRIs) with 23 bearer channels each, either ISDN or what was originally analog. The PRIs terminate on Ascend MAX concentrators, which are attached to the FDDI rings via Catalyst Ethernet switches.

- *Access Routers and Multicast Service Router:* Between the two FDDI rings are the Cisco 47xx access routers and the multicast router. If the analog and ISDN customer concentrators are in the same hub, the FDDI ring will be within the hub facility, but if the dial fabric is remote, the interconnection facility, if needed, will be metropolitan area in scope and not in the same room.

- *XR Routers:* The XR routers are Cisco 7500 routers that provide cross-connection to the FDDI rings supporting the connection to the dial fabric as well as T3 links to the non-ATM "old hub." This architectural element allows the interconnection of the new and old technologies and a smooth, case-by-case migration until the old systems are no longer needed. This allows the migration to be noncritical path, both for UUNET and their customers, and allows the migration to take place over long periods of time, which is desirable for UUNET because it retains the investment in the old equipment longer.

- *Core Routers:* The core routers are the "brains of the backbone" and are logically connected to the other core routers in other cities in the UUNET network. It is these routers between which the pre-ATM T3 frame relay backbone PVCs exist. Information is delivered efficiently between city pairs using the Layer 2 frame relay switching fabric implemented on the transit frame switches, which are also Cascade 9000s.

■ *Border Router:* The border router allows connection to the Internet as well as other peers and private networks as needed.

Logical architecture   The post-frame-relay logical architecture is the same as the pre-frame-relay logical architecture (see Figure 12.3): access to Internet/intranet services, such as World Wide Web browsing, electronic mail, file transfer services, remote access services such as Telnet, and other file management and information retrieval services such as Archie, Veronica, and Gopher.

Operations and Network Management

UUNET has designed, engineered, built, and evolved their network to be managed remotely. UUNET has no remote network management personnel: all network management personnel are concentrated in Fairfax, Virginia.

Network management architecture   The UUNET network management architecture has three tiers: in-band, frame relay PVC based out-of-band, and dial-up. All of the console ports of all devices in the network are Ethernet connected to Cisco 2511 routers that allow access from any network management position in Fairfax to any remote device in the network.

The first tier of the UUNET network management architecture uses in-band network management, which utilizes the UUNET backbone to allow network management systems to communicate with the standards-based native Simple Network Management Protocol (SNMP) agent in each Cascade switch, Cisco router, and Fore Systems ATM switch.

UUNET also uses out-of-band network management utilizing a frame relay PVC provided by an alternate frame relay network service provider, ordinarily their colocation host. This provides network management connectivity that is independent of the UUNET network so that problems in the network being managed do not adversely affect the ability to manage the network.

A dial-up capability is also maintained as a last fallback position in case the in-band and out-of-band network management paths fail.

Operations   Day-to-day operations, administration, provisioning, and maintenance are performed with a combination of CascadeView, Cisco-Works, HP OpenView, and a suite of UNIX-based applications developed by UUNET for their own internal use to supplement and complement the operation of the other systems. UUNET has also implemented the Net-Cool product, a rules-based expert system that helps UUNET technicians coordinate and clarify alarm status based upon experience and reduce network disruption and downtime even further.

12.4 Living with Frame Relay

While deploying over $75 million worth of ATM technology, for tactical reasons UUNET remains enamored with frame relay and other frame-based protocols for their IP-only environment. UUNET's $300 million vote for the future of ATM was made reluctantly to allow them to take advantage of a great leap to OC-12 technology; had OC-12 frame relay been available, it would have been the technology of choice. UUNET continues to reap the benefits of frame relay because of the simplicity and elegance of frame relay itself as well as how it has been architected and implemented.

12.5 Lessons Learned and Future Plans

As far as "future plans" are concerned, UUNET is already so far out on the technology curve that they are several generational steps ahead of most other IP networks. UUNET makes a strong point of the fact that they do not back specific technologies, but rather work closely with their technology partners to use what is available and, to the extent possible, shape it for their own specific needs. The only definitive thing UUNET is willing to share about their future plans, and something with which their technology partners are apparently very familiar, is that UUNET anticipates growing 10-fold by the turn of the century.

12.6 Conclusion

To witness the technology deployed in UUNET and to hear such remarkably large numbers is to see the future. Information—from the Internet, intranets, and other sources—continues to drive humankind in new directions, continues to fuel growth in research in many fields, and, when done over great distances ignoring national boundaries and time zones, continues to bring people together. When we see huge, multigigabit demands and fiber optic connections pulsing with ruby light connecting megahubs that contain as much networking equipment as was previously required to operate the entirety of the UUNET network, it is fascinating not only from a technology viewpoint, but also from a human one. Every information exchange, every email, every home page, every digital photo, every voice clip, and every sonogram picture made available only further feeds our curiosity about our neighbors, wherever they may live, and only drives demand up more and more. And for each upward step in the demand curve, the Earth we all occupy gets just a little bit smaller.

In the next case study, we will learn about a very successful implementation of voice-over-frame-relay technology and find out how voice-over-frame-relay technology has fostered increased internal communication within a company while saving a substantial amount of money.

CHAPTER THIRTEEN

Data and Voice over Frame Relay

In this case study we will look at one of the early pioneers in adoption of voice over frame relay. Initially, Allen Lund Company installed voice over frame relay strictly for its cost-saving aspects, but as the technology has matured and improved, ALC has begun relying on it more and more until it has become an important business tool and almost indistinguishable from traditional "plain old telephone service" except, of course, for the cost.

13.1 Case Study Background

Caliber Technology, in the case study about the traditional IBM environment, was in the transportation industry, as was Greyhound, in the X.25 migration case study. So, too, is the subject of this case study: the Allen Lund Company (ALC). This was not by design as much as it was by coincidence. But this coincidence does highlight one of the most important aspects of why companies are adopting frame relay at such a rapid pace:

cost savings. In the trucking industry in particular, an industry characterized by rising personnel and fuel costs and myriad other barriers to profitability, the cost savings and bottom-line contribution of frame relay are critical to overall company success. It is not the technology but the business aspects that make frame relay such a success in these organizations.

Allen Lund Company, Inc., based in La Cañada, California, near Los Angeles, is a transportation broker dealing with over 5000 shippers and 6,000 carriers. Incorporated in 1978, the Allen Lund Company currently has 17 offices in 13 states. This broad geographical coverage allows ALC to manage the movement of customer freight anywhere in the United States and Canada, including complete truckloads or less-than-load (LTL) quantities of refrigerated, van, or flatbed freight. In 1996, Allen Lund Company brokered approximately 47,000 truckloads with a revenue of $72 million.

ALC has foregone complexity for simplicity, state of the art for what works well, and has kept costs to a bare minimum, even though network voice calls and data processing costs are still their number two budget item, after personnel costs. The ALC network consists of a central Integrated Business Computer (IBC) host, similar in size and function to an IBM AS/400, but substantially lower in initial and operating costs and faster, with twin mirrored 4-GB hard drives and over 100 MB of main memory. The IBC host uses the SCO UNIX operating system and Thoroughbred, a Business BASIC programming language variant, to support about 120 local and remote $100–150 WYSE 60 asynchronous ASCII terminals and printers star-configured back to headquarters via a public frame relay network provided by MCI.

Most of the programming has been developed by ALC. The central system is now over a decade old and has undergone multiple upgrades, from the previous REXON system with a 10-MB disk and an initial capability of supporting only a single terminal, soon upgraded to a half dozen terminals. ALC has been automated for almost 15 years of their 20-year life span and has no immediate plans to dump their tried-and-true IBC and 15-year-old BASIC computer code in favor of any fancy, expensive, modern HTML, client-server, or intranet-type solution. And this is not due to any particular nostalgia as much as it is a flat refusal to change from something that is stable, low cost, and working to something new and different simply based on promises. This is one reason why ALC has embraced frame relay, a newborn technology by ALC standards, and integrated it into their network: frame relay works, it is simple, it is a cost-effective alternative to their expensive, distance-sensitive leased lines, and it provides "free" in-company voice and fax.

Like the transportation industry itself, ALC is experiencing tremendous growth and is opening offices around the United States at a fast pace. In addition to the simplicity and cost benefits, frame relay also allows more flexibility and shorter lead times for bringing up new offices than do traditional leased lines, and this is very key when the normal lead time for a new office opening, anywhere in the continental United States, is about two weeks.

In the computer and communications industries, it is almost impossible to keep up with the latest technology trends, acronyms, fads, and gimmicks. Reading about companies who do keep up with these trends, or better yet, who stay ahead of the trends, is very interesting stuff indeed. In many cases, the failures are as interesting, or even more interesting, to read about than the successes. But it is also refreshing to read about a company that embraces simplicity, low cost, and what works, and that is successful in these endeavors as well. And this is just such a case study.

13.2 Before Frame Relay

In the late 1980s, Allen Lund Company was a beta-test site for MCI's Sub-Rate Digital Multiplexing (SRDM) service, one of only four in California. SRDM allowed ALC to connect each of their 10 remote offices to the central host site via 9.6-Kbit/second digital lines. Each of the remote offices' leased lines were routed to MCI's point-of-presence (POP) in Los Angeles, where they were combined onto a single DS0 for each group of five and put on the T1 that connected ALC to MCI's voice service. This meant that ALC was able to afford the 9.6-Kbit/second lines because they only used 2 of the 24 DS0 channels on their T1 access, but saved an average of almost $700 per remote site per month. Although the SRDM service never became commercially viable for MCI, ALC continued to use the service until they converted to frame relay. ALC also watched the cost of 56-Kbit/second leased lines fall, and when the cost of 56-Kbit/second circuits was equal to the cost of their 9.6-Kbit/second lines, ALC evaluated a move to the higher-speed service.

13.2.1   Business Aspects

About the time ALC undertook an evaluation of the move from 9.6-Kbit/second digital service to 56-Kbit/second digital service, one of the consultants with whom ALC had been working for a number of years presaged the use of frame relay at ALC. The consultant identified frame relay, quite accurately, as a technology that would soon be available nationwide and that would allow ALC to provide higher-speed connections to their remote offices on a distance-insensitive pricing basis and at a lower cost than the 56-Kbit/second service. All of these aspects of frame relay were very attractive to ALC, and with the added benefits of configuration flexibility and possibly adding voice, frame relay sounded as though it would meet ALC's needs perfectly.

Requirements

Allen Lund Company's primary requirement was to save money, but not with a reduction in service or reliability because their data and voice network are the veins through which the lifeblood of their organization pulses. A secondary consideration, but still an important one, is enhanced configuration flexibility. We see these recurring themes in many organizations that use frame relay: lower costs, maintain reliability, increase flexibility.

Lower costs   Allen Lund Company's simplified view of network costs works well with frame relay's distance-insensitive pricing structure. ALC's formal pricing comparisons for network services look at each site's costs, and the individual components of that cost, independently and roll those details up to an overall corporate total. Monthly management reporting, however, is based upon an average cost per site, derived by taking the total networking costs and dividing by the number of remote sites. The distance insensitivity aspect of frame relay connections *inside* the network gives an approximately equal per-month cost, but there is some distance-based variation by site for access charges. Under their present MCI price structure, there is a monthly fixed cost for access that can vary by site. For example, monthly access charges from MCI, which include the distance-sensitive LEC access and port charges, are $402 per month for their new Baltimore, Maryland, office; $367 for Memphis, Tennessee; and $214 for San Francisco, for port charges only and no local LEC access, because the San Francisco frame relay connections ride along on the access T1 that is already installed to support MCI long-distance voice access.

Table 13.1   **ALC Payback Analysis**

Item	Amount
Leased-line monthly charges	$10,000
Frame relay monthly charges	4,300
Monthly data savings with frame relay	5,700
Monthly voice savings with frame relay	2,000
Total monthly savings with frame relay	7,700
Hardware charges to go to frame relay (charges include installation)	80,000
Payback period (months)	10.4

Another cost aspect of their MCI service that ALC finds very attractive is the usage-based billing option. With the usage-based billing option, ALC has a 32-Kbit/second CIR, but only pays for a 24-Kbit/second CIR if their average utilization during a monthly billing cycle does not exceed 24 Kbits/second. This allows ALC to have the comfort of knowing that they can present up to 32 Kbits/second of data to the network for delivery and that there is a very high likelihood that it will be delivered, but they can pay the lower price if they do not use the 32-Kbit/second capacity very often and the average falls below 24 Kbits/second.

ALC has found that a combination of falling prices for frame relay and the efficiencies of frame relay multiplexing and bandwidth allocation have combined to drop their networking bill from $10,000 per month for their initial 10 sites to $4,300 per month. This cost savings figure does not take into account the cost of the additional hardware required to support frame relay data, voice, and fax (approximately $80,000), nor does it take into account the cost savings for putting their private voice and fax traffic across their frame relay network (approximately $2,000 per month). Including those figures, as indicated in Table 13.1, gives a payback period of less than 11 months, after which time the $7,700 per month savings goes directly to the bottom line.

To take this analysis one step further, we could look at the $7,700 per month savings as a profit contribution and determine the actual effect of the savings in a different manner. If ALC were to sell additional brokerage services each month sufficient to make a profit of $7,700, what would the dollar volume of sales need to be? For example, if ALC's profit margin were 25%, then the $7,700 profit would require sales four times that number, or at least $30,800 per month. Multiplying this figure by 12 months per year gives us yearly sales of $369,600 needed to generate the additional profit represented by the $92,400 in annual savings. In other terms, after the initial 10.4 months, during which the equipment and installation is paid for, the bottom-line contribution of the frame relay savings would be the same as a .5% increase in sales, not an insubstantial number when multiplied by $72 million in 1996 revenues. If, of course, ALC's profit margin is less than 25%, the savings profit contribution would be more substantial; if ALC's profit margin is more than 25%, then the contribution would be less substantial.

Voice over frame relay has been seen widely in the U.S. market only very recently compared to the length of time it has existed in the international marketplace, mainly because users internationally have been willing to accept lower levels of voice quality for cost savings because the cost savings on international toll calls can be very high. One of the first geographic areas to see widespread use of voice over frame relay was the Pacific Rim, and many technology advances are a direct result of product acceptance in that area. Voice over frame relay, like voice over IP on the Internet, still has some way to go before it matches the quality of public switched telephone network (PSTN) voice, but the gap is closing rapidly. Voice over frame relay is definitely ready for serious consideration by companies anywhere in the world: the quality of voice over frame relay will be affected, positively or negatively, by many of the same things that affect PSTN voice.

Maintain reliability   ALC's intention to save money was not at the risk of network reliability or maintainability, and they have not been disappointed. ALC's carrier has provided proactive frame relay service monitoring and automatic trouble ticket generation that far exceeds the levels of responsiveness available with the prior leased-line system. With the proactive frame relay monitoring arrangement, it is not uncommon for MCI to notify ALC about an outage before the outage has been reported internally within ALC. This is even more important because the frame relay service carries both data and internal voice/fax traffic and any system outage diminishes the remote sites' ability to report problems themselves to headquarters.

Increase flexibility   In as dynamic an industry as transportation, flexibility is important—the flexibility to enter a new market, to relocate or add an office, and to have data, voice, and fax service in place when that new office is opened. It had been ALC's experience that a 30- to 45-day lead time was required in even the best of cases for the installation of a private 9.6-Kbit/second leased line from a new remote site to headquarters. A new site can be added or an existing site relocated on the frame relay service in as little as 14 to 21 days, half the time of a leased line.

The primary reason for this increased flexibility is that with a frame relay network it is not necessary to engineer a complete end-to-end circuit, as it is with a leased line. With frame relay, a local access line is installed that carries the remote site's traffic to the nearest public network POP, where it is terminated on a port on a frame relay switch. The bandwidth is then allocated inside the frame relay transport network, or cloud, on a dynamic basis. In the case of adding additional sites, it is a very simple matter to reconfigure the access T1 at the headquarters site if more bandwidth is needed.

Because of the statistical multiplexing aspects of frame relay, it is not necessary to reserve bandwidth for each site, but rather it is possible in many cases, as it is in ALC's, to oversubscribe the bandwidth of the access line at the headquarters office. Oversubscription is simply utilizing the probabilities that a permanent virtual circuit will need all of its bandwidth at a moment in time to more efficiently use the access bandwidth; a similar oversubscription is done by the carrier in the transport backbone. If a 56-Kbit/second DS0 access channel is reserved within a T1 and it is utilized 100% of the time by a PVC with a 56-Kbit/second CIR, for instance, the frame relay access is said to be subscribed at 100%, with an oversubscription of 0%. If the same frame relay access, however, is shared by two PVCs, each with a 56-Kbit/second CIR, but each PVC only transmits information at 56 Kbits/second half of the time, then the port is said to be oversubscribed by 100% because two 56-Kbit/second PVCs, representing a potential traffic of 112 Kbits/second, are defined for the port. If we take a closer look at oversubscription, we see that it is really no different from what an airline does in overbooking seats, and there are only four situations that must be dealt with. To use our airline analogy, if there are 100 seats on the airplane and the airline books 200 people into those seats, the four possible situations that can occur are the following:

- *Situation 1:* No one shows up for the plane, in which case there is no problem with capacity, but a problem with cost because a plane is being flown empty.
- *Situation 2:* Fewer than 100 passengers show up for the plane, in which case the plane is operated at a level of efficiency below 100%, but all passengers are accommodated.

- *Situation 3:* Exactly 100 passengers show up for the plane, and while this is good from an efficiency standpoint (in that the plane's capacity is 100% utilized), it is too close for comfort statistically because only one more passenger would cause Situation 4.
- *Situation 4:* More than 100 passengers show up for the flight. Some passengers will have to wait for the next plane in order to get to their destination. In frame relay networking, the penalty is usually the same as well, reduced performance, and rarely results in truly discarded data, though in cases of extreme oversubscription or of unusually high instantaneous load on the network, discarded data is possible, but the discarded data is usually retransmitted by a higher OSI layer, again resulting in diminished performance rather than true discard. In airline terms, these passengers are normally sorted out on some priority scheme (such as major frequent fliers first, minor frequent fliers next, and infrequent fliers last), issued denied boarding compensation of some type, and asked to wait in the airline's lounge until the next flight. In frame relay terms, the frames are sorted out based upon some industry standard or proprietary prioritization scheme, with higher-priority packets going first and those not able to go now being buffered by the router or other type of frame relay access device at the edge of the network.

ALC presently has four 56-Kbit/second DS0 data channels defined on their access T1 for use by frame relay. This 4 × 56-Kbit/second, or 224-Kbit/second, channel is being used by 12 remote sites whose access rates are 56 Kbits/second, but whose CIRs are lower. This creates a situation where the remotes can burst, but it is statistically unlikely that they will require more than 224 Kbits/second at an instant in time. And this contributes to ALC's flexibility because they may add a remote site without always changing the DS0 allocation on the access line at the headquarters site, but when they need to do so, it is easily accomplished.

13.2.2 Technical Aspects

The applications of Allen Lund Company consist of voice and data applications, both of which are mixed successfully on their frame relay network.

Applications

ALC's network is a star configuration in terms of its physical arrangement, with all frame relay connections going from the remote offices back to the headquarters. But, in terms of its logical arrangement, ALC must provide any-to-any voice and data connectivity in order to provide the logistical and tactical support for truckloads from any customer to any other location in the system. The any-to-any data coordination is facilitated by everyone in the company accessing a single centralized computer system and all reviewing or modifying a central file system. Any-to-any voice coordination is provided inside the company using a fairly simplified internal voice switching capability that switches all calls via the headquarters office and the frame relay star. Both voice and data, as well as fax, are provided using the MICOM Marathon customer premises multiplexers with frame relay interfaces.

Traditional ASCII/asynchronous terminal data   The use of older, traditional ASCII asynchronous data terminals in the ALC environment has the benefit of placing a terminal on a user's desk for $60 to $100 per unit, about the cost of a discounted Ethernet card for an IBM PC, but it has the drawback of providing a communications environment where each user keystroke, or set of keystrokes, must be acknowledged by the central computer. No programs can execute locally, as they might in a PC, and this creates an even stronger reliance on the communications system.

These older systems, where the error checking and correction is performed by a user at a screen seeing a problem with displayed data, are not really ideal for frame relay because frame relay is based largely on the assumption that end systems (that is, the systems ultimately communicating with each other; in ALC's case, the IBC host and the asynchronous ASCII terminal) have enough intelligence to recover from a discard of data by frame relay. Frame relay has no internal error correction or retransmission capability; it simply does error checking and discarding. For this reason, additional steps must be taken in these types of systems to ensure there are no discards in the frame relay network. ALC, for instance, has made sure that their CIRs are well below the access rate so that no discards will occur at the point of network ingress—the place where information enters the network—and it has actually experienced fewer problems with the frame relay system than with the prior leased-line system.

Voice   The second application for the ALC frame relay network is voice communications. ALC desired to move their internal voice requirements to the frame relay network to reduce costs for intracompany calls and also to encourage the different offices to communicate more because voice communication would be "free."

Fax   Fax, which is essentially voice band data, similar to modem traffic or any other analog-to-digital technology, was the third application for ALC's frame relay network. ALC wished to also move internal faxing to the frame relay network, thereby lowering their costs and increasing the chances that this form of communication would be utilized between their offices.

Communications Environment

The ALC communications environment, as we will see, is a very unique one. Much of its uniqueness comes from its cost-reduction approach and its reliance on less expensive asynchronous terminal equipment.

Physical architecture   The ALC pre-frame-relay communications environment was a very simple one: digital 9.6-Kbit/second leased lines connecting asynchronous ASCII remote terminal and printer devices to a central host (Figure 13.1). The telephony environment was typical PSTN connectivity, with key systems at the remote offices and a Nortel Meridien SL/1 PBX at headquarters.

At ALC's remote sites, an Astrocom 4100 multiplexer allowed attachment of multiple asynchronous ASCII terminals and printers to the leased line via a DSU/CSU or to a T1 access circuit via a synchronous port connection on the T1 channel bank. At the host side, an Astrocom 8100 multiplexer with connections to five Astrocom 4100 multiplexers with 64 asynchronous ports allowed direct one-to-one assignment of remote terminals and printers to IBC host ports.

The key systems at the remote ALC offices have multiple buttons on each phone, one assigned to each incoming/outgoing phone line, a technology that is fairly old-fashioned, but that also works and will be retained for a number of years at ALC.

Logical architecture   In the pre- and post-frame-relay logical architectures (Figure 13.2), there are no changes from the user's standpoint in the data area. In the voice and fax area, the dialing arrangements are a bit different, but the equipment is the same.

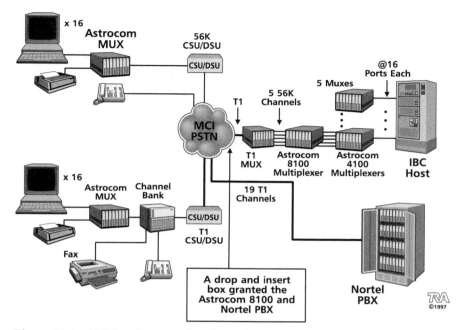

Figure 13.1   ALC Pre-Frame-Relay Physical Architecture

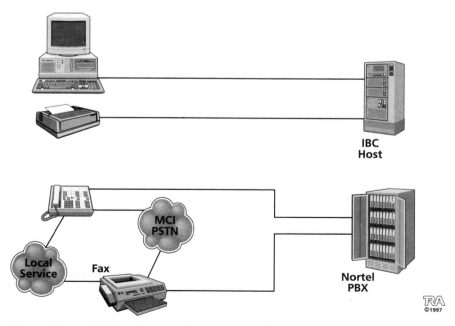

Figure 13.2   ALC Pre-Frame-Relay Logical Architecture

13.3   Frame Relay: Selection and Migration

At the time that Allen Lund Company evaluated a move to frame relay, they were actually contemplating a move from 9.6-Kbit/second digital leased lines to 56-Kbit/second digital leased lines and reviewed frame relay and ATM as future technologies in which they had no particular immediate interest. The efficiencies and pricing of frame relay, however, were too good to ignore, and ALC was soon soliciting bids from three vendors for frame relay.

13.3.1   Business Aspects

ALC has historically tried to avoid expensive, new high-tech solutions in lieu of tried-and-true, already-paid-for but admittedly lower-tech solutions that are already understood by the staff and work well. The main driver for a move to frame relay was to save money but without too great a risk to the systems that keep their business alive.

Expectations

ALC expected that a move to frame relay would cut their $10,000-per-month telecommunications bill in half with a modest investment in equipment. ALC found that the $10,000-per-month cost was slashed to $4,300 per month with an additional $2,000 savings on intercompany voice and fax, with an initial hardware and installation investment of about $80,000. ALC also expected the move to frame relay to be somewhat technically challenging and underestimated the substantial cost savings and high quality they achieved. The original plan was to migrate to frame relay in a little over a year, but in light of the high quality and cost savings, ALC accelerated the migration process to three months.

Alternatives Considered

Allen Lund Company looked at three alternatives to their 9.6-Kbit/second digital line network: 56-Kbit/second leased lines, frame relay, and ATM.

Leased lines   ALC's first step was to look at leased-line alternatives. The leased-line alternative was to replace the existing 9.6-Kbit/second digital leased lines with 56-Kbit/second digital leased lines, replace all 9.6-Kbit/second DSU/CSUs with new DSU/CSUs, and abandon the MCI

SRDM system. It would also have been possible to share an access T1 with voice and 56-Kbit/second leased lines, but this alternative would have required approximately half of the access T1's 24 DS0 channels and reduced the number of available voice channels to 12 at the headquarters office. ALC also realized that their growth would have mandated the addition of an expensive access T1 sooner or later anyway with this channelized 56-Kbit/second solution.

Frame relay Even though frame relay was not in the original plans, ALC felt it would be a good idea to evaluate this new technology anyway; as long as they were going to make a change, they wanted to be assured they were getting all of the benefit they could from their investment. ALC found frame relay to be a viable technology alternative and pursued this avenue.

ATM After only the most cursory examination, ALC was able to determine that not only was ATM not right for them, they were not right for ATM—and they might never be. The high costs of the service and required customer premises equipment and the lack of an ATM service offering in all of their locations discouraged them from looking further at ATM as an alternative.

Carrier Selection Process

ALC entertained formal proposals from three different carriers: Sprint, WilTel (now WorldCom), and MCI. The key points of ALC's evaluation were

- saving money
- maintaining quality and reliability
- ease of support

Saving money While all of the base proposals from the three carriers were fairly close in price for similar services, Sprint additionally offered a zero CIR service. Sprint's zero CIR service was priced lower than the competitive offering, or their own service with a guaranteed CIR, and provided no guarantee, but rather allowed ALC traffic to ride on "spare" network bandwidth at a substantial savings. Based upon ALC's desire to save money without risking network reliability and quality, they did not consider zero CIR a viable alternative, in much the same way as a cost-conscious traveler who does not wish to ruin their trip might consider a low-cost, no-frills airline, but will still not fly standby.

Maintaining quality and reliability   ALC felt that the various carriers' offerings were probably similar in terms of quality and reliability because they were all proposed by large, capable, reliable communications carriers, but MCI was the only one of these carriers with whom ALC had had any experience. In the absence of overwhelming cost savings, ALC was reluctant to go with any other carrier than MCI, which was for ALC the tried-and-true carrier choice.

Ease of support   All carriers proposed similar capabilities in terms of proactive monitoring of the frame relay service, automatic trouble ticketing, management reporting, and mean-time-to-service-restoral (MTTSR) times. Again, lacking overwhelming reasons to not use MCI, ALC chose to go with their existing carrier. In frame relay, as well as with other technology decisions, it is often the case that the incumbent carrier is almost impossible to unseat, unless the incumbent carrier has caused a major trauma for their customer, either in the area of price or support.

Migration

Migration planning was performed so as to minimize costs and negative impact on remote operations. Originally the migration was to occur over a 12- to 13-month period, but this cycle was accelerated, mainly to achieve cost savings sooner.

13.3.2 Technical Aspects

After choosing the frame relay service provider, the next step for ALC was to choose the provider of the customer premises equipment that would integrate data, voice, and fax at the remote sites to be transported and demultiplexed at headquarters. As MICOM was one of the early entrants into the market and had a product based upon an existing platform that was working in the leased-line environment, ALC felt comfortable enough to initiate a first installation of MICOM equipment. ALC uses the MICOM 5K and 2K multiplexers at remote offices and a MICOM 20K and 5K Turbo with redundancy and alternative power features at headquarters.

The MICOM Marathon 5K and 20K provide the basic data/voice/fax capabilities that ALC currently needs with the ability to expand into LAN interconnection if they should ever decide to install LANs. The Marathon 5K Turbo supports up to three leased-line WAN links or up to 20 frame relay WAN links, or a combination of both, for cost-effective internetworking. For public frame relay access, the Marathon 5K Turbo allows integrated communications traffic to travel over a common PVC to its destination. Multiple frame relay links can be configured to segment traffic for access to multiple public frame relay carriers. The Marathon 5K Turbo also allows locally attached frame relay devices, including those that support RFC 1490 encapsulation, token ring, and SNA applications, to transparently pass traffic to the public frame relay network.

The Marathon 5K Turbo handles virtually all legacy data including DEC VT100, HP ENQ/ACK, and SNA/SDLC. A five-slot modular design allows expansion for up to 41 asynchronous channels or 12 synchronous channels. Other optional data modules provide remote users with access to Ethernet LAN-based services or Ethernet LAN routing capabilities.

The high-performance Marathon 20K supports up to six private leased lines or public frame relay service WAN links, or a combination of both, and provides similar capabilities to the 5K in terms of connecting locally attached frame relay devices and ClearVoice technology. It has a five-slot modular design, which allows expansion for up to 41 asynchronous channels and 18 synchronous channels. Optional modules also provide remote users with access to Ethernet LAN-based services and Ethernet LAN routing capabilities.

Planning

The planning process was a fairly simple one. The biggest decisions had to do with whether ALC should maintain their star configuration or should use a fully meshed configuration, thereby taking advantage of the MICOM Marathon's capabilities to perform voice switching and providing a modest performance improvement for calls made between offices located at some distance from headquarters. For instance, a voice call made over a star-configured network from the Atlanta office to the Boston office would travel approximately 2,000 miles from Atlanta to La Cañada, California, and back 2,600 miles from La Cañada to Boston, a total trip of 4,600 miles. If, on the other hand, ALC chose to implement a mesh network, PVC connections would be established between all offices, and the MICOM Marathon would simply route the call directly to Boston from Atlanta, a distance of only about 950 miles, a savings of 3,650 miles with a higher-quality call because of reduced propagation delay. But when confronted with the additional cost of $15 per month per PVC times the number of PVCs needed—$((n \times (n-1))/2) - 10$ are required for a star network, which for 10 sites would be 35 PVCs—ALC decided that the additional $525 per month was not justified. ALC planned the phase-in of their frame relay system over a 12- to 13-month time frame and planned to do the migration as they went out to the remote sites for routine maintenance or other regularly planned visits. The great success of their first site, however, caused ALC to accelerate the implementation process. The initial installation was done in Los Angeles with a local network integration firm, Datalink Associates, and ALC learned from them. Then ALC shipped the new equipment to the sites and did subsequent installations themselves on regular visits.

Voice over frame relay   In order to better understand the issues associated with voice communications across a digital frame-based communications system, it is important to understand traditional digital voice transmission, telephony principles, and their historical background.

From the day when the first words were transmitted via an analog signal over a length of copper wire until the early 1960s, telephony technology changed very little, with the exception of the distance the signal traveled and the invention of dialing to connect a call. Entering the decade of the 1960s, it was apparent that a more efficient method of voice communications was needed, an alternative to using pairs of copper wire and dedicating each pair to a single conversation.

The original idea had been to send waves representing the tones of human speech across the wires in an analog, or wave, format, but increasingly the idea of digital networks (networks that use the same "1" and "0" digits of computers to represent the waveforms of human speech) was emerging, and with it a new way of representing speech. The original standard algorithm for digital transmission was pulse code modulation (PCM), and it is still used as the basis for digital telephony today. PCM utilizes a system that measures the height of the analog wave above a baseline or the depth of the analog signal below the baseline and encodes the height or depth number as an 8-bit digital sample, which is transmitted from transmitter to receiver. The originators of PCM at Bell Laboratories determined that an 8-bit sample was sufficient to represent the height or depth of the signal from the baseline and that the difference between subsequent samples would be sufficiently close that the human brain would create a smooth, continuous waveform in the receiver's mind, even though the received signal actually had very small stair steps. The next issue was to determine how often the samples were to be taken, or the frequency of the samples. It was decided that 8,000 samples per second would be sufficient

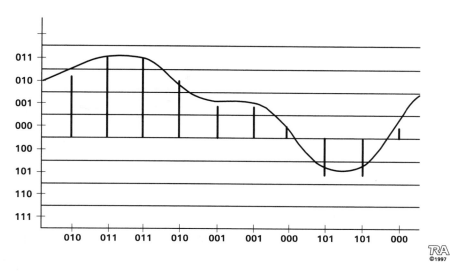

Figure 13.3   PCM Voice Encoding and Transmission

to provide a very high quality of voice reproduction and that the technology was sufficiently simple that it could operate this quickly. As Kosek (1995, p. 45) relates:

> Analog voice communication by telephone was designed as a bandpass filter, allowing a frequency range from 300 Hz [cycles per second] and 3,000 Hz. A basic law of 8-bit PCM states that the sample rate must be at least two times the highest frequency allowed—this means the minimum allowable sample rate is 6,000 times per second. The engineers chose 8,000 times per second to ensure the delivery of excellent quality voice.

The transmission of 8-bit samples, taken at a frequency of 8,000 per second, determined the bandwidth required to transmit digital voice: 8 bits/sample × 8,000 samples/second, or 64 Kbits/second.

PCM (Figure 13.3) provided very good voice quality, but network bandwidth is expensive and the search was on to find a digital telephony standard that could provide reasonably high quality but use less than 64 Kbits/second of bandwidth. The result of this process was the development of many variations of adaptive differential pulse code modulation (ADPCM). Where PCM measured the *absolute* height of the voice wave above a reference line, ADPCM measured the *relative* height of the wave from the height of the prior sample. ADPCM's first pass was to use samples that could be encoded in 4-bit samples, thereby halving the amount of

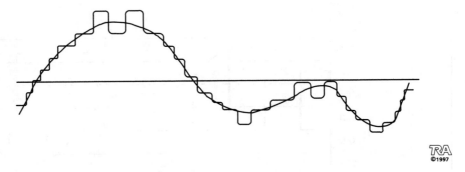

Figure 13.4   ADPCM Voice Encoding and Transmission

bandwidth needed to 32 Kbits/second, but keeping the frequency of samples constant at 8,000 times per second. Subsequent ADPCM algorithms have been developed that use 24 Kbits/second and 16 Kbits/second with lower voice quality for less bandwidth utilized, but still within a marginally acceptable range of quality.

PCM and ADPCM, while originally created for use in the telephone company networks, are a mainstay of corporate networking today. PCM and ADPCM technologies (Figure 13.4) are found extensively in corporate PBX and T1/E1 time division multiplexing (TDM) networks around the globe. The time division multiplexing networks allow voice and data to travel in separate predefined channels within the T1 or E1 circuits. TDM is a good choice for circuit-type networking where delay (or as network engineers prefer to call it, latency) needs to remain constant and low, but TDM networking lacks the efficiency of instantaneous bandwidth allocation possible with packet- and frame-switching technologies, like X.25 and frame relay, respectively.

Two closely related new technologies for voice encoding that have emerged in voice over frame relay products are code-excited linear prediction (CELP) and algebraic code-excited linear prediction (ACELP). ACELP grew out of years of study at various research institutions using CELP and CELP-like coders. CELP provides high-quality voice compression, with its only real limitations being the time required to perform compression and decompression, which can introduce undue delay into the speech stream. This problem is being solved with faster microprocessors and better, more efficient algorithms. CELP compression is achieved by mapping incoming speech onto a mathematical model of human voice and

Table 13.2   **Mean Opinion Score (MOS) Definitions**

Score	Quality
4.0 to 5.0	toll quality
3.0 to 4.0	communication quality
< 3.0	synthetic quality

sending only the model parameters as they change. Products based upon currently available CELP chip sets can provide understandable, though low-quality, voice down to approximately the 4-Kbit/second range. A variation of the ACELP algorithm is currently being reviewed by the ITU for recommendation G.729 at 8 Kbits/second. The newer 8-Kbit/second ACELP part of G.729 is the standard upon which the MICOM Marathon voice products used in the ALC network are based.

Many products attempting to put voice over X.25 have come and gone, and early attempts to do so over frame relay appeared to be doomed to failure as well. The biggest problem was that because packet and frame-based networks use variable-length data transport units (packets or frames), the predictability of network performance was low, and the range of possible latency values was very wide; therefore, there was no hope of emulating circuits for data within the X.25 or frame relay network.

Frame relay, unlike X.25, offers a relatively high backbone transport speed, up to 45 Mbits/second, and could potentially combine a bursty, rather than circuit-oriented, voice connection with the high-speed 45-Mbit/second backbone to achieve a very desirable performance level. The biggest questions are how to create bursty voice connections and how to keep latency low and constant. But first we will take a look at what "acceptable voice quality" actually means.

Although perceptions of voice quality vary by individual, the mean opinion score (MOS) is a widely accepted measure of voice quality. MOS ratings provide a subjective quality score averaged over a large number of speakers and listeners. Table 13.2 shows the voice quality associated with various MOS scores. The most desirable, and rarely achieved with anything but PCM or 32-Kbit/second ADPCM, is "toll quality," which used to be the quality objective for all telephony systems, but which has been largely abandoned, especially in packet and frame-based voice, in lieu of greater cost savings. Most packet and frame-based products deliver voice quality in the "communication quality" bracket.

There are a number of techniques and technologies that can be employed to deliver an acceptable level of voice quality across frame relay networks. These techniques and technologies are usually a combination of network-provided capabilities (or network shortcomings) and capabilities enabled or provided by the customer premises equipment.

- *Small buffers:* Keep buffers small to avoid long wait times at the ingress and egress points in the network and at intermediate points. Reducing the amount of time that frames containing voice samples will sit in each buffer reduces the maximum latency that a frame containing voice samples can accumulate on its trip through the network. Often keeping buffers small is a function of configuration parameters inside a public network, over which the end user has no control, and the management of buffers and configuration parameters in customer premises equipment, over which the customer does have some control.

- *Predictive congestion management:* The forward explicit congestion notification (FECN) and backward explicit congestion notification (BECN) bits provided for in frame relay standards provide a closed-loop congestion mechanism that signals the presence of congestion in the network. The BECN bit is set to notify the source of the frame containing the FECN bit that congestion was encountered in at least one intermediate switch on the path from source to destination. BECN bits are not set on a one-for-one basis, but rather on a statistical basis after a certain number, or percentage, of the most recent n FECN bits have arrived set to 1. It is possible to look at trends in FECN/BECN bits and to predict when congestion might occur, because simply knowing that congestion has occurred is not sufficient. Predictive congestion management techniques vary queue depths and the mix of more delay-tolerant bursty data versus less delay-tolerant voice traffic before congestion occurs.

- *Jitter buffers:* Because frame relay is bursty in nature, variable delays between consecutive packets will result. The time difference between each arriving frame is called *jitter,* and jitter can impede the ability of the receiving end to smoothly regenerate voice. Since voice is inherently a continuous analog waveform, a large gap between the regenerated voice packets will result in gaps, drops, and other sounds that are annoying to the listener. These problems can be minimized by using a jitter buffer with a slight compensatory delay prior to playing out received voice. It is also important that the backbone transport network have a large bandwidth in relationship to the bandwidth requirement of the voice connection.

■ *Fragmentation/segmentation:* Fragmentation, or segmentation, refers to the parsing of long frames presented to the network into shorter frames for transmission across the network and possibly the reassembly of the smaller units at the receiving end. Fragmentation/ segmentation, or at least the enforcement of a small maximum transfer unit (MTU) size, ensures that a single long frame will not monopolize the transport infrastructure: access lines, buffers, trunks, ports, buses inside network switches, and so on. Fragmentation/segmentation minimizes end-to-end delay through network switching equipment, ensuring the timely delivery of voice and fax, as well as data. Specifically, the fragmentation of data packets ensures that voice and fax packets are not unacceptably delayed behind large data packets.

■ *Variable voice compression rates:* Many sophisticated customer premises devices that provide data, voice, and fax multiplexing across frame relay PVCs can vary the compression rates applied to the voice stream. While the more sophisticated compression schemes use less of the precious and costly frame relay network bandwidth, they also require more time to execute and are therefore more delay sensitive than straight PCM coded voice. There are two schools of thought in this area: One says, use the less sophisticated methods, but more bandwidth, during times of congestion because there will be more delay and the method with least delay sensitivity should be utilized. The other says, the more delay there is likely to be, as a function of network congestion, the more sophisticated compression techniques should be used because more bandwidth for voice traffic will only intensify the congestion and use bandwidth at a time when it is least available.

Another aspect of compression is that the higher the compression ratio, the lower the voice quality, and many systems will adjust the voice compression to use the higher-quality/higher-bandwidth schemes in the absence of any congestion to provide the best possible voice quality, all the way up to 64-Kbit/second PCM.

■ *Prioritization:* Many customer premises data/voice/fax multiplexers prioritize input traffic via multiple input queues and complex queue management techniques. Some of these techniques leverage frame relay's FECN/BECN and discard eligibility (DE) schemes, and others use entirely proprietary techniques, but their order of prioritization seems to be consistent: Circuit-type data is prioritized first because it is least tolerant of delays and lost bits, and there is no absolute guarantee that an error recovery or retransmission scheme is built in. Fax is typically second because it is exactly as intolerant as circuit data but is guaranteed to have a built-in retransmission mechanism. Voice is usually third because voice also has almost zero delay tolerance. Bursty data is fourth because it has the greatest delay tolerance. One type of information that was not mentioned is network control and signaling traffic, which may be given a priority 0, even ahead of circuit-type data.

■ *Silence detection and digital speech interpolation:* Voice communication, by nature, is half-duplex, with pauses between sentences. The net effect is that network capacity is used to transmit normal two-way conversational speech only about 38% of the time. Advanced voice-processing algorithms take advantage of these two characteristics in silence processing, which significantly improves system performance in frame relay networks. The extra bandwidth saved from the silent period of one voice channel is allocated to other channels. This technique is called digital speech interpolation and can improve bandwidth utilization by 35% or more.

Another issue that affects speech quality in silence suppression systems is the proper matching of background noise between the ends: noise is inserted so that the speaker will know that the listener is still present and that the connection is still "up."

Migration

Migration was accomplished over the course of three months using a combination of headquarters ALC support and MCI field personnel. The first site installation took 1½ days and used a local Los Angeles firm to share frame relay installation expertise with ALC staff. Subsequent installations require approximately one-half day each.

After the local exchange carrier turns the line over to MCI, ALC stressed the importance of MCI's testing the line again prior to deploying installation personnel. After a line has been in service, it is possible to also use a loop-back capability within the MICOM Marathon combined with a Fire-Berd or other similar bit error rate tester (BERT) to do remote troubleshooting, problem isolation, and resolution. After the line is in place and verified, the MICOM Marathon at the remote office is installed. ASCII asynchronous terminals and printers are configured on the ports and appropriate parameters are set for those ports (number of data bits, number of stop bits, parity, port speed, etc.). A typical remote site has a 56-Kbit/second access rate with either a 16- or 32-Kbit/second CIR. A 16-Kbit/second CIR would be used to support one voice or fax connection

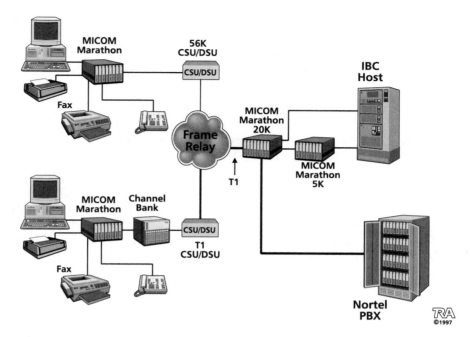

Figure 13.5 ALC Frame Relay Configuration

and up to 14 terminals and printers; a 32-Kbit/second CIR would be used to support two voice or fax connections and up to 24 terminals and printers. It is possible to configure voice for 4, 8, or 16 Kbits/second, and it has been ALC's experience that 8 Kbits/second produces the best voice quality and "perfect faxes."

Configuration after Migration

In the post-frame-relay migration environment, ALC has maintained their cost-effective hardware, added voice over frame relay, and saved even more money.

Physical architecture   After the migration to frame relay, each office has a MICOM Marathon connected to the MCI frame relay network service. The MICOM Marathons replace the Astrocom muxes in their respective positions in the configuration, with a similar tiered arrangement being used at the headquarters office (Figure 13.5).

Logical architecture   The logical architecture has not changed as a result of the migration to frame relay.

Operations and Network Management

Even though MICOM offers a sophisticated network management system called NetMan, which runs on a UNIX workstation, ALC does not use it. ALC prefers to use an ASCII asynchronous terminal interface that allows the scrolling of alarms and accompanies new alarm messages with an audible beep. While ALC agrees that the MICOM NetMan product offers some very nice features, the combination of the ASCII terminal display and calls from MCI's network operations center are enough to keep the ALC network running smoothly. MCI also provides a series of monthly performance reports, which ALC uses to evaluate performance at their remote sites and to identify sites where parameter changes, such as increasing CIR, might be needed. Generally, though, the MCI reports are used to confirm what they have already learned from their remote office staff about performance.

13.4 Living with Frame Relay

Now that ALC has been living with frame relay for a while, they just cannot imagine their lives without it. Lower costs, improved manageability, network reliability, improved in-company dialing and access—all of the benefits they wanted have been achieved.

13.4.1 Anticipated Benefits

ALC surpassed their goal of 50% savings on network costs, provided enhanced internal voice, fax, and data services, and did so in a shorter time frame than they had thought possible. Frame relay has clearly exceeded ALC's expectations.

13.4.2 Unanticipated Benefits

ALC expected that their employees would communicate more because the interoffice calls are now "free" and because the new dialing arrangement is more efficient than the old system, and they have. ALC has been pleasantly surprised at how much additional communication occurs, including by their headquarters personnel back to the office when they are at field locations. The "free voice" aspect of the systems has caused the traveling headquarters personnel to access home office voice mail, personnel, and local out-dial lines more from the field than they previously had. The net effect of all of this increased communication has been improvements in levels of customer service, better cooperation between ALC offices, and faster access to critical noncomputer information. The ALC system is now handling 700 calls per day, which translates to roughly 22 call hours per day, or at only 10 cents per minute, to $132 per day, or almost $3,000 per month in savings.

13.5 Lessons Learned

Initial voice quality left a lot to be desired. One of the most important aspects of the Marathon 5K Turbo to ALC, in terms of keeping it in their voice network, is that the Marathon 5K and 20K now support ClearVoice technology, which is based on the International Telecommunications Union's G.729 standard for wide area voice compression. A new, more powerful digital signal processor and advanced algorithm provide toll-quality voice at 8-Kbit/second compression rates. Silence suppression and other bandwidth efficiencies reduce the average consumed bandwidth by more than half. Prior to the implementation of ClearVoice technology, ALC rated on-network voice as a "5 to 6" on a 10-point scale. With the implementation of ClearVoice technology, ALC now rates on-net voice "about a 9+, where the public switched phone network is a 10." The reason given for the 9+ rating rather than a 10 was that the MICOM systems still have a very brief decompression delay prior to speech actually starting.

ALC's migration was without major incident, their cost savings are substantial, and the network works well. ALC is very pleased with their data/voice/fax network.

13.6 Future Plans

ALC sees frame relay in their network for many years to come. They can anticipate no event in which they will move to a new networking technology for their data/voice/fax needs. The present solution is highly scalable in terms of their anticipated future size, and they can foresee no reason to change technologies. The next logical technology step is ATM, which is too expensive and delivers huge bandwidths that they do not anticipate ever needing for their applications.

13.7 Conclusion

By any measure, ALC has had very good success with their frame relay implementation: voice, data, and fax are now available cost-effectively companywide; ALC has become self-sufficient in terms of installation, support, and ongoing management; and the configuration ALC has built can grow as they grow.

This is the last frame relay case study in this book, but certainly not the last case study you will encounter. Frame relay case studies are very common and can be found in magazines, newspapers, and journals and in real life. You should now be sufficiently familiar with the business and technical aspects of frame relay to know what questions to ask, to understand the different aspects of frame relay and their interrelationships, and to appreciate some of the finer points of frame relay implementation.

PART FIVE

The Future

CHAPTER FOURTEEN

The Future of Frame Relay

As the primary organization driving frame relay advances, the Frame Relay Forum is the group to watch for future changes. This chapter will cover the anticipated changes as well as some thoughts on the evolution of the frame relay market.

14.1 Frame Relay: Past, Present, and Future

Frame relay, which began its life as a "high-speed" interconnection technology, with maximum speeds of 2.048 Mbits/second, and was positioned by its early marketers as *"The* WAN for LANs," has come a long way toward being the be-all and end-all of networking for many users—a role that more conventional wisdom seems to say is the domain of ATM. While frame relay still lacks the inherent quality-of-service (QoS) capabilities, firmware-based switching speed, and multimedia fairness characteristics that are fundamental to ATM, the new higher speeds at which frame relay is being operated have eliminated many of the traditional ATM versus frame relay arguments. Frame relay is being used increasingly for transport of not only traditional data and highly bursty LAN interconnection but also for traditional constant bit rate data types such as voice and video. And a notable number of high-profile networks are adopting frame relay as a backbone switching technology, and not just for the network interface role for which it was originally envisioned and standardized.

This is not to say that the original performance and bandwidth efficiency arguments about small, efficient, fixed-length units (i.e., ATM's cells) versus variable-length transport units (i.e., frame relay's frames), especially for unpredictable multimedia traffic mixes, are not valid. They still are. What has happened, however, is that the differences have blurred somewhat due to the high speeds of frame relay and the relatively small differences between the new frame relay speeds and ATM speeds. In years gone by, for instance, it was not uncommon to compare 2-Mbit/second frame relay speeds to 45- or 155-Mbit/second ATM and thereby show substantial discrepancies in performance. Not so with 45-Mbit/second ATM versus 45-Mbit/second frame relay, where issues like ATM's adaptation delays for parsing frames into cells and reassembling frames at the destination become an important part of the latency and performance formula.

Many originally viewed frame relay as an interim solution on the road to ATM, many viewed it as the heir apparent to X.25 public networking, and still others simply viewed frame relay (as it was originally defined) as a data transport option for use with ISDN. Few envisioned that frame relay would have established itself as strongly as it has or that it would be such a clear choice for such a variety of information transport missions. As we have described exhaustively in the earlier chapters, the main reason for this wide adoption is the simplicity and ubiquity of frame relay, which translates to low cost. Frame relay is available in both public and private implementations, can be implemented in a very reliable fashion, and can replace many older technologies.

Two very important technological innovations have, in fact, been the cause of many organizations' rethinking of their long-term networking strategies. In no particular order of preference, they are 100 megabit/gigabit Ethernet for the LAN and campus area backbone networks, and high-speed frame relay for the WAN. Both are very attractive in terms of low cost, high capacity, and broad product availability, both are based upon technologies that are considered to be proven core technologies, and both are based upon the movement of variable-length units at OSI Layer 2—units called "frames."

14.2 Frame Relay Forum Developments

The Frame Relay Forum has identified six primary areas that will receive its near and mid-term focus:

- Switched virtual circuits at the NNI
- Voice-over-frame-relay de facto standards
- Frame relay fragmentation
- Multilink frame relay at the UNI
- Frame-relay-to-ATM SVC service interworking
- Frame relay network service-level definitions

One of these initiatives, voice-over-frame-relay standards, will clarify a standardized approach for a capability that is already widely offered. Two initiatives, switched virtual circuits at the NNI and multilink frame relay at the UNI, are intended to broaden the effectiveness of frame relay. One, frame relay network service-level definitions, is aimed at providing standard metrics for performance and service compliance. One project, frame-relay-to-ATM SVC service interworking, is intended to make another key aspect of the interworking of frame relay and ATM possible, in a standards-based manner. The final project, frame relay fragmentation, has as its goal allowing frame relay to adopt some of the more desirable characteristics of ATM, to blur the distinction between the two, and thereby to extend the life cycle and market acceptance of frame relay even further. We will now look at each of these much more closely.

14.2.1 Switched Virtual Circuits at the NNI

Both switched virtual circuits (SVCs) at the network-to-network interface (NNI) and voice-over-frame-relay de facto standards should be available by the time this book is in print. SVCs at the NNI is described in the Frame Relay Forum Implementation Agreement FRF.10 and was generally available in the spring of 1997.

The original designers of frame relay were intent on providing a universally applicable interface definition, free of any specific backbone transport constraints. For this reason, the frame relay interface definitions, as the X.25 interface definitions before them, were written to be independent of the backbone transport. This is why the manufacturers of circuit-switched TDM systems could provide frame relay interfaces for their systems, just as ATM switch manufacturers and frame switch and router manufacturers could provide frame relay interfaces for their systems. One aspect of frame relay networks that is almost universal is that frame relay networks will provide alternate routing around failures inside the transport backbone. This is not, however, specified anywhere in the frame relay interface standards because it is related to the backbone transport, and not to the interface. This is also why there are no standards for rerouting, because the implementation of rerouting is within a single manufacturer's proprietary switching fabric and does not require standards.

The NNI has historically been the weak point in any frame relay implementation. A failure at the NNI is usually service affecting because there is no way to route around the failure, especially in a situation where the two interconnected systems are from different manufacturers. This problem has been solved as well as possible by reducing the number of events that could cause the NNI to not operate, but has not been completely solved until the introduction of SVCs at the NNI, as described in FRF.10. Prior to FRF.10, frame relay implementers would put the two NNI-interconnected frame relay switches in one cabinet (or two cabinets bolted together), provide redundant logic and redundant interface cards, put yellow emergency tape on interconnecting cables, and provide uninterruptible power supplies. There were still several things that could go wrong, and when they did, there was no practical way of reestablishing connections.

The use of SVCs at the NNI will allow the SVCs to be reestablished in the case of a failure because the SVC signaling has been standardized and will operate regardless of which pair of manufacturers' frame switches exist at the NNI. It is also possible to reestablish NNI connections over geographically diverse NNIs, and not just within the same physical facility. This capability offers the most comprehensive possible combination of options.

As shown in Figure 14.1, a single nonresilient NNI with permanent virtual connections offers no alternatives in the case of a failure. Any failure that affects either of the frame relay switches providing NNI in either network is service affecting. It is very common to have multiple NNIs for reasons of capacity, but the PVC approach has no method to switch the PVCs to an alternate NNI in case of problems. While many manufacturers have worked on solutions for specific pairs of products, such as Cisco/StrataCom and Bay Networks, which utilize a high-level network management system to coordinate PVC movement after a failure, no workable long-term solutions have been forthcoming.

The alternative provided by FRF.10, shown in Figure 14.2, allows the NNI connections to be reestablished in the case of a service-affecting

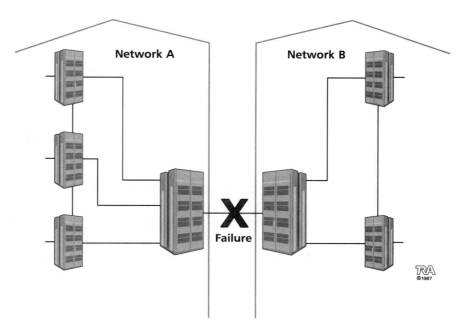

Figure 14.1   Nonresilient NNI with PVCs

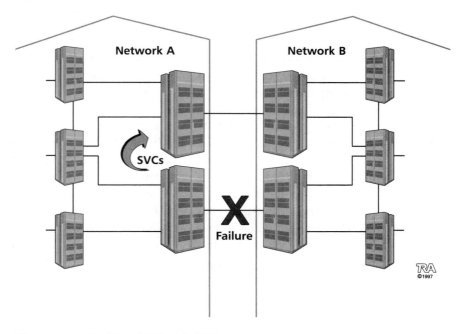

Figure 14.2   Resilient NNI with SVCs

outage using standard SVC signaling with a minimal service disruption. When the NNI fails, the connections across the NNI are simply reestablished and information transfer goes on. Even though frame relay will not perform any retransmission of frames affected during the switchover, higher-layer protocols will do so if needed, at only a small degradation in performance. Voice connections may hear a brief pause, or silence, during service reestablishment, but the delays will be negligible and should not be long enough to cause people to terminate and reestablish the calls.

14.2.2 Voice-over-Frame-Relay De Facto Standards

For quite a large part of frame relay's life cycle, multimedia applications such as voice were thought to be impractical and not technically feasible. But market demand (and market acceptance of poor voice quality in early products in exchange for low voice costs) has created a very viable set of products, and now standards, for voice over frame relay.

The first step was to simply get anything resembling a voice connection to work over frame relay. The second step was to enhance the quality to a generally acceptable level. The third step was to use some of the revenues generated by the increasing market acceptance to improve the product and establish some proprietary methods that work well. The fourth step is to standardize those methods that work best and to ensure interoperability between manufacturers who adhere to the standards.

The next step is to position frame relay along with the traditional telephony infrastructure and the Internet as viable transport choices for voice traffic. There have been many arguments, both technical and legal, surrounding the use of anything other than the traditional carrier telephony networks for carrying voice traffic. And, although the final word in this argument has not yet been heard, the consensus seems to be that anything coded in bits can be carried over any medium that provides the appropriate quality-of-service and delay characteristics for the information stream being transported. Increasingly this will mean carrying voice over frame relay, and this will also mean driving voice costs down.

Carriers are already anticipating voice tariffs to be driven down to several cents per minute in the traditional telephony space, but Internet and frame-relay-based voice could go well below that, depending upon call patterns and call volumes. Companies who require a lot of additional equipment and bandwidth will not achieve as low a cost per minute as those companies who are successful at multiplexing more voice calls into their existing bandwidth, but both will see costs per minute well below the one-cent mark.

As with any standards, whether de facto such as those defined in the Frame Relay Forum's Implementation Agreements or de jure such as those published by ANSI or ITU, the voice-over-frame-relay Implementation Agreement only defines a set of minimum capabilities for interworking between products from different manufacturers. In many cases, manufacturers will use, or continue to use, proprietary capabilities or supersets of the standards and will strictly adhere to standards only where their interfaces must be interconnected to those of other manufacturers. Among other things, the intent of an FRF voice-over-frame-relay Implementation Agreement is to provide information on packetizing voice data for interoperability with a reduced amount of overhead, voice compression algorithms to use for interoperating at various speeds, and end-to-end voice signaling.

14.2.3 Frame Relay Fragmentation

At the risk of oversimplification, it is possible to say that broadband frame switching and cell switching are both fundamentally standardized statistical multiplexing capabilities based upon the same philosophical model. The one significant difference is the size and variability of the transport unit. Frame relay utilizes frames of varying lengths, which Frame Relay Forum Implementation Agreement 1 (FRF.1) has put at a maximum of 4,096 octets. Standard ATM uses a fixed-length unit of 53 bytes: 48 bytes of payload with a 5-byte header. It is not only the size, but the range of possible frame sizes, that makes the performance of frame relay variable and makes assignment of absolute QoS metrics elusive. The more uniform the distribution of frames, the more possible it becomes to predict performance (and the more frame relay will perform like ATM). And, if the frames are not only uniform in length but are also short, near-ATM-like performance and QoS can be achieved.

The solution to this problem, and one that many manufacturers have solved with proprietary capabilities, is to provide network-based segmentation and reassembly of incoming frames. A frame of any size can be presented to the network for transport. At the edge of the network, it can be modified for transport. If the frame is larger than the maximum transmission unit length, the frame is parsed into two or more shorter frames for transport. The shorter frames are transported through the network and are reassembled into their full length at the destination and forward-ed. In this scenario, there is no risk of network trunks, buffers, switching capabilities in intermediate frame switches, and so on being monopolized by single large frames, and the performance is much more predictable—much like ATM.

The most important aspect of having an agreed-upon method of how to perform the segmentation and reassembly is that incompatibilities due to proprietary methodologies are avoided, yet the benefits can be realized. The more frame relay can adopt the characteristics of predictable perfor-mance and minimum delay and QoS variation, the more it will be utilized for a wider range of applications.

14.2.4   Multilink Frame Relay at the UNI

While the majority of frame relay UNIs are 64 Kbits/second, there are still a growing number of sites that require connections at bandwidths greater than the 1.5 Mbits/second of T1 or 2 Mbits/second of E1. The primary rea-son for this is aggregation: many 64-Kbit/second connections from remote sites are aggregated into a host, headquarters, or data center. The next prac-tical step above the 1.5-Mbit/second T1 in the North American Digital Hierarchy is the 45-Mbit/second T3; the next step above the 2-Mbit/second E1 is the 34-Mbit/second E3. This is usually too much bandwidth and/or is usually too costly. What is needed is some middle ground or com-promise. T2 and E2 are rarely used in the engineering of subscriber connections (instead they are reserved for some intra-central-office engi-neering and some arcane microwave systems), which leaves no practical traditional interim step. Multilink frame relay UNIs solve this problem.

A multilink frame relay UNI is a super-T1/E1-rate UNI built in incre-ments of T1/E1 that uses inverse multiplexing technology to preserve tim-ing and bit alignment and to give the appearance of a single $n \times$ T1 or $n \times$ E1 aggregate. Customers using multilink frame relay UNIs can build UNIs in these simple increments up to the point that a full T3 or E3 becomes economical and then switch over.

The primary benefit of the multilink approach versus several individual T1s or E1s is that multilink UNIs are treated as a single UNI connection from a bandwidth management and frame relay configuration standpoint. It is possible, therefore, to assign more than 1.5 Mbits/second to a single

SVC or PVC. The other good news is that the actual implementation by most carriers will allow the UNI to continue to function, even if one or more of the T1s or E1s on the UNI fail.

14.2.5 Frame-Relay-to-ATM SVC Service Interworking

Definitions have already been established to assure the interworking of frame relay and ATM permanent virtual connections. The frame-relay-to-ATM SVC service interworking Implementation Agreement and associated standards will assure the same level of interworking for switched virtual connections. The definitions will assure that frame relay or ATM originated information can traverse and/or terminate on the other service with minimum loss of meaning in the parameters and minimum loss of information.

These definitions are very important to any organization that has adopted a mixed frame relay/ATM networking strategy or that is looking for a smooth transition from frame relay to ATM as part of a migration strategy.

14.2.6 Frame Relay Network Service-Level Definitions

At the present time there are only some very sketchy guidelines for how to measure service levels and contract compliance. BellCore has published a set of guidelines that are, at best, somewhat vague and ambiguous and that require a great deal of work to tailor them to a specific customer instance. Magazines have furnished several different approaches, and of course carriers are a great source of information about how you should measure them and administer their contracts. The Frame Relay Forum is initiating the first real concerted effort, which will take into account both user concerns and carrier/service provider concerns.

This is an important effort for all frame relay users because of the lack of true guidelines and the necessity for them. Unlike a leased line, availability is only one of the service parameters, and CIR compliance, delay, delay variation, prioritization by traffic type, handling of DE versus non-DE traffic, and many other factors all come into play in the overall service definition and compliance measurement.

14.3 Frame Relay and Multimedia Applications

Multimedia networks are designed (or at least used) to carry a mixture of information types, including data, voice, image files, and video. Although frame relay was positioned initially to carry bursty packet/frame-type data, it is seeing some of its biggest growth as a result of the ability to carry other types of information and increasingly to carry multiple types simultaneously as a part of a multimedia application.

14.3.1 Traditional and Bursty Data

Traditional data includes all forms of computer data that have been carried by leased lines. In many cases, this has meant bursty data, with its potentially high peak-to-average ratio and delay insensitivity, which could be carried by other means, such as X.25 packet-switching networks, but is carried by leased lines because of availability, cost, or other issues. In many more cases, however, traditional data means traffic that is carried by circuits because delay sensitivity and delay variation must be minimized, even though the actual information is delimited by a frame based upon the High Level Data Link Control protocol (including X.25, SDLC, and most other bit-oriented protocols). As frame relay achieves higher and higher speeds, the delays that will cause problems for circuit-type data will not be a problem, and frame relay will find wider utilization in these areas.

Increasingly, frame relay users will move traditional leased-line connections over to frame relay, and the carriers and service providers will be positioned to handle this type of traffic. This will also represent the greatest area of revenue growth, especially for carriers without existing leased-line revenues, as more and more of the multibillion dollar leased-line market shifts to broadband services, with frame relay getting the lion's share of low- to medium-speed business and a great deal of the higher-speed business as well.

14.3.2 Voice

Voice will continue to be an important traffic type for frame relay, and a great deal of growth will be seen in this area. With the finalization of Frame

Relay Forum interoperability definitions and the possibility of standards organizations and traditional telephony carriers becoming more involved, the idea of which network (traditional telephony, frame relay, the Internet, etc.) carries voice becomes more a question of the availability, cost, and utilization levels of the respective networks than it does an either/or technology choice. Much of the research and development done on Internet/intranet voice has direct applicability to frame relay, and there will continue to be a boom in both areas.

14.3.3 Image

Because images are really nothing more than really large files, image applications on frame relay networks will benefit from standardized frame fragmentation because they can be done without negatively impacting other applications. Prior to either proprietary or standardized frame fragmentation, a very large frame (for example, associated with an image file) could monopolize resources and cause undue delays for other applications.

For these and other performance-related reasons, image applications today in many cases utilize separate dedicated leased lines or other transport capability besides the frame relay service. Improving image compression technologies, coupled with the fragmentation (parsing) of very long frames into shorter frames for transmission, will make image applications perform better on multimedia networks and have a less detrimental effect on other users' connections.

14.3.4 Video

Video is widely acknowledged to be a very difficult application for frame relay because of the real-time, delay-sensitive, constant-bit-rate nature of current video transmission techniques. The advent of real-time video compression and use of other technologies has given all but the highest-bandwidth video applications a bursty aspect and has improved their sensitivity to delay to the point that, coupled with higher frame relay speeds, video in many forms is becoming a suitable application for frame relay.

From a transmission point of view, video can be divided into three categories. The first category is high-bandwidth broadcast-quality or near-broadcast-quality real-time video. This is not a good frame relay application, and that will remain true for many years to come. The second category is real-time or near-real-time video that can be compressed or otherwise modified so that it does not require a substantial amount of bandwidth, and which, as a result of variations in compression, exhibits a bursty traffic profile and may be productively multiplexed with other information. This type of video has great promise for use on frame relay, and there are a number of products on the market that already create these types of output streams. The third category, and one that is akin to image in its characteristics, is stored video. Stored video can be video programming or other video "clips" that have the benefit of being compressed once, stored, and played back across the network many times. While there are many very innovative and powerful video compression algorithms available on the market today, most are not usable for real-time or near-real-time video because they take too much time to perform their compression magic. With video that will be stored, on the other hand, it does not matter if they require many minutes to do their job because it may be days, weeks, or months before the compressed and stored image is required.

14.3.5 Multimedia

Since multimedia is a mixture of various types of information, and the transfer of that information across the network, multimedia takes into account all of the information transport discussions in the foregoing paragraphs. To the extent that "multimedia," per se, is an important application, because the multimedia nature of the communication enriches its information content, we will be seeing more and more multimedia applications using frame relay.

14.4 Evolution of the Frame Relay Market

The success of frame relay continues to draw attention from users and suppliers. The continued attention from users (in terms of product and service revenues) and from suppliers (in terms of new products and services) also ensures frame relay's continued success. It is unlikely that ATM sales will overtake frame relay sales until well after the turn of the century. Manufacturers, carriers, and service providers continue to redirect research and development and expansion funds to frame relay that were originally earmarked for ATM and other networking technologies.

It is likely that the price of frame relay products and services will continue to drop for some time, especially for large or high-visibility customers, and that services will continue to get better as a result of a focus on service-level agreements and performance and availability objectives. Although many experts see the frame relay market beginning to flatten out during the 1998–1999 time frame, it is also possible to predict a continued growth in frame relay services until the shift from leased lines to frame relay has occurred. And if switched virtual circuits are implemented as widely as carriers and service providers claim they will be, it is also easy to forecast continued growth in the frame relay market until most X.25 services are migrated to frame relay. At the end of this great shift, frame relay will have reached predominance in terms of customer connections, and ATM will have been implemented, in many cases, in high-speed backbones to accomplish the transport of information for these millions of frame relay users because yesterday's frame-based network problems will have scaled to tomorrow's frame-based network problems. Or gigabit frame relay may surface and push the need for ATM out another decade or two.

14.5 Frame Relay versus ATM

Just before or during the Warring States period in China, approximately 480 to 220 BC, a very important and often quoted military text was written by a philosopher named Sun (pronounced Swun) Tzu. Master Sun, in writing *The Art of War*, put forth a tightly compressed set of principles for achieving triumph over opposition. What is most remarkable about this book, drawn from philosophy and observation, is that the central premise is that a true victory can be won only with a strategy of tactical positioning, so that the moment of triumph is effortless, and destructive conflict is averted. In *The Art of War* Sun Tzu states: "Those who win one hundred triumphs in one hundred conflicts do not have supreme skill. Those who have supreme skill use strategy to bend others without coming into conflict." Using 2,300-year-old Chinese philosophy, we can hope to make sense out of the telecommunications marketplace—a battlefield where ideas, products, standards, and companies struggle for supremacy and where the stakes are very high.

In looking, for instance, at frame relay and ATM, it is possible to visualize a true battle between ideologies and organizations, in which one must triumph and one must perish. It is equally possible to envision a symbiotic relationship, where frame relay performs the interface job for which it was originally designed and ATM performs the high-speed transport of a variety of information types. And it is also possible to construct a highly believable story of the Frame Relay Forum's carefully positioning their ideas and philosophies into the marketplace in such a way that the market has adopted them and shunned the ways of other approaches. In fact, all three are true, but it is the third, the Frame Relay Forum's careful positioning strategy, that is the closest to the truth. And while it is also true that many of the larger companies will benefit regardless of which approach users take (because they have products that will do either, and in many cases will do both, frame relay and ATM), there is still the supremacy of individuals and departments within those organizations to consider. One trip to a major Frame Relay Forum meeting will convince even the most skeptical that there is merit to this view.

But, regardless of which of the philosophical models you believe, the reality for most medium to small users is that frame relay will suffice for today and for the foreseeable future and that ATM, if it figures into the picture at all, will be in carrier backbones, where it is as invisible to the frame relay user as the pulse code modulation algorithm used in today's telephony systems is to the user of the telephone. The people left caring about ATM, beyond just curiosity, are the very large users, who are themselves effectively carriers for their own organizations, or the true carriers and service providers, for it is these people who, at least in the long term, will be using ATM for backbone or access or both.

14.5.1   Frame Relay and ATM Interworking

Frame relay and ATM interworking is being done to some extent in most frame relay networks today, either using a proprietary prestandard approach or based upon the work of the Frame Relay Forum. A vast majority of frame relay frames traversing frame relay networks today are parsed into cell payloads, their header bits are mapped to the ATM header, and they are transported across the long distance as cells. Many of the largest carriers have always done frame relay that way. Many are also just now offering network access using ATM UNIs. In the future, it will not be uncommon for organizations with a large number of sites to have all of the low-speed sites connected to the backbone transport network via frame relay and the large host or data center sites connected via ATM. This will be an important future model because it will leverage the lower speeds of frame relay for the many and get the most from the higher-speed ATM UNIs where the costs are justified.

Additionally we will increasingly see carriers and service providers placing a new type of customer-located equipment on the premises of medium- to large-scale users. There are scattered examples today, but in the future we will see more and more premises multiplexers (or service multiplexers, as they are often called), which have a high-speed ATM umbilical cord to the backbone network but which provide everything from traditional T1 and E1 telephony connections, RS232 and V.35 circuit data ports, Ethernet, token ring, ATM, SMDS, and, of course, frame relay. This strategy places the most flexibility in the hands of the customer and puts the carrier in the business of selling cells, allowing the leveraging of ATM for a variety of services (whatever the customer needs) and providing instantaneous bandwidth-on-demand, quick service turn-up, ease of migration between technologies, and to-the-premises remote provisioning, monitoring, and testing.

14.6 Conclusion

Although this book strongly advocates a highly customized patchwork quilt approach to networking, in which a variety of transport methods, each appropriate to the narrow job that it is defined to do, are stitched together in a useful and beautiful whole by network management and tight network monitoring and operations procedures, many organizations seem bent on the search for a single all-encompassing network transport technology. And it seems that these organizations are willing to make the occasional sacrifice in cost or performance for a single, unified transport strategy.

Many of these single-solution organizations have been finding that when it comes to frame relay a single, flexible solution can, in fact, be made to fit all of their needs. These organizations cite the variety of suppliers of public, private, and public/private hybrid solutions; the wide and increasing range of speeds at which frame relay is available; the availability of switched virtual connections promised by carriers; the option of dedicated or switched access to frame relay; and the many special variations now available in frame relay access devices to do everything from traditional LAN routing to voice over frame relay to SNA poll spoofing to encryption—and the list goes on and on.

Many organizations have cast, or are now casting, their votes with budget dollars. And the reality of the marketplace is that these organizations, for reasons of network stability and fiscal prudence, will stay with their chosen solutions for some number of years before even considering a substantial change.

Is frame relay the alpha and omega of networking? Is frame relay the last network transport technology you will ever use? For most applications, for most organizations, the answer is an unqualified "no," even though frame relay is entrenched for quite some time and many organizations cannot foresee a time when frame relay will not fulfill their wishes.

Regardless of what the future holds, one thing is clear: frame relay is going to be an important part of the networking future for years to come.

Frame Relay Resources

The following page is available on the Web at `http://www.mot.com/MIMS/ISG/tech/frame-relay/resources.html`.[1]

Frame Relay Resources

This page is mostly a collection of pointers to Frame-Relay-related information on the Web. If your favorite online source of Frame Relay information is not listed here, send Steve Neil some email at `<LSN001@email.mot.com>`. This page is sponsored by Motorola ISG as a service to the frame relay industry.

This page was inspired by Dan Kegel's excellent ISDN page `<http://alumni.caltech.edu/~dank/isdn/>`.

---

[1] Copyright 1996, Motorola Inc. Reprinted with permission. The author of this Web page is Steve Neil. Steve is a networking technologist at Motorola's Network System Division.

Table of Contents

- Basics of Frame Relay
- Frequently Asked Questions (FAQ)
- Frame Relay Access Devices (FRADs)
- Bridges/Routers with Frame Relay Support
- PC Cards with Frame Relay Support
- DSU/CSUs
- Frame Relay Switches
- Voice over Frame Relay Products
- Data Encryption over Frame Relay Products
- Host Equipment Supporting Direct Frame Relay Connections
- Frame Relay Network Management
- Frame Relay Test Equipment and Suppliers
- Frame Relay Network Providers
- Internet Service Providers with Frame Relay Connectivity
- User Groups and Standards Bodies
- Non-RFC Standards Related to Frame Relay
- Internet RFCs and Drafts Related to Frame Relay
- White Papers and Articles
- Usenet News Groups and Related Archives
- On-Line News Services
- Magazines
- Books
- Courses

Basics of Frame Relay

- Frame Relay: Networks for Tomorrow and Today
  `<http://www.frforum.com/4000/4001.html>`
- Application Guide
  `<http://www.frforum.com/4000/4002/4002index.html>`
- Frame Relay Glossary
  `<http://www.frforum.com/4000/4003.html>`
- Special Report: Frame Relay 1994 and Beyond
  `<http://www.frforum.com/4000/4004/home.html>`

Frequently Asked Questions (FAQs)

Authors Note—It appears as though there is no up-to-date FAQ for the comp.dcom.frame-relay news group. This is the only FAQ I have been able to find on the Web. If anyone knows of a more recent version of this document, please let me know <mailto:LSN001@email.mot.com>.

- FAQ dated Feb 25, 1995
  <http://netlab.ucs.indiana.edu/hypermail/frame-relay/9502/0023.html>

Frame Relay Access Devices (FRADs)

- ACT Networks
  <http://www.acti.com/>
  - SDM-FP and SDM-JFP Integrated FRADs
    <http://www.acti.com/sdmfp.html>
- Ascom Timeplex
  <http://www.timeplex.com/>
  - Branch Nodal Processor (BNP)
    <http://www.timeplex.com/bnp/bnp_intro.html>
  - Integrated Access Node (IAN)
    <http://www.timeplex.com/ian/ian_intro.html>
- BBN
  <http://www.bbn.com/>
  - BBN T/10(TM) FRAD
    <http://www.bbn.com/iad.frad.html>
- Cisco
  <http://www.cisco.com/>
- Data Comm for Business
  <http://www.dcbnet.com/>
- Dynatech Communications Inc.
  <http://www.dynatech.com/>
- Eicon
  <http://www.eicon.com/>
- FastComm
  <http://www.fastcomm.com/>
  - MonoFRAD—One serial port, optional integral 56K CSU/DSU
    <http://www.fastcomm.com/frads.html>
  - QuadFRAD—Four serial ports, optional integral 56K CSU/DSU
    <http://www.fastcomm.com/frads.html>
  - EtherFRAD—One Ethernet port, up to 3 serial ports, optional integral 56K CSU/DSU
    <http://www.fastcomm.com/frads.html>

- Hughes Network Systems
  `<http://www.hns.com/>`
- Jupiter Technology
  `<http://www.jti.com/>`
  - Voyager tFRAD supports a Token Ring LAN and up to four serial sync/async ports.
    `<http://www.jti.com/market/voyager/tfrad.htm>`
  - Voyager eFRAD supports an Ethernet LAN and up to three serial sync/async ports.
    `<http://www.jti.com/market/voyager/efrad.htm>`
  - Voyager kFRAD supports up to four serial sync/async ports.
    `<http://www.jti.com/market/voyager/kfrad.htm>`
  - Voyager hFRAD will typically be deployed as a concentration node and can support up to 7 LAN interfaces, 13 high-speed serial interfaces, 31 low-speed sync ports and 127 async ports.
    `<http://www.jti.com/market/voyager/hfrad.htm>`
- Memotec
  `<http://www.memotec.com/>`
  - FR 870
    `<http://www.memotec.com/MEMFR870.html>`
  - FR 970
    `<http://www.memotec.com/970.html>`
- Micom
  `<http://www.micom.com/>`
  - Marathon 2K, 5K Turbo, 10K, 20K
    `<http://www.micom.com/product/marathon.html>`
- Microtronix Datacom
  `<http://www.microtronix.com/mdlprod/>`
- Motorola Information Systems Group
  `<http://www.mot.com/MIMS/ISG/>`
  - Vanguard 100—One or two serial ports, optional integral 56K CSU/DSU, ISDN BRI (U or S/T)
    `<http://www.mot.com/MIMS/ISG/Products/Vanguard100/>`
  - Vanguard 100PC—One serial port, optional integral 56K CSU/DSU, ISDN BRI (U or S/T)
    `<http://www.mot.com/MIMS/ISG/Products/Vanguard100PC/>`
  - Vanguard 200—Five serial ports, optional 56K CSU/DSU
    `<http://www.mot.com/MIMS/ISG/Products/Vanguard200/>`
  - Vanguard 300—One or two serial ports, ethernet, optional integral 56K CSU/DSU, ISDN BRI (U or S/T)
    `<http://www.mot.com/MIMS/ISG/Products/Vanguard300/>`

- Vanguard 305—One or two serial ports, token ring, optional integral 56K CSU/DSU, ISDN BRI (U or S/T)
    `<http://www.mot.com/MIMS/ISG/Products/Vanguard305/>`
- 6500PLUS—6 to 54 serial ports, optional token ring, optional 56K CSU/DSU
    `<http://www.mot.com/MIMS/ISG/Products/6500plus/>`
- 6520 MPRouter—5 to 19 serial ports, one optional ethernet or token ring port, optional ethernet hub, optional 56K CSU/DSU, optional ISDN BRI
    `<http://www.mot.com/MIMS/ISG/Products/6520m/>`
- 6560 MPRouter Pro
    `<http://www.mot.com/MIMS/ISG/Products/6560/>`

■ Netlink
`<http://www.netlink.com/>`
- TurboFRAD
    `<http://www.netlink.com/turbo.htm>`
- OmniLinx 4000
    `<http://www.netlink.com/4000.htm>`
- OmniLinx 8000
    `<http://www.netlink.com/8000.htm>`

■ Netrix
`<http://www.netrix.com/>`
- Netrix 2210
    `<http://www.netrix.com/products/net2210.html>`

■ Newbridge
`<http://www.newbridge.com/>`

■ Racal-Datacom
`<http://www.racal.com/>`
- EAN 4200 FN—One serial port
    `<http://www.racal.com/racal/products/dap/ean4000/e4000.html>`
- EAN 4400 FN—One or three serial ports, optional ethernet or token ring
    `<http://www.racal.com/racal/products/dap/ean4000/e4000.html>`

■ RAD Data Communication
`<http://www.rad.co.il/>`

The following companies are known to have FRADs, but they do not appear to have servers on the Web:

■ Hypercom

- NetLink
- Sync Research

Bridges/Routers with Frame Relay Support

- 3Com
  <http://www.3com.com/>
- ACC
  <http://www.acc.com/>
  - Amazon
    <http://www.acc.com/Products/amazon.html>
  - Colorado
    <http://www.acc.com/Products/colorado.html>
  - Danube
    <http://www.acc.com/Products/danube.html>
  - Nile
    <http://www.acc.com/Products/nile.html>
  - Yukon Frame Relay
    <http://www.acc.com/Products/yukon-frame.html>
- Ascend Communications, Inc.
  <http://www.ascend.com/>
  - Pipeline 50 EtherFrame
    <http://www.ascend.com/products/P50/P50EFindex.html>
  - Pipeline 400 BRI
    <http://www.ascend.com/products/P400/P400briindex.html>
  - Pipeline 400 T1/E1
    <http://www.ascend.com/products/P400/P400T1index.html>
  - MAX 4000
    <http://www.ascend.com/products/max4000/max4000index.html>
- Ascom Timeplex
  <http://www.timeplex.com/>
  - Access Router
    <http://www.timeplex.com/ar/ar_intro.html>
  - Access Router 150
    <http://www.timeplex.com/ar/ar150_intro.html>
  - Access Router 350
    <http://www.timeplex.com/ar/ar350_intro.html>
  - Integrated Access Node (IAN)
    <http://www.timeplex.com/ian/ian_intro.html>
  - Router-Bridge
    <http://www.timeplex.com/rb/rb_intro.htm>

- Enterprise Router (ER)
  `<http://www.timeplex.com/er/er_intro.html>`
- Bay Networks
  `<http://www.baynetworks.com/>`
  - AN—Access Node
    `<http://www.baynetworks.com/Products/Routers/Systems/AN>`
  - ANH—Access Node Hub
    `<http://www.baynetworks.com/Products/Routers/Systems/AN>`
  - ASN—Access Stack Node
    `<http://www.baynetworks.com/Products/Routers/Systems/ASN>`
  - BLN—Backbone Link Node
    `<http://www.baynetworks.com/Products/Routers/Systems/BLN BCN>`
  - BCN—Backbone Concentrator Node
    `<http://www.baynetworks.com/Products/Routers/Systems/BLN BCN>`
- Cisco
  `<http://www.cisco.com/>`
  - 5000 Series
    `<http://cio.cisco.com/warp/public/641/10.html>`
  - 4000 Series
    `<http://cio.cisco.com/warp/public/563/1.html>`
  - 2500 Series
    `<http://cio.cisco.com/warp/public/563/4.html>`
  - 1005 Synchronous Router
    `<http://cio.cisco.com/warp/public/558/58.html>`
  - AccessPro PC Card
    `<http://cio.cisco.com/warp/public/563/8.html>`
- Compatible Systems
  `<http://www.compatible.com/>`
  - 3400R
    `<http://www.compatible.com/Spec_Sheets/3400R_Spec/RISC_Router_3400R>`
  - 1000R
    `<http://www.compatible.com/Spec_Sheets/1000R_Spec/MicroRouter_1000R>`
  - 900I
    `<http://www.compatible.com/Spec_Sheets/900i_Spec/MicroRouter_900i>`

- Cray Communications
  <http://www.craycom.com/>
  - DCP4802 and DCP4802LE Ethernet FRADs
    <http://www.craycom.com/prodinfo/4802.html>
  - MatchBox Router
    <http://www.craycom.com/prodinfo/matchbox.html>
- Digital Networks
  <http://www.networks.digital.com/>
  - DECNIS Backbone Router
    <http://www.networks.digital.com/npb/html/products_guide/
    routers1.html>
  - RouteAbout Access Router
    <http://www.networks.digital.com/npb/html/products_guide/
    routabot.html>
- Engage Communications
  <http://www.engage.com/engage/>
  - ExpressRouter
    <http://www.engage.com/engage/html/prod2.html>
- Hewlett Packard
  <http://www.hp.com/>
- Hughes Network Systems
  <http://www.hns.com/>
- IBM
  <http://www.ibm.com/>
- Imatek Inc.
  <http://www.imatek.com/>
  - OnRamp DSU-Router
    <http://www.imatek.com/DSU-data-sheet.html>
  - OnRamp V.35 Router
    <http://www.imatek.com/V.35-data-sheet.html>
- ISDN Systems Corporation
  <http://www.infoanalytic.com/isc/>
  - MPAX Multi-Protocol Access Node
    <http://www.infoanalytic.com/isc/mpax.htm>
- Livingston Enterprises Inc.
  <http://www.livingston.com/>
- Memotec
  <http://www.memotec.com/>
  - CL 2500
    <http://www.memotec.com/MEMCL25.html>

- Micom
  <http://www.micom.com/>
  - NetRunner 75E, 500ET, 1000E, 2000E
    <http://www.micom.com/product/netrunner.html>
- Morning Star Technologies
  <http://www.morningstar.com/>
  - Express Router Family
    <http://www.morningstar.com/MorningStar/MST-Express.html>
- Motorola Information Systems Group
  <http://www.mot.com/MIMS/ISG/>
  - Vanguard 300—One or two serial ports, ethernet, optional integral
    56K CSU/DSU, ISDN BRI (U or S/T)
    <http://www.mot.com/MIMS/ISG/Products/Vanguard300/>
  - Vanguard 305—One or two serial ports, token ring, optional
    integral 56K CSU/DSU, ISDN BRI (U or S/T)
    <http://www.mot.com/MIMS/ISG/Products/Vanguard305/>
  - Vanguard 310—ISDN Bridge/Router which supports Frame Relay
    on the B channel(s)
    <http://www.mot.com/MIMS/ISG/Products/Vanguard310/>
  - 6500PLUS—6 to 54 serial ports, optional token ring, optional 56K
    CSU/DSU
    <http://www.mot.com/MIMS/ISG/Products/6500plus/>
  - 6520 MPRouter—5 to 19 serial ports, one optional ethernet or
    token ring port, optional ethernet hub, optional 56K CSU/DSU,
    optional ISDN BRI/U
    <http://www.mot.com/MIMS/ISG/Products/6520m/>
  - 6560 MPRouter Pro
    <http://www.mot.com/MIMS/ISG/Products/6560/>
- Proteon
  <http://www.proteon.com/>
- RAD Data Communication
  <http://www.rad.co.il/>
- Skyline Technology
  <http://www.skylinetech.com/>
  - Veloce
    <http://www.skylinetech.com/Skylinetech/veloce.html>
  - Avanta
    <http://www.skylinetech.com/Skylinetech/avanta.html>
  - Matera
    <http://www.skylinetech.com/Skylinetech/matera.html>

- Telebit
  <http://www.telebit.com/>
  - NetBlazer Product Family
    <http://www.telebit.com/ProductS/nbdescription.html>
- Triticom
  <http://www.triticom.com/>
  - BRouteIT!
    <http://www.triticom.com/triticom/broe/broe.htm>
- Xyplex
  <http://www.xyplex.com/>

PC Cards with Frame Relay Support

- Cisco
  <http://www.cisco.com/>
  - AccessPro PC Card
    <http://cio.cisco.com/warp/public/563/8.html>
  - LAN2LAN
    <http://cio.cisco.com/warp/public/662/index_data.shtml>
- ISDN Systems Corporation
  <http://www.infoanalytic.com/isc/>
  - FX-56 & FX-T1 Frame Relay PC Adaptors
    <http://www.infoanalytic.com/isc/fx56t1.htm>
  - FX-PRI ISDN/Frame Relay PC Adaptor
    <http://www.infoanalytic.com/isc/fxpri.htm>
- Motorola Information Systems Group
  <http://www.mot.com/MIMS/ISG/>
  - Vanguard 100PC
    <http://www.mot.com/MIMS/ISG/Products/Vanguard100PC/>
- Sangoma Technologies Inc.
  <http://www.sangoma.com/>
  - FPIPE Frame Relay Pump for TCP/IP
    <http://www.sangoma.com/fpipe.htm>
- SDL Communications Inc.
  <http://www.sdlcomm.com/>
- The Software Group (TSG)
  <http://www.group.com/>
  - NetcomHighway
    <http://www.group.com/prods/netcomhw.html>

DSU/CSUs

- **American Technology Labs**
  <http://www.fred.net/atl/>
- **AT&T Paradyne**
  <http://www.paradyne.att.com/>
- **ADC Kentrox**
  <http://www.kentrox.com/>
  - D-SERV
    <http://www.kentrox.com/dserv.html>
  - DataSMART Single-Port
    <http://www.kentrox.com/ds.single.html>
  - DataSMART Dual-Port
    <http://www.kentrox.com/ds.dual.html>
  - DataSMART Add/Drop
    <http://www.kentrox.com/ds.adddrop.html>
  - DataSMART Quad-Port
    http://www.kentrox.com/ds.quad.html>
  - DataSMART T1 SMDSU
    <http://www.kentrox.com/t1smdsu.html>
  - WANCard NW1544
    <http://www.kentrox.com/wancard.html>
  - WANCard NW56
    <http://www.kentrox.com/wancard56.html>
- **Adtran**
  <http://www.adtran.com/>
  - DSU III AR, DSU III S4W, DSU III S2W, DSU III DBU, DSU III TDM, 56/64 DSU, DSU 5600, DSU III DBUc, DSU III ARc, DSU III S4Wc
    <http://www.adtran.com/cpe/dsu/descr.html>
- **Cray Communications**
  <http://www.craycom.com/>
- **Data Comm for Business**
  <http://www.dcbnet.com/>
- **Digital Link**
  <http://www.dl.com/>
- **General Datacomm**
  <http://www.gdc.com/>
  - Manages and Non-managed DSU/CSUs
    <http://www.gdc.com/access.html#link4>

- Memotec
  <http://www.memotec.com/>
- Motorola
  <http://www.mot.com/>
  - 3512—1, 2 or 4 channel DSU/CSU
    <http://www.mot.com/MIMS/ISG/Products/3512/>
  - 3512SDC—Bandwidth Expander, sync up to 256K
    <http://www.mot.com/MIMS/ISG/Products/3512sdc/>
  - 3520—2 or 8 channel DSU/CSU
    <http://www.mot.com/MIMS/ISG/Products/3520/>
  - DA 56 DSU/CSU
    <http://www.mot.com/MIMS/ISG/Products/da56/>
  - DM170 Hybrid, SW56 DSU/CSU and Data/Fax Modem
    <http://www.mot.com/MIMS/ISG/Products/dm170/>
  - DU170 and DU56 switched 56 2-wire DSU/CSUs
    <http://www.mot.com/MIMS/ISG/Products/du170/>
  - FT100 Family of T1 DSU/CSU
    <http://www.mot.com/MIMS/ISG/Products/ft100/>
  - FT100M T1 DSU/CSU, network managed
    <http://www.mot.com/MIMS/ISG/Products/ft100m/>
  - MR64 DSU/CSU
    <http://www.mot.com/MIMS/ISG/Products/mr64/>
  - SW56II—Switched 56 4-wire DSU/CSUs
    <http://www.mot.com/MIMS/ISG/Products/sw56ii/>
  - T1 CSU
    <http://www.mot.com/MIMS/ISG/Products/t1esf/>
- Racal-Datacom
  <http://www.racal.com/>
- TyLink
  <http://204.178.65.252/>
- Verilink
  <http://www.verilink.com/>
- Visual Networks
  <http://www.visualnetworks.com/>

Frame Relay Switches

- ACT Networks
  <http://www.acti.com/>

- MS-2000 Frame Relay Switch
  `<http://www.acti.com/ms2000.html>`
- Alcatel Data Networks
  `<http://www.adn.alcatel.com/>`
  - Avanza
    `<http://www.adn.alcatel.com/docs/factsht.html>`
- Ascom Timeplex `<http://www.timeplex.com/>`
  - ST-1000 Integrated Transport Node
    `<http://www.timeplex.com/st/st1000_intro.html>`
  - ST-50 Multi-Service Backbone Switching Node
    `<http://www.timeplex.com/st/st50.html>`
  - Enterprise Router (ER)
    `<http://www.timeplex.com/er/er_intro.html>`
- AT&T
  `<http://www.att.com/>`
- Cascade
  `<http://www.casc.com/>`
  - STDX 6000
    `<http://www.casc.com/products/stdx6000/>`
  - B-STDX 8000 & 9000
    `<http://www.casc.com/products/stdx9000/>`
- Eigentech
  `<http://www.eigentech.com/eigentech/>`
  - uFRX*4 Frame Relay Branch Exchange
    `<http://www.eigentech.com/eigentech/frx.html>`
- Hughes Network Systems
  `<http://www.hns.com/>`
- Memotec
  `<http://www.memotec.com/>`
  - CX 1000
    `<http://www.memotec.com/CX1000.html>`
- Motorola Information Systems Group
  `<http://www.mot.com/MIMS/ISG/>`
  - Vanguard 100—One or two serial ports, optional integral 56K CSU/DSU, ISDN BRI (U or S/T)
    `<http://www.mot.com/MIMS/ISG/Products/Vanguard100/>`
  - Vanguard 100PC—One serial port, optional integral 56K CSU/DSU, ISDN BRI (U or S/T)
    `<http://www.mot.com/MIMS/ISG/Products/Vanguard100PC/>`

- Vanguard 200—Five serial ports, optional 56K CSU/DSU
  <http://www.mot.com/MIMS/ISG/Products/Vanguard200/>
- Vanguard 300—One or two serial ports, ethernet, optional integral 56K CSU/DSU, ISDN BRI (U or S/T)
  <http://www.mot.com/MIMS/ISG/Products/Vanguard300/>
- Vanguard 305—One or two serial ports, token ring, optional integral 56K CSU/DSU, ISDN BRI (U or S/T)
  <http://www.mot.com/MIMS/ISG/Products/Vanguard305/>
- 6500PLUS—6 to 54 ports, optional token ring, optional 56K CSU/DSU
  <http://www.mot.com/MIMS/ISG/Products/6500plus/>
- 6520 MPRouter—5 to 19 ports, one optional ethernet or token ring port, optional ethernet hub, optional 56K CSU/DSU, optional ISDN BRI/U
  <http://www.mot.com/MIMS/ISG/Products/6520m/>
- 6560 MPRouter Pro
  <http://www.mot.com/MIMS/ISG/Products/6560/>
- Netrix
  <http://www.netrix.com/>
  - #1-ISS Series 10
    <http://www.netrix.com/products/ser10.html>
  - #1-ISS Series 1000
    <http://www.netrix.com/products/ser1000.html>
  - Netrix 200
    <http://www.netrix.com/products/net200.html>
  - Netrix 2210
    <http://www.netrix.com/products/net2210.html>
- Network Equipment Technologies (NET)
  <http://www.net.com/>
- Newbridge
  <http://www.newbridge.com/>
  - 36120 MainStreet
    <http://www.newbridge.com/marccom/Products/datasheets/169.html>
- Northern Telecom
  <http://www.nortel.com/>
  - Magellan Passport
    <http://www.nortel.com/english/magellan/architecture/frame_relay.html>

- RAD Data Communication
  `<http://www.rad.co.il/>`
- Stratacom
  `<http://www.strata.com/>`
  - BPX/AXIS
    `<http://www.strata.com/corporate/products/bpxaxis.html>`
  - IGX
    `<http://www.strata.com/corporate/products/igx.html>`
  - IPX
    `<http://www.strata.com/corporate/products/ipx.html>`

The following companies are known to make Frame Relay Switches, but they do not appear to have servers on the Web:

- Andrews

Voice over Frame Relay Products

The following companies make products that can transport voice traffic over frame relay networks:

- ACT Networks
  `<http://www.acti.com/>`
  - SDM-FP and SDM-JFP Integrated FRADs
    `<http://www.acti.com/sdmfp.html>`
- Memotec
  `<http://www.memotec.com/>`
  - CX 1000
    `<http://www.memotec.com/CX1000.html>`
- Micom
  `<http://www.micom.com/>`
  - Marathon 2K, 5K Turbo, 10K, 20K
    `<http://www.micom.com/product/marathon.html>`
  - NetRunner 75E, 500ET, 1000E, 2000E
    `<http://www.micom.com/product/netrunner.html>`
- Motorola Information Systems Group
  `<http://www.mot.com/MIMS/ISG/>`
  - 6520 MPRouter
    `<http://www.mot.com/MIMS/ISG/Products/6520m/>`
  - 6560 MPRouter Pro
    `<http://www.mot.com/MIMS/ISG/Products/6560/>`

- Voice Relay Product Overview
    `<http://www.mot.com/MIMS/ISG/Products/voice_relay/>`
■ Netrix
  `<http://www.netrix.com/>`
  - RLX-246
    `<http://www.netrix.com/products/rlx246.html>`
  - RLX-416
    `<http://www.netrix.com/products/rlx416.html>`
■ Scitec
  `<http://www.scitec.com.au/>`

Data Encryption over Frame Relay Products

The following companies manufacture equipment that can be used to encrypt the data being passed over a frame relay network:

■ Cray Communications
  `<http://www.craycom.com/>`
  - FPX4802/DES Frame Relay Encryptor
    `<http://www.craycom.com/prodinfo/4802des.html>`
■ Cylink
  `<http://www.cylink.com/>`
■ Semaphore Communications Corporation
  `<http://infolane.com/infolane/semaphore/>`
  - NEU-ST
    `<http://infolane.com/infolane/semaphore/semdtsfr.html>`

Host Equipment Supporting Direct Frame Relay Connections

■ IBM
  `<http://www.ibm.com/>`
  - AS/400—requires 2666 High Speed Communications Adaptor and OS/400 Version 2 Release 3 or later
  - 3172 Interconnect Controller
    `<http://www.raleigh.ibm.com/312/312prod.html>`
  - 3174 Network Processor
    `<http://www.raleigh.ibm.com/314/314prod.html>`
  - 3745 Communications Controller
    `<http://www.raleigh.ibm.com/375/375prod.html>`
  - 5494 Communications Controller
    `<http://www.raleigh.ibm.com/549/549prod.html>`

Frame Relay Network Management

- Visual Networks
  <http://www.visualnetworks.com/>
  - Visual UpTime
    <http://www.visualnetworks.com/vuptime/vuptime.htm>

Frame Relay Test Equipment and Suppliers

- NCC—Network Communications Corporation
  <http://probe.netcommcorp.com/>
  - Network Probe 7000 Series
    <http://probe.netcommcorp.com/general/np7000.htm>
- Odin TeleSystems
  <http://www.pic.net/~jari/odin.html>
- Telenex Corporation, AR Test Systems
  <http://www.ar.telenex.com/>
- TTC
  <http://www.ttc.com>
- Wandel & Goltermann
  <http://www2.interpath.net/interweb/wg/homepage.html>

Frame Relay Network Providers

- AmeriCom
  <http://www.xmission.com:80/~americom/>
- Ameritech
  <http://www.ameritech.com/>
  - Ameritech Frame Relay Service
    <http://www.ameritech.com/solutions/business/
    asg-ds-dds-afrs.html>
- AT&T
  <http://www.att.com/>
- Bell Canada
  <http://www.bell.ca/>
- Bell Atlantic
  <http://www.ba.com/>
- Bell South
  <http://www.bst.bls.com/>
- British Telecommunications (BT)
  <http://www.bt.net/>

- Cable & Wireless Inc.
  `<http://www.cwi.net/>`
- GTE Communications Corp
  `<http://www.gtecc.com/>`
- InComA Ltd.
  `<http://www.incoma.com/>`
- Intermedia Communications
  `<http://www.intermedia.com/>`
- LDDS WorldCom (formerly WilTel)
  `<http://www.wcom.com/>`
  - WilPak Frame Relay Services
    `<http://www.wiltel.com/services/bband/wilpak.html>`
- Lincoln Telephone
  `<http://www.ltec.net/>`
  - Frame Relay Services
    `<http://www.ltec.net/Ltec/Prod/doc00049.htm>`
- MCI
  `<http://www.mci.com/>`
- MFS Datanet
  `<http://www.mfsdatanet.com/>`
- Nippon Telegraph and Telephone (NTT)
  `<http://www.ntt.jp/>`
- Pacific Bell
  `<http://www.pacbell.com/>`
- scruz-net Frame Relay Connections
  `<http://www.scruz.net/frame.html>`
- Southwestern Bell
  `<http://www.sbc.com/>`
- Sprint
  `<http://www.commerce.com/sprint/sprint_top.html>`
- Structured Network Systems Inc.
  `<http://www.structured.net/>`
- Telstra (Australia/International)
  `<http://www.telstra.com.au/>`
  - Telstra's Frame Relay Services
    `<http://www.telstra.com.au/prod-ser/dataservices/frame.htm>`
- ThoughtPort Authority
  `<http://www.thoughtport.com/>`

- UniSPAN Frame Relay Consortium
  `<http://www.unispan.com/>`
  - EMI Communications Corporation
    `<http://www.emi.com/>`
  - Sprint Canada Inc. (Formerly INSINC)
  - Intermedia Communications (ICI)
    `<http://www.intermedia.com/>`
  - MRC Telecommunications, Inc(NorLight, Inc.)
    `<http://www.norlight.com/>`
  - PACNET Inc. (MIDCOM Communications Inc.)
  - TeleMedia International, Inc. (TMI)
- US West
  `<http://www.uswest.com/>`
  - Frame Relay Service
    `<http://www.uswest.com/products/intprs/frs.html>`

Resellers and Consultants

In addition to the above list, there are also resellers and consultants that can help you obtain Frame Relay services. Here are some that I've come across. There are probably lots more. If you come across any others that have Web sites, please let me know.

- Digital Access
  `<http://www.intense.com/digital-access/>`
  - Frame Relay
    `<http://www.intense.com/digital-access/frame.html>`
  - ISDN
    `<http://www.intense.com/digital-access/isdn.html>`
  - SMDS
    `<http://www.intense.com/digital-access/smds.html>`

Internet Service Providers with Frame Relay Connectivity

There are a lot of internet providers that provide frame relay access. Here are some that I've come across. There are probably lots more. If you come across any others, please let me know.

- ABSNET Internet Services
  `<http://www.abs.net/>`

- ABWAM
  `<http://www.abwam.com/>`
- Aimnet
  `<http://www.aimnet.com/>`
- Alternate Access
  `<http://www.aa.net/>`
- ARInternet
  `<http://www.ari.net/>`
- Bay Area Internet Solutions
  `<http://www.bayarea.net/>`
- BBN Planet
  `<http://www.bbnplanet.com/>`
- Best Internet Communications
  `<http://www.best.com/>`
- CompuServe
  `<http://www.compuserve.com/>`
- Connectivity Solutions
  `<http://www.connection.net/>`
- Creative Friendly Technologies
  `<http://www.cftnet.com/>`
- CrossLink Internet Services
  `<http://www.crosslink.net/>`
- Databank
  `<http://www.databank.com/>`
- DIGEX
  `<http://www.digex.net/>`
- digitalNATION
  `<http://www.dn.net/>`
- DigiLink Network Services
  `<http://www.DigiLink.net/>`
- Direct Network Access
  `<http://www.dnai.com/>`
- EarthLink Network
  `<http://www.earthlink.net/>`
- ElectriCiti
  `<http://www.electriciti.com/>`
- emf.net
  `<http://www.emf.net/>`
- Foothill-Net
  `<http://www.foothill.net/>`

- Future Net
  `<http://www.fn.net/>`
- General Internet
  `<http://www.general.net/>`
- GetNet International
  `<http://www.getnet.com/>`
- GTE.NET
  `<http://www.gte.net/>`
- HarvardNet
  `<http://harvard.net/>`
- Harborside Internet
  `<http://www.harborside.com/>`
- HoloNet
  `<http://www.holonet.net/holonet/>`
- INTAC Access Corporation
  `<http://www.intac.com/>`
- InteleNet Communications Inc.
  `<http://www.intelenet.com/>`
- Intelligence Network Online
  `<http://www.IntNet.net/>`
- Intellitech Walrus
  `<http://www.walrus.com/>`
- Internet Access Group
  `<http://www.iag.net/>`
- Internet Direct
  `<http://www.indirect.com/>`
- Internex Information Services
  `<http://www.internex.net/>`
- InterWorld Communications
  `<http://www.interworld.net/>`
- IXA
  `<http://www.ixa.net/>`
- Jet.Net Internet Services
  `<http://www.jet.net/>`
- Keyway Network Systems
  `<http://www.keyway.net/>`
- Lincoln Telephone
  `<http://www.ltec.net/>`
  - Navix Internet Access Service
    `http://www.ltec.net/Ltec/Prod/doc00048.htm>`

- MCI
  `<http://www.mci.com/>`
- MegaNet
  `<http://www.mega.net/>`
- MGL Systems
  `<http://www.mgl.ca/>`
- MIDnet
  `<http://www.mid.net/>`
- MV Communications
  `<http://www.mv.com/>`
- NETCOM On-Line Communications Services
  `<http://www.netcom.com/>`
- NETPLEX
  `<http://www.ntplx.net/>`
- Network 99
  `<http://www.net99.net/>`
- Networks Online
  `<http://www.nol.net/>`
- NICOH Net
  `<http://www.nicoh.com/>`
- North Shore Internet Services
  `<http://www.nsis.com/>`
- Northwest Link
  `<http://nwlink.com/nwlink/pbs.html>`
- Northwest Nexus
  `<http://www.nwnexus.com/>`
- Pacific Bell
  `<http://www.pacbell.com/>`
  - Dedicated Internet Access
    `<http://www.pbi.net/publicInfo/dedicated/>`
- PSINet
  `<http://www.psi.net/>`
- Random Access
  `<http://www.randomc.com/>`
- RealNet
  `<http://www.reallife.com/>`
- SoftAware
  `<http://www.softaware.com/>`
- SourceNet
  `<http://www.source.net/>`

- Structured Network Systems Inc.
  `<http://www.structured.net/>`
- The Destek Group
  `<http://www.destek.net/>`
- ThoughtPort Authority
  `<http://www.thoughtport.com/>`
- Thurber Technology Group
  `<http://www.fta.com/>`
- UltraPLEX Information Systems
  `<http://www.uplex.net/>`
- US Internet
  `<http://www.usit.net/>`
- UUNET Technologies
  `<http://www.uu.net/>`
- Value Net Internetwork Services
  `<http://www.value.net/>`
- Wintek
  `<http://www.wintek.com/>`
- Wolfe Internet
  `<http://www.wolfe.net/>`
- WorldNET Internet Access Service
  `<http://www.wn.net/>`
- wyoming.com
  `<http://www.wyoming.com/>`
- Zocalo
  `<http://www.zocalo.net/>`

User Groups and Standards Bodies

- ATM Forum
  `<http://www.atmforum.com/>`
- Cell Relay Retreat
  `<http://cell-relay.indiana.edu/cell-relay>`
- Frame Relay Forum
  `<http://www.frforum.com/>`

Non-RFC Standards Related to Frame Relay

- Frame Relay Forum Implementation Agreements (Ias).

The Frame Relay Forum maintains a number of online specifications. These are also available in PostScript or Adobe Acrobat.
`<http://www.frforum.com/>`

- FRF.1 User-to-Network (UNI) Implementation Agreement
  `<http://www.frforum.com/5000/Approved/FRF.1/FRF1.TOC.html>`
- FRF.2 Network-to-Network (NNI) Phase 1 Implementation Agreement
  `<http://www.frforum.com/5000/5001-approved.html>`
- FRF.3 Multiprotocol Encapsulation Implementation Agreement (MEI)
  `<http://www.frforum.com/5000/Approved/FRF.3/FRF3.TOC.html>`
- FRF.4 Switched Virtual Circuit Implementation Agreement (SVC)
  `<http://www.frforum.com/5000/Approved/FRF.4/FRF4.TOC.html>`
- FRF.5 Frame Relay/ATM Network Interworking Implementation Agreement
  `<http://www.frforum.com/5000/Approved/FRF.5/FRF5.TOC.html>`
- FRF.6 Frame Relay Service Customer Network Management Implementation Agreement (MIB)
  `<http://www.frforum.com/5000/Approved/FRF.6/FRF6.TOC.html>`
- FRF.7 Frame Relay PVC Multicast Service and Protocol Description
  `<http://www.frforum.com/5000/Approved/FRF.7/FRF7-TOC.html>`
- FRF.8 Frame Relay/ATM PVC Service Interworking Implementation Agreement
  `<http://www.frforum.com/5000/5001-approved.html>`
- FRF.9 Data Compression Over Frame Relay Implementation Agreement
  `<http://www.frforum.com/5000/5001-approved.html>`

■ ANSI Standards
`<http://www.ansi.org/>`
ANSI has a number of specifications pertaining to Frame Relay. These are not available online on the Web. These must be purchased from ANSI. The following ANSI specifications pertain to Frame Relay:

- T1.606, ISDN—Architectural Framework and Service Description for Frame Relay Bearer Service
- T1.606 Addendum, Frame Relay Bearer Service: Architectural Framework and Service Description
- T1.617, ISDN: DSS1—Signaling Specification for Frame Relay Bearer Service

- T1.617, Annex D Additional Procedures for PVCs Using Unnumbered Information Frames
- T1.618, ISDN—Core Aspects of Frame Protocol for use with Frame Relay Bearer Service

■ ITU Recommendations
`<http://www.itu.ch/>`
The ITU has a number of specifications pertaining to Frame Relay. These are not available online on the Web. These must be purchased from ITU. The following ITU-T specifications pertain to Frame Relay:

- I.122 Frame Relay Framework
- I.233.1 Frame Relay Bearer Services
- I.370 Congestion Management in Frame Relay Networks
- I.555 Frame Relay Bearer Service Interworking
- Q.933 DSS1 Signaling Specification for Frame Mode Bearer Service
- Q.933, Annex A Additional Procedures for PVCs Using Unnumbered Information Frames
- Q.922, Annex A Core Aspects of Q.922 for Use With Frame Relaying Bearer Service
- X.76 NNI between Public Data Networks providing the Frame Relay Data Transmission Service

Internet RFCs and Drafts Related to Frame Relay

- RFC1604 PS T. Brown, "Definitions of Managed Objects for Frame Relay Service," 03/25/1994. (Pages=46) (Format=.txt) (Obsoletes RFC1596)
- RFC1596 PS T. Brown, "Definitions of Managed Objects for Frame Relay Service," 03/17/1994. (Pages=46) (Format=.txt) (Obsoleted by RFC1604)
- RFC1586 I O. deSouza, M. Rodrigues, "Guidelines for Running OSPF Over Frame Relay Networks," 03/24/1994. (Pages=6) (Format=.txt)
- RFC1490 DS T. Bradley, C. Brown, A. Malis, "Multiprotocol Interconnect over Frame Relay," 07/26/1993. (Pages=35) (Format=.txt) (Obsoletes RFC1294)
- RFC1483 PS J. Heinanen, "Multiprotocol Encapsulation over ATM Adaptation Layer 5," 07/20/1993. (Pages=16) (Format=.txt)
- RFC1315 PS C. Brown, F. Baker, C. Carvalho, "Management Information Base for Frame Relay DTEs," 04/09/1992. (Pages=19) (Format=.txt)

■ RFC1294 PS T. Bradley, C. Brown, A. Malis, "Multiprotocol Interconnect over Frame Relay," 01/17/1992. (Pages=28) (Format=.txt) (Obsoleted by RFC1490)

White Papers and Articles

■ *Migrating An AS/400 Network to Frame Relay or ISDN.* The demand for Frame Relay services is exploding, and for two very good reasons—speed and economics. Frame Relay is consistently less expensive than equivalent leased services and provides the bandwidth needed for other services like LAN routing, voice, and fax. Contrary to rumor, the AS/400 environment can be migrated easily to Frame Relay and at the same time provide new value-added services for the network user.
`<http://www.mot.com/MIMS/ISG/Papers/as400_wp/>`

■ *Low Cost Frame Relay Access for IP and IPX Networks using SLIP and PPP* by James Sturgess. This white paper discusses the use of SLIP and PPP to efficiently transport IP and IPX traffic across Frame Relay networks. Alternatives to the use of a router for this purpose are discussed, which can save a lot of money.
`<http://www.mot.com/MIMS/ISG/Papers/SLIP_WhitePaper/`
`SLIP_WhitePaper.html>`

■ *Frame Relay: Playing a Lead Role in SNA and LAN Internetworking* by Rocco DiCarlo. This white paper discusses how Frame Relay networks can be used to efficently transport both LAN and SNA traffic, and also how Frame Relay can play a lead role in the internetworking of SNA and LAN networks.
`<http://www.mot.com/MIMS/ISG/Papers/FR_WhitePaper/`
`FR_WhitePaper.html>`

■ *SNA Capabilities of Motorola Network Access Products* by John Rolfe. This paper describes the rich SNA feature set of the Motorola Network Access Product line.
`<http://www.mot.com/MIMS/ISG/Papers/SNA_Paper/>`

■ *Efficiently Transporting SNA Traffic across Frame Relay and X.25 Networks* by James Sturgess. This white paper discusses how to efficiently transport SNA traffic across Frame Relay or X.25 networks using Motorola Vanguard and 6500 products.
`<http://www.mot.com/MIMS/ISG/Papers/SNA_WhitePaper/`
`SNA_WhitePaper.html>`

- *Semaphore Global Data Communications Security Architecture.* This white paper discusses the need for network security and the use of the encription to provide security.
  `<http://infolane.com/infolane/semaphore/semwp.html>`
- *SNA Battle Royal* by Anura Guruge. This article compares RFC1490 and Data Link Switching (DLSw) for the transportation of SNA/SDLC traffic across Frame Relay networks. This article appeared in the May 1, 1995 issue of *Network World.*
  `<http://www.mot.com/MIMS/ISG/reprints/network-world-950501/>`
- *Importance of Data Compression in Branch Office Networks* by Jim Mello and Nav Chander. This paper outlines where the use of data compression makes most sense and discusses the benefits it can provide in various network environments. It discusses the more commonly implemented forms of data compression and outlines the advantages and shortcomings of each. It discusses the differences between internal and external data compression solutions. In addition, it suggests the most efficient data compression options for environments with mixed public and private framed data networks.
  `<http://www.mot.com/MIMS/ISG/Papers/Data_Compress/>`
- *Voice over Frame Relay* by Ross Kocen. This paper describes how ACT Networks combines voice, fax, and data traffic using Frame Relay Access Devices (FRADs).
  `<http://www.acti.com/vofr.html>`
- *Introduction to SNA* by Howard Gilbert. To make the transition to Client/Server technology, it will still be necessary to communicate to legacy systems. To make the transition from Research to Production, networks have to achieve a high level of management and reliability. SNA provides mainframe and corporate access, and it has evolved to provide more flexibility. Unfortunately, it is still almost impossible to understand the key concepts within the mass of standard documentation.
  `<http://pclt.cis.yale.edu/pclt/comm/sna.htm>`

Usenet News Groups and Related Archives

- comp.dcom.frame-relay
  `<news:comp.dcom.frame-relay>`
  - Charter for the comp.dcom.frame-relay news group
    `<http://www.frforum.com/archives/FR-Charter.html>`

- Subscribing to the comp.dcom.frame-relay mailing list
  `<http://www.frforum.com/archives/subscribing.html>`
- Hypermail archive of the comp.dcom.frame-relay news group:
  1996

    March 1996 `<http://netlab.ucs.indiana.edu/`
    `hypermail/frame-relay/9603/subject.html>`
    February 1996 `<http://netlab.ucs.indiana.edu/`
    `hypermail/frame-relay/9602/subject.html>`
    January 1996 `<http://netlab.ucs.indiana.edu/`
    `hypermail/frame-relay/9601/subject.html>`
  1995

    December 1995 `<http://netlab.ucs.indiana.edu/`
    `hypermail/frame-relay/9512/subject.html>`
    November 1995 `<http://netlab.ucs.indiana.edu/`
    `hypermail/frame-relay/9511/subject.html>`
    October 1995 `<http://netlab.ucs.indiana.edu/`
    `hypermail/frame-relay/9510/subject.html>`
    September 1995 `<http://netlab.ucs.indiana.edu/`
    `hypermail/frame-relay/9509/subject.html>`
    August 1995 `<http://netlab.ucs.indiana.edu/`
    `hypermail/frame-relay/9508/subject.html>`
    July 1995 `<http://netlab.ucs.indiana.edu/`
    `hypermail/frame-relay/9507/subject.html>`
    June 1995 `<http://netlab.ucs.indiana.edu/`
    `hypermail/frame-relay/9506/subject.html>`
    May 1995 `<http://netlab.ucs.indiana.edu/`
    `hypermail/frame-relay/9505/subject.html>`
    April 1995 `<http://netlab.ucs.indiana.edu/`
    `hypermail/frame-relay/9504/subject.html>`
    March 1995 `<http://netlab.ucs.indiana.edu/`
    `hypermail/frame-relay/9503/subject.html>`
    February 1995 `<http://netlab.ucs.indiana.edu/`
    `hypermail/frame-relay/9502/subject.html>`
    January 1995 `<http://netlab.ucs.indiana.edu/`
    `hypermail/frame-relay/9501/subject.html>`
  1994

    December 1994 `<http://netlab.ucs.indiana.edu/`
    `hypermail/frame-relay/9412/subject.html>`

November 1994 `<http://netlab.ucs.indiana.edu/`
`hypermail/frame-relay/9411/subject.html>`
October 1994 `<http://netlab.ucs.indiana.edu/`
`hypermail/frame-relay/9410/subject.html>`

On-Line News Services

- NewsPage—an information service from Individual Inc.
  `<http://www.newspage.com/NEWSPAGE/newspagehome.html>`
  - Frame Relay News
    `<http://www.newspage.com/NEWSPAGE/cgi-bin/walk.cgi/`
    `NEWSPAGE/info/d7/d9/d3/>`
  - ISDN News
    `<http://www.newspage.com/NEWSPAGE/cgi-bin/walk.cgi/`
    `NEWSPAGE/info/d4/d3/d5/>`

Magazines

- *Communications Week* `<http://techweb.cmp.com/cw/current/>`
- *Computer Life* `<http://www.zdnet.com/~complife/>`
- *Data Communications* `<http://www.data.com/>`
- *Electronic Engineering Times* `<http://www.wais.com:80/eet/>`
- *HotWired* `<http://www.hotwired.com/>`
- *InformationWeek* `<http://techweb.cmp.com/iw/current/>`
- *Interactive Age* `<http://techweb.cmp.com/ia/>`
- *MacUser* `<http://www.zdnet.com/~macuser/>`
- *Macworld* `<http://www.macworld.com/>`
- *MacWEEK* `<http://www.zdnet.com/~macweek/>`
- *Network World* `<http://www.nwfusion.com/>`
- *PC Computing* `<http://www.zdnet.com/~pccomp/>`
- *PC Magazine* `<http://www.zdnet.com/~pcmag/>`
- *PC Week* `<http://www.zdnet.com/~pcweek/>`
- *Telecommunications Magazine*
  `<http://www.telecoms-mag.com/tcs.html>`
- *TidBITS*
  `<http://www.dartmouth.edu/pages/TidBITS/TidBITS.html>`
- *Web Week* `<http://pubs.iworld.com/ww-online/>`
- *Windows Sources* `<http://www.zdnet.com/~wsources/>`

Books

There are a number of books that deal directly or indirectly with frame relay:

- *Analyzing Broadband Networks: Frame Relay, SMDS and ATM,* by Mark A. Miller
- *ATM Networks—Concepts, Protocols, Applications, Second Edition,* by Ranier Handel, Manfred N. Huber, and Stefan Schroder, 308 pages (Addison-Wesley, 1994, ISBN 0-201-42274-3)
- *Broadband Communications: A Professional's Guide to ATM, Frame Relay, SMDS, SONET and B-ISDN,* by Balaji Kumar, 513 pages (McGraw-Hill, 1995, ISBN 0-07-035968-7)
- *Emerging Communications Technologies, Third Edition,* by Uyless Black, 448 pages (Prentice Hall, 1993, ISBN 0-13-203464-6)
- *Frame Relay: Principles and Applications,* by Philip Smith, 268 pages (Addison-Wesley, 1993, ISBN 0-201-62400-1)
- *Frame Relay Specifications and Implementations,* by Uyless Black (Addison-Wesley, 1993)
- *Frames, Packets and Cells for Broadband Networking,* by Williams Flanagan, 242 pages
- *ISDN and Broadband ISDN with Frame Relay and ATM, Third Edition,* by William Stallings (Prentice Hall, 1995, ISBN 0-02-415513-6)
- *ISDN: Concepts, Facilities, and Services,* by Gary C. Kessler, 454 pages (McGraw-Hill, 1993, ISBN 0-07-034247-4)
- *Networking Standards—A Guide to OSI, ISSN, LAN, and WAN Standards,* by William Stallings, 672 pages (Addison-Wesley, 1993, ISBN 0-201-56357-6)
- *SMDS—Wide Area Data Networking with Switched Multi-Megabit Data Service,* by Robert W. Klessig and Kaj Tesink (Prentice Hall, 1995, ISBN 0-13-814807-4)
- *SNMP, A Guide To Network Management,* by Dr. Sidnie Feit, 674 pages
- *The Basics Book of Frame Relay* (Motorola University Press, 1993, ISBN 0-201-56377-0, MUP-56-377)
- *The Basics Book of ISDN* (Motorola University Press, 1992, ISBN 0-201-56374-6, MUP-56-368)
- *The Basics Book of Information Networking* (Motorola University Press, 1992, ISBN 0-201-56372-X, MUP-56-370)
- *The Guide to Frame Relay and Packet Networking,* by Nathan J. Muller and Robert Davidson, 232 pages

- *The Guide to Frame Relay Networking—How to Evaluate, Implement and Maintain a Frame Relay Network,* by Christine A. Heckart (Flatiron Publishing, 1-800-LIBRARY)

To order any of these books, you can contact the publishers through the following Web sites:

- Addison-Wesley <http://www.aw.com/>
- McGraw-Hill <http://www.mcgraw-hill.com/>
- Motorola University Press <http://www.mot.com/MU/Press/>
- Prentice Hall <http://www.prenhall.com/>

The Internet Book Shop <http://www.bookshop.co.uk/> is also a good place to search for information about a particular book.

Courses

The following companies offer courses on various data communications related technologies, including frame relay.

- Net Guru Technologies Inc. <http://www.ngt.com/>
- Hill Associates Inc. (HAI) <http://www.hill.com/>
- Motorola University East
  <http://www.mot.com/MIMS/ISG/Training/>
- Teletutor <http://www.teletutor.com/>

Author: Steve Neil <LSN001@email.mot.com>
Addition of <web links> in text by Jim Cavanagh, June 1, 1997.

Bibliography

Cisco Systems. 1996 (date accessed). `www.cisco.com/warp/public/608/1.html`.

Comer, D. 1988. *Internetworking with TCP/IP: Principles, Protocols, and Architectures.* Englewood Cliffs, NJ: Prentice-Hall.

Frame Relay Forum. 1995a. "Frame Relay and Frame-Based ATM: A Comparison of Technologies." *Frame Relay Forum White Paper* (June).

Frame Relay Forum. 1995b. "Frame Relay/ATM PVC Service Interworking Implementation Agreement." *Frame Relay Forum Implementation Agreement Number 8 (FRF.8)* (Apil).

Gareiss, R. 1996. "Don't Take No for an Answer." *Data Communications* (November):67–82.

Guruge, A. 1996. "SNA Battle Royal: RFC 1490 vs. DLSw." *Network World* (May).

Heckart, C. 1994. *The Guide to Frame Relay Networking.* New York: Flatiron Publishing Company.

Hedrick, C. L. 1991. *An Introduction to IGRP.* New Brunswick, NJ: Rutgers, The State University of New Jersey, Center for Computers and Information Services.

Kosek, D. 1995. *Multimedia Networking Handbook.* New York: Auerbach Publishers.

Lieberman, R., and P. Szoke. 1996. "How to Size Frame Relay Access for Interconnecting Local Nets." *Network World* (May).

McQuillan, J. M. 1990. "Broadband Networks, The End of Distance?" *Data Communications* (June):48–55.

Taylor, S. 1995. *Report on Frame Relay Customers and Carriers.* Commissioned by the Frame Relay Forum.

Vertical Systems Group, Inc. 1995. *Data Communications* (May)

Index

Telecommunications Research Associates

Since 1985, more than 200,000 communications professionals, globally, have benefitted from the finest communications training available –TRA classes. TRA works closely with our customers, and our public and private classes are designed to meet the unique needs of today's communications students. In fact, TRA classes (both "off-the-shelf" classes as well as customized sessions) are components of the internal curricula of many large communications companies.

Perhaps the single greatest distinguishing factor separating TRA from other training companies is our faculty. TRA faculty members have helped create the very technologies they teach: our faculty members currently hold 24 patents in communications and information-processing technologies and have served in the industry's leading research and development facilities (such as Bell Labs) and as "frontline engineers" in developing and deploying emergent technologies.

www.tra.com

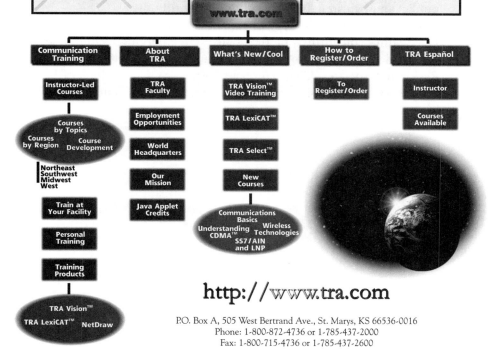

Communication Training
- Instructor-Led Courses
  - Courses by Topics
  - Courses by Region
  - Course Development
    - Northeast
    - Southwest
    - Midwest
    - West
  - Train at Your Facility
  - Personal Training
  - Training Products
    - TRA Vision™
    - TRA LexiCAT™
    - NetDraw

About TRA
- TRA Faculty
- Employment Opportunities
- World Headquarters
- Our Mission
- Java Applet Credits

What's New/Cool
- TRA Vision™ Video Training
- TRA LexiCAT™
- TRA Select™
- New Courses
  - Communications Basics
  - Understanding CDMA™
  - Wireless Technologies
  - SS7/AIN and LNP

How to Register/Order
- To Register/Order

TRA Español
- Instructor
- Courses Available

http://www.tra.com

P.O. Box A, 505 West Bertrand Ave., St. Marys, KS 66536-0016
Phone: 1-800-872-4736 or 1-785-437-2000
Fax: 1-800-715-4736 or 1-785-437-2600

About the Author

Jim Cavanagh has been in the computing and telecommunications industry for over 15 years. Jim has been involved in the engineering, implementation, marketing, and sales of a variety of technologies from the asynchronous terminal networks of the 1970s to X.25, SNA, and the emerging frame relay, SMDS, and ATM networks of the 1990s. Jim is the author of over 40 technical articles, editor of the *Multimedia Networking Handbook, Internet and Internetworking Security Handbook,* and *Guide to the Telecommunications Act of 1996,* and author of four computer-based training packages on telecommunications topics. Jim has done over three dozen presentations at trade shows and technical symposia and is the recipient of the International Communications Association 1994 Citation of Merit for contributions to global telecommunications. Jim spent five years at StrataCom where he designed, engineered, and implemented WilPak, the world's first public frame relay network, in addition to providing support for ATM-based integrated voice, data, and video, private, public, and hybrid networks around the world.

Jim is presently an independent consultant, based in Atlanta, Georgia, U.S.A. Jim's consulting practice focuses on emerging technologies planning and implementation. Jim is on the faculty of Telecommunications Research Associates (TRA) and has consulting clients, which include carriers, service providers, manufacturers, end users, and governmental organizations.